Joseph Hall, John Joseph Hornyold

The Grounds of the Christian's Belief

Joseph Hall, John Joseph Hornyold

The Grounds of the Christian's Belief

ISBN/EAN: 9783337028220

Printed in Europe, USA, Canada, Australia, Japan

Cover: Foto ©Lupo / pixelio.de

More available books at **www.hansebooks.com**

THE GROUNDS OF THE CHRISTIAN'S BELIEF;

OR THE

Apoſtles Creed Explained;

IN A

Concife, eaſy, and familiar Manner.

IN

Twenty-three moral Diſcourſes.

※✧※✧※✧※✧※✧;✧※✧※✧※✧※✧※

By J----H---- C. A. D. S,

※✧※✧※✧※✧※✧;✧※✧※✧※✧※✧※

Be always ready to give an Account of the Faith that is in you. 1 *Pet.* c. iii. v. 18.

For if any Man knows not, he ſhall not be known. 1 *Cor.* c. xiv. v. 38.

※✧※✧※✧※✧※✧;✧※✧※✧※✧※✧※

BIRMINGHAM:
Printed and ſold by T. Holliwell, at No. 32, in Moor-ſtreet; and J. P. Coghlan, in Duke-Street, Groſvenor-Square, LONDON.

M,DCC,LXXI.

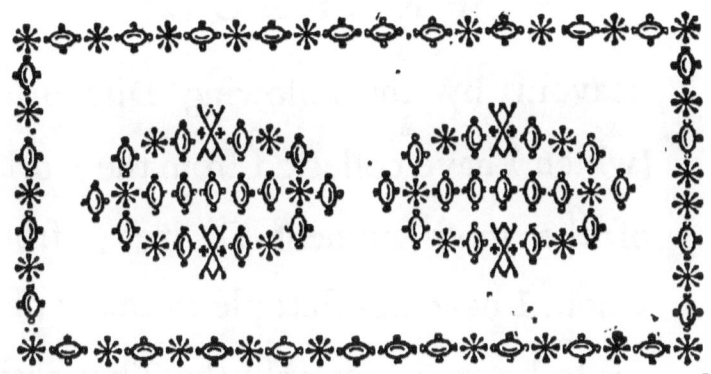

THE
PREFACE.

IF we examine into the Cause of so much Infidelity, Immorality and Wickedness, reigning in this Age; we may justly attribute it to the want of Faith, or ignorance of the Christians *Belief.* In order then to remove the Cause, or put a stop to the ruinous progress, which Immorality and Infidelity are making upon us; I shall endeavour

PREFACE.

deavour by the following Difcourfes (which I have collected from the works of the moſt eminent Divines; from whom I have not Scruple in many places to borrow, not only the Thoughts, but even the Expreſſions of ſome of them, who have treated on the like Subject) to lay before you the great and important Truths of our Chriſtian Religion; by explaining to you in the moſt eaſy, clear, and familiar manner the *Apoſtles Creed*; which is ſo called, as being generally aſcribed or attributed to the Apoſtles, as St. Ambroſe; (*a*) Rufinus; (*b*) S. Leo the great; (*c*) St. Jerome; (*d*) St. Auguſtin; (*e*) and Caſſian;

(*a*) in Serm. xxxviii. (*b*) in expoſi. Symb. Apoſt. §. 2. (*c*) in Epiſt; c. xiii, (*d*) adverſ, error, Joan, Hieroſol. Apoſt.

PREFACE.

fian ;(*f*) and innumerable other authors affirm.

But notwithstanding these primitive Vouchers; there are some who dispute whether this Creed was composed by the Apostles, before their dispersion from Jerusalem; for if so say they, how can it be imagined that St. Luke in his History of the Acts of the Apostles, would have totally omitted so considerable a Fact as this; neither can it be conceived that several Councils, and Synods, amongst the primitive Christians, or at least some of them, would in their Decisions of Faith and Doctrine, have had some reference to this Creed,

Apost. 61. Cap. 9. (e) Serm. de Temp. 115. *(f)* De Incar. Dom. L. 5.

as their ſtandard, and baſis, if any ſuch had been at that time; whereas no ſuch thing appears: Beſides if the Apoſtles had at that time really framed and delivered this Creed to their Succeſſors, then every Church would have agreed therein.

Now in anſwer to all this, it may be replied, that tho' the ancient Councils and Synods make no mention of it, yet, this is no abſolute proof, that there was not then ſuch a Creed in being; for no one can deny, but that it is very ancient and *Apoſtolical;* ſince it is certain that the greater part of it, if not all, as to the chief Articles or Subſtance thereof was compoſed by the Apoſtles, and left

left by them to their Successors, and was always made use of in Baptism from the very beginning, tho' not perhaps in the same Form as we find it at present; some parts being changed or added by the Church in opposition to certain Heresies as they sprung up.

Again we find in a Creed, which *St. Irenæus* (Bishop of Lyons, who lived in the Second Century, and was Scholar of *St. Polycarp*, the Disciple of St. John) repeats, not much unlike to ours, where he assures us that *the Church dispersed throughout the whole World, had received this Faith from the Apostles and their Disciples* (g) And *Tertullian* affirms the same in one of his Creeds, where he

(g) Lib. 1, c. ii,

he says that, that rule of Faith has been current in the Church from the beginning of the Gospel. *Hanc regulam ab initio Evangelii decucurrisse* (h). And it is very remarkable altho there was so great a diversity of Creeds, yet the Form and Substance of every Creed was in a great measure the same; so that unless there had been from the beginning of Christianity a Form or System of Faith delivered by the Apostles, it is not easy to conceive, how all Churches should agree, not only in the Articles themselves, but also in a great measure in the Method and order of them.

All that I shall farther affirm is, that this Creed, which contains the Summary,

(h) advers. Praxeam.

PREFACE.

mary, or chief Articles of the Christians Belief, has always been held in the greatest veneration in all Christian Churches, and has been generally looked upon in all Ages, to have been compiled by the Apostles themselves. The ancient Fathers and Doctors of the Catholick Church make frequent mention of it, as a sacred Depositum of Faith, which the Catholick Church received from the Apostles, or Disciples of Christ, and carefully transmitted to Posterity. " Let credit be given, says " St. Ambrose (i) to the Apostles Creed, " which the Catholick Church has al- " ways preserved and kept inviolable. " And again in his 38 Sermon, he says, " that

(i) Epist. 81. ad Siric. Pap.

PREFACE.

" that our *Faith* is comprised in the
" *Symbol* of the Apostles, who compos-
" ed it by mutual consent, that it might
" serve as a Key to exclude the Dark-
" ness of Hell, and make way for the
" light of Christ.

St. Augustin likewise asserts the same thing; " the holy Apostles, says he,
" have delivered a set form of *Faith*,
" comprised in twelve Articles which
" they called a Symbol; as being a
" Token of union amongst true belie-
" vers, and a certain Rule for the dis-
" covery, and condemnation of such
" as are misled by Heresy. (*k*)"

Cassian says that this Creed comprehends in itself, tho' in few words, " the
" Faith

(*k*) Serm. de Temp. 181.

PREFACE.

"Faith of both Testaments and the
"sense of the whole Scripture. (*l*) And
"St. Peter Chrysologus, says, that it is
"the entrance into Life, the Gate of
"Salvation; a peculiar, innocent, and
"pure Confession. (*m*) And many o-
ther such like noble Expressions were
made use of by the primitive Writers
to declare their Esteem of this Creed.

Now what I chiefly intend or design
by the following Discourses, is to explain and deliver to you the true sense
and meaning of each Article of the
Creed, and to shew what those Truths
are, which we are obliged to believe;

(*l*) De Incarn. Dom, L. 5. (*m*) In Symb. Apost. Serm. 65.

PREFACE.

and how far they ought to have an Influence over our Lives and Actions; and I shall also endeavour to defend our Christian *Belief* from any Evil or disagreeable Impression which those Blasphemous and insidious Writings (that have been published in this our present Age) might cast upon the Minds of unwary Christians; and I shall endeavour to obviate those Evils by letting them see the weakness of human *Reason* in Matters of Faith.

And if no more than one single Person should hereby receive either a Defence, Assistance, or a Comfort from this my Labour, I should then bless and praise God who made me his Instrument

of

PREFACE.

of that Good; and highly rejoice in the succefs of this my undertaking. For is it not enough to draw Tears from the Eyes of every thinking Chriftian? Who has any bowels of compaffion for his fellow Creatures, or his poor deluded Country Men, to fee fuch Floods of Infidelity daily pouring in upon us, when he knows from Truth itfelf, that he who does not believe fhall be condemned. St. Mar. c.xvi.v.16 And to fee fuch Crowds of new invented fects, and pretended Religions thrufting themfelves in among us, when he feels from his own inward Confcioufnefs, that there can be but one *Truth* or *Faith*.

Some

RREFACE.

Some of thefe, the produce in appearance, only of a diftempered Imagination, while others, more flagitious, are Herefies revived from many ages ago, then condemned, rejected, and after a time, almoft entirely obliterated, whofe very Tenets are now fcarce any where to be found, but in the Triumphant Arguments of thofe great Men, who oppofed, confuted, and filenced them,

Good God! when will thy anger ceafe! or when fhall an End be put, to this the fevereft of all thy Scourges.— But what am I faying? Let us not lofe Confidence in Him, fince it has been long ago foretold us, this was to be; and

; Cor. c. xi. v. 19.

PREFACE.

and that Men would one Day turn their Ear from Truth to Fables. Let us ^{2 Tim. c. iv. v. 4.} therefore comfort ourselves in the certain assurance, that these also shall vanish in their turn, for we are assured, that Heaven and Earth shall pass away, before one single title of God's Word. No, No! Christ has built his Church upon a ^{St. Mat. c. v. v. 18} Rock, and in spite of all the Malice of ^{St. Mat. c. xvi. v. 18} Men and Devils, the Gates of Hell shall not prevail against it.

A DIS-

A DISCOURSE
SHEWING THE
Necessity of Faith, &c.
By way of
INTRODUCTION.
Without faith it is impossible to please God. Heb. xi. 6.

AS it is a certain Truth, that *Faith* alone cannot save a man without good works, so it is no less certain that good works cannot save a man without *Faith;* this made St. Paul, in the words of my text, say, that without faith it is an impossible thing to please God.

Divis.

Before I enter on the Explanation of the Creed, it will not be improper to lay before you, *first,* The Necessity and Nature of Faith; *secondly,* The inward Properties; and, *thirdly,* The outward Requisites thereof.

P. I.

The *Necessity* of Faith is a truth so universally received, that it may seem a needless trouble to offer any thing by way of proof, but because the most obvious duties are often neglected, it will not be unseasonable in a few words to explain the Ground of this obligation; and, in the first place, the Scriptures are very distinct in pressing the necessity of faith. There we are told that *without faith it is impossible to please God;* that *he who does not believe is already judged;* that *the just man lives by faith,* with many other passages

Heb. c. xi. v. 6.
John c. iii. v. 18.
Gal. c. iii. v. 11.

passages to the same purpose. Now the reason of this obligation is, because faith is in some degrees the only way, whereby we become acquainted with the duties of the Christian Religion; and as no man can become Master of any Art or Science, unless he has beforehand obtained a sufficient knowledge of the principles from which they are derived, so unless we learn by Faith which are the respective duties of a Christian, it seems impossible to comply with them. If we proceed farther, and enquire after the more particular Reasons of this obligation, we may be informed from the nature and definition of faith. Faith in the view we here look on it may be considered in two lights, either as *an assent of the mind in yielding belief*, or as *the object or thing we believe*. In the first acceptation it imports no more than the bare assent we give to all those truths which God has revealed. In the other acceptation, it is a collection of all those Articles, both speculative and practical, which are designed to make us happy in a future Life: where we may observe that several of the truths proposed to us are Mysterious points, which appear to have no immediate relation to practice; but they give us an idea of God's greatness and incomprehensibility; they convince us of our own weakness and infirmity in being incapable of comprehending his divine Perfections; they render us humble and submissive to the Church; it being the business of a Christian, as St. Augustin says, not to dispute but believe, and obey those who are placed over us as God's representatives. Again, in regard of practical Articles, it

was

INTRODUCTORY DISCOURSE.

was highly requisite that God should reveal his will to mankind, and in what manner he would be served; for tho' we are acquainted with many things regarding a good Life, by the sole light of Reason, yet the world was become so corrupted and so blinded with ignorance, that the law of nature was almost defaced; the divine goodness therefore was pleased to revive it by a revealed Law, which should furnish us with more plain and distinct Rules of a good Life, as in effect we find them laid down both in the old and new Scriptures.

From hence we may infer, that *faith* is the only foundation of man's future Happiness. If we are ignorant, Faith is our instructor; if we are weak, Faith is our support; it is the Guide that leads us through the dangers of life, and the only thing that can improve the soil for true virtue, for without it, the soil of man's heart can produce nothing conducive to our eternal salvation. You may easily perceive, that when I urge the necessity of Faith, I mean the true Catholick Faith, delivered by Christ and his Apostles, and handed down to the present age by an uninterrupted succession; for though there are many Faiths, that is, many Sects or Religions, who lay claim to the name of *Christians*, yet as there is only *one* God, so there is only *one* Baptism, and *one* true Faith. It is not my present purpose to discuss which is the true Faith: I shall only take notice of that pernicious notion of a great many Libertines, Enemies to the Church of Christ, who wanting proofs to justify their separation, pretend it is not material what they believe, provided they live moral good Lives; because, say they, it is not a man's Faith that will save him. I own it is not Faith *alone* that will save a man, yet no man can be saved without it. To enter into any other way of thinking is to destroy the whole frame of Christianity. Christ came not into the world to establish different Faiths, or different Churches, but only one Church, and at the same time he established this Church, he prescribed Rules, both as to what was to be believed, and what was to be practised, which all were to comply with, under pain of Damnation. To say that we may believe what we please, is to destroy one half of the divine Law; for he that said Thieves, Murderers, and Adulterers, shall not enter into the kingdom of Heaven, tells us, that he who does not believe is already condemned. A person may believe several Articles of the Christian Religion, but if he does not believe all, he denies Christ to be the Author of Truth, since he equally revealed and commanded all to be believed.

Again the pretence of a good Life is altogether frivolous; for how can they lead good Lives, who deny the authority of God and his Church? One single deformity spoils the beauty of the Face, one mortal Sin destroys charity, and makes a person liable to Hell, as St. James c. ii. v. 10 assures us, *he that offends in one point, becomes guilty of all.* In the same manner to reject one Article, destroys all Faith. I own it has the appearance of a charitable Disposition to save persons of all Religions, and it is to be hoped the mercies of God extend to great numbers, where *invincible* Ignorance may take place, and no obstacle is put by a wicked Life: but these

are

are out of the cafe, I only fpeak of thofe who *knowingly*, and *willingly*, reject the Rule eftablifhed by Chrift in points of belief.

I come now to the fecond Point, which will bring more light to the matter, where it will appear by the true Properties of Faith, what is required to lay a juft claim to that divine Gift. Though there are feveral excellent properties belonging to Faith, I fhall only mention one or two, which are abfolutely neceffary to preferve its effence, and render it ferviceable to all true Believers. The one is an humble Mind; the other is a lively Apprehenfion of the truth of what we believe. The Humility required is nothing elfe, but the fubmiffion we pay to Almighty God, and to the Authority he has eftablifhed on earth to recommend and explain the Articles of our Belief: A behaviour fo conformable to the holy Scriptures that wherever they make mention either of Faith in general, or any particular Functions belonging to it, they are always preffed upon mankind as a Duty belonging to Humility, and Obedience. This was the notion St. Paul had of Faith, which he frequently inculcates in his Epiftle to the Romans, and calls the converfion both of Jews and Gentiles *an obedience to faith*, fignifying upon all occafions, that Errors and Herefies were the effect of Pride, and Difobedience: and the fame Apoftle where he gives the Reafon of this humble and fubmiffive behaviour, tells us, that, *faith is the argument of things not appearing*, and a means of *bringing into captivity all underftanding unto the obedience of Chrift*. Wherein we are not to depend upon the wit, knowledge, wifdom, or experience of men,

P. II.

Heb. c. xi. v. 1.
2. Cor. c. x. v. 5.

men, but upon the Power, Authority, and Promises of God, who has appointed Persons to govern his Church, and pronounce upon all religious Controversies to the same effect, as if he himself personally stood among them. This is the teachable disposition so much extolled by our blessed Saviour, when he reprehended St. Thomas for his incredulity. *Because thou hast seen me, Thomas, thou hast believed, blessed are they that have not seen, and have believed.*

<small>John c. xx. v 29.</small>

But there are still other Circumstances to be considered, which are a farther Proof of the Necessity of an humble and obedient behaviour in matters of Faith. What idea can you form of those great Mysteries that are proposed to the Faithful, and inserted in the Creed? Who can conceive a Being infinite as to duration without either beginning or end? How all things could be made of nothing? With the several Mysteries of the Trinity, Incarnation, Passion, Resurrection, and other points of our belief, which surpassing our Reason, we must forbear being too inquisitive, or asking how? Or why? But humbly submit to the Authority of the Revealer, and the methods he has left to keep the belief alive. And indeed considering the weakness of man's Capacity, it is the highest Presumption imaginable to think of bringing the divine Perfections, and the Mysteries of Religion within the compass of our poor Understanding. We who are at a stand, and obliged to acknowledge the insufficiency of Reason when we pretend to enquire into the secrets of Nature; we who are baffled and struck dumb in every trivial enquiry about the objects of our Senses; we who are subject to so many mistakes

takes and Errors in the common occurrences of Life, how can we pretend to penetrate into the hidden Mysteries of Heaven, or hope to conclude them within our scanty Notions? I appeal to the most ingenious, and greatest wit of the present or past Ages, what account they can give of the nature of man's Soul? Of it's surprising union with the Body? Of the divisibility of Matter? Of the magnitude, composition, and motion of the Sun, Moon, and Stars? Of the ebbing and flowing of the Sea? The attracting qualities of the Loadstone? And a thousand other Mysteries of Nature? Are we not obliged to humble ourselves upon these Enquiries? Are we not puzzled and forced to confess our Ignorance, when we consider the products of the Creation? Every Insect that crawls on the Earth, every Herb that grows in the Fields, every Flower that adorns our Garden, every Bird that flies in the Air, every Fish that swims in the Water, every Fly that sticks in our Window, the Bee, the Ant, and Spider proclaim our Ignorance, when we set about to enquire into their Nature, Structure, Properties, and Effects. If we are at a loss in contemplating these seemingly contemptible Creatures, what likelihood is there of comprehending the sublime Mysteries of Religion?

'Tis true, our Reason suggests that there is a God or supreme Being, but if we proceed much farther, we wade beyond our depth, we have but a very confused Knowledge of the infinite Perfections that belong to the Deity. It is here we must humble ourselves; it is here we must submit our Judgment; it is here we must rely entirely on the Authority of God, who has revealed such

Mysteries,

INTRODUCTORY DISCOURSE.

Mysteries, and upon the Authority of those who are commissioned by him to explain them, that they may not be misrepresented by false Glosses, and Interpretations of private Reason. I am not ignorant of what a great many (who call themselves *Christians*) do often alledge against the Submission which is due to the Church in Mysteries of Faith; they pretend it is renouncing their Reason, which God has bestowed upon man for his Guide; and so traduce it with the name of *implicit faith*, blind Obedience, and pinning their Faith upon another man's sleeve. But these are all suggestions of the Devil, in favour of Licentiousness and Error. I own God has provided mankind with Reason for his Direction both in Civil, and Religious Matters: But then it is often blinded and seduced by Passion, and carried out of the way by human considerations. I do not deny the use of Reason even in the case of Mysteries; for what is more conformable to Reason, than to believe God in things that are above our Reason? What is more conformable to Reason, than to submit to the highest Authority on Earth, supported by the strongest Arguments, and Motives, in opposition to private Authority, or private Reason? A contrary way of proceeding brings nothing but confusion both in Church and State, and a down-right Anarchy in all Societies. Reason is our Guide as well in Civil, as Religious Matters; Shall therefore every private Person, or Subaltern branch of a Community, upon pretence of following their Reason, withdraw themselves from the Obedience that is due to the Supreme civil Power? No, the Consequences are too pernicious to insist upon any such Plea.

Providence

Providence has provided againſt Inconveniences in one Caſe, by eſtabliſhing a Power without appeal in Temporal Controverſies, and Chriſt has conferred a Power upon his Church to avoid Inconveniences in the other.

As for blind Obedience, implicit Faith, and pinning our Faith to another man's ſleeve, where is the abſurdity of ſuch a Submiſſion when terms are rightly underſtood? Does not all this happen when private Reaſon is obliged to ſubmit to public Authority in Controverſies of a civil kind? Reaſon is at Liberty to perform her Functions when ſhe approves of thoſe Arguments which are brought to confirm the Myſteries of Religion in general; but it is an abuſe of Reaſon either to reject ſuch Myſteries becauſe they are above a Man's private Reaſon or Conception, or not to ſubmit to that Authority which is empowered to enforce a Belief. Is not our Faith implicit, when no explicit Conception can be had of the Myſteries we believe?

As to pinning our Faith upon another Man's ſleeve, the meaning of the Words muſt be, that we are not to hear the Church, which Chriſt has recommended, and obliged us to adhere to, or otherwiſe to be looked upon as Heathens, and Publicans. On the other hand, whoſe ſleeve do they pin their Faith upon, who follow their own Opinion in oppoſition to God's Authority, and make their own Fancy, the Rule of expounding his Law? A Method which plainly ſhews they want Humility, and have thrown off that Obedience which St. Paul requires in all thoſe who pretend to be Members of God's Church.

What I have said hitherto, is sufficient to demonstrate that Humility and Submission of Judgment, is requisite to be esteemed a Christian; another inward Property of Faith, is to make a good Christian, which is not only to believe; but to believe with a strong and lively Faith; when we speak of strength with regard to human Bodies, those are said to be strong, who are able to bear heavy Burdens; if we speak of the Mind, those are said to be strong Reasoners, who having laid a Foundation of good Principles. draw such Consequences as naturally follow from them; and when we speak of the strength of Faith, it is said to be strong, when the assent we give to the Truth of our Religion, so enlivens our Behaviour, as to influence every Action to the purposes for which it was designed. It is this strength of Faith which is so frequently recommended in the holy Scriptures under several Figures, and by several Instances of it's prevailing Power. Faith is that small Seed, which grows up into a large and spreading Tree; It is that handful of Leaven, which seasoned the whole Mass of Bread; Faith is that Shield which St Paul advices all the Faithful to cover themselves with in the time of Temptation; It was by Faith, that Abraham was encouraged to Sacrifice his only Son, in opposition to the promise of a numberless Issue (which in all appearance depended entirely upon the preservation of his Life) as knowing and believing with a Strong Faith, that God was able to make good his Promise by raising him to Life again, as St.

Heb. c. xi. v. 19.
Paul seems to say. In fine it is by the same strength of Faith, that our Blessed Saviour assures

sures us we may be enabled to remove Mountains, and perform any other miraculous Work, which is out of the reach of natural Causes: But as these are uncommon Experiments of the Strength of Faith, let us consider what force it ought to have in the common Duties of a Christian.

To this purpose, we may compare it to a Master Wheel upon which all the rest depend in their Motion; for if this be out of order, all the rest must of necessity move irregularly. In like manner, if Faith (which is the Foundation of all other Christian Duties) is defective in it's Influence, all the other concurring Duties, which ought to contribute towards Man's Happiness, will be in a languishing Condition. But if our Faith be strong and lively, the work is carried on with all imaginable Hopes of Success. It clears our Understanding, it discovers the Infirmities of our corrupt Nature, and force of Divine Grace; It inclines the Will to embrace all the methods of the Gospel, and gives a Singular relish to Duty. In a word, it makes us go on with Speed, and play as it were with the Burdens of Life, while our Eyes are continually fixed upon the Pleasures of a future State.

On the other hand, what is it but the Weakness of Faith, that occasions the present feeble State of Christianity? We glory in the Title of being Christians, and part of Christ's Church, above those that are out of the Pale of the Church; but how does it appear by the strength of our Faith, that we have any advantage over Heathens? The Heathens reproach us very deservedly, with an inconsistency of Behaviour:

Did you believe, say they, that Eternal Punishments and Rewards, were the Consequences of a Good and Bad life, you must be more then mad Men to live in the Manner you do. All that we can say by way of Excuse (but it is far from an Excuse) is, that we have Faith, tho' a weak and languishing Faith, as it is indeed, a Faith that has no influence upon our Behaviour; a Faith unprofitable to ourselves, and scandalous to our Neighbour. Let none therefore value themselves for the advantages of their Faith, unless they are better qualified to recommend it by Practice. We daily see a great many express their Zeal with remarkable warmth in maintaining the Tenets of their Religion against all opposers, but they can quietly pass over any indignity offered to Almighty God in the way of Practice. They have not Patience to hear any of the Articles of their Belief run down and exposed to ridicule; and yet they stick not to attack all those Articles by their immoral Lives. They Scruple not to disobey the Church, whose Authority they otherwise maintain, to affront those Ministers whose Character they look upon to be Divine, and are as careless in other Duties of Religion, as if they had not the least Belief in them.

Take a view therefore of Faith as it is serviceable to the Ends for which it was designed; as you are humble in Submitting to the Judgment of the Church, Shew the like Submission, when you are called upon to practise what you believe. If Faith be necessary to make you a Christian, a strong and lively Faith is necessary to make you a *good* Christian; were
Faith

INTRODUCTORY DISCOURSE.

Faith languishes, all other Duties are carelesly performed; a lively Faith solves all Objections, removes all Difficulties, and comes off victorious in every Temptation. The Saints never went to battle without their Armour, and whatever they did, was done with a lively Faith.

P. III

The last point we have to consider, are the outward requisites to Faith; which in general is a Life conformable to what we believe as to all the practical Duties of Religion. If we examine the tendency of those false Doctrines, which have been propagated by Hereticks, since the first establishment of Christianity, we shall find, that tho' they were set on foot with plausible Pretence of reforming Errors, and redressing Abuses, yet they always favoured Licentiousness, and tended to the corruption of Men's Morals. This never appeared more visibly, than when those Errors were spread a broad concerning Merit, and good Works; for by extolling Faith, and ascribing Merit to it *alone*, it plainly appeared to be a Stratagem of the Devil, in order to have the practical Duties of Religion neglected.

Now, tho' it is an unquestionable Truth, that the Life of a Christian ought to be conformable to his Belief, yet considering the irregular Lives of a great many Christians, they act as if they were really of Opinion that Faith *alone* was Sufficient without good Works. What I have to suggest in order to cure this common Error in Behaviour, may be collected from what the holy Scriptures have declared in the Case from the Nature and Properties of Faith, from the Exigency of the thing itself, and from the Punishment nifhment thofe are threatened with, whofe Lives are contrary to their Belief.

Our Bleffed Saviour in the firft place, tells us, that *not every one that fays Lord Lord, fhall enter into the Kingdom of Heaven, but only thofe that do the Will of the Father;* That he, who intends to *enjoy Life everlafting, muft keep the Commandments;* That befides believing in Chrift, we muft endeavour to follow his Example. St Paul in like manner, tho' he greatly extolls Faith and excludes fuch Works from juftification, as proceeding from Nature or the old Law, yet fpeaking of the good Works enjoined by the Law of Chrift, he talks in a different manner, and conftantly requires good Works effential to man's juftification, *for it is not the hearers of the Law, but the doers that fhall be juftified;* He tells us alfo, that there is a kind of falfe nominal Chriftians, who believe and confefs there is a God, but deny him by their Actions; and St. Peter advifes all Perfons to make fure their Election by good Works. But no one is more diftinct in defcending into particulars than St. James, who wrote an Epiftle that was defigned to fhew the Neceffity of good Works, and the Infignificancy of Faith, when they are neglected; He diftinguifhes two forts of Faith, a living Faith, and a dead Faith; one vain and idle, the other a working and beneficial Faith. At the fame Time, St Paul declares that, tho' we fhould have all Faith, and fo ftrong, as even to remove Mountains, yet without Charity and good Works, it would avail us nothing. Shew me, fays St. James thy Faith, by thy Works;

Mat. c. vii. v. 21.

Mat. c. xix. v. 17

Rom. c. ii. v. 13

Ep. Jam. c. ii.

Works; thou fayeft thou believeft, don't the Devils alfo believe and tremble?

Again, if we confider Faith, as it is enjoined by the Gofpel, and as a Duty regarding a good Life, what does it import? It is an Application to the *practical* parts, as well as a Belief of the *Speculative* parts of Religion, and an Omiffion in either kind, deprives us of the Bleffings of the Gofpel. Hence a true Believer is compared to a Steward, who is to give up his Accounts; to a Merchant, who is to multiply and increafe his Stock; to thofe, who labour in a Vineyard, and fuch like Perfons, where a bare Knowledge of one's Duty without Application is infignificant, goes unrewarded, and demonftrates them to be only half Chriftians: And indeed the nature of the thing itfelf declares this Conformity of Belief and Behaviour. There is no Art or Science whatever, that can bring any Profit to the pretender, without applying the Rules that are prefcribed; and can we imagine, that Religion is only a Scheme of idle Notions to be gazed upon, and never reduced to practice? Confider the Threats that are pronounced againft thofe, who conform not their Lives to their Belief, and you will be convinced of the ftrict Account, that is to be given, and that Punifhments will be propottioned according to the neglect; it being juft and reafonable, that fuch as have been favoured with more Opportunities of practifing their Religion, fhould meet with a Chaftifement suitable to their Offence. Thefe Threats are fignified plainly in the Gofpel by thofe Words of our Bleffed Saviour; *Wo be to thee Corazain, Wo to thee Bethfaida;* Mat. c. xi. v. 21.

saida; for if in Tyre and Sidon had been wrought the Miracles that have been wrought in you, they had long ago done penance in Sack-cloth and Ashes.---It shall be more tolerable for the land of Sodom in the Day of Judgment, than for thee. The impartiality of the Divine justice requires this kind of Punishment, for as there is an equality of Capacities, and Conveniences, so there is of Punishments and Rewards. Sins of Ignorance are not to be considered in the same way, as those that are attended with more aggravating Circumstances, where Neglect, Disrespect, Ingratitude, and Contempt are thrown into the Scales, infinitely to the disadvantage of those, who have been favoured with peculiar Blessings.

v. 24.

In this Glass, the Libertine, the tepid Christian, nay even the strictest Livers, may take a view of themselves, and be struck with Confusion, when they consider, what it is they profess, and what it is they have practised; how much they have promised at their Baptism, and how little they have performed? It is an unspeakable Blessing to be a Member of the Church of God, and to be provided with all the helps it affords to make us Happy: But do you imagine, that God does not require from us a suitable return? If many whole Nations are still intangled in the Errors of Idolatry; if the Jews have still a Veil over their Eyes; certainly God requires from us performances answerable to the Advantages we enjoy above them, and that we give the same Test of our Faith, which the primitive Christians produced, when they demonstrated the Truth of their Religion by the Innocence of their Lives: But

now

INTRODUCTORY DISCOURSE.

now it is much to be feared the Rule will not hold, for there is very little difference in outward appearance between many true Believers and Heathens, as to their Morals; are not their Hearts equally bent upon the World? Do they not give the same Liberty to their Tongues in Lying, Swearing, Backbiting, Detracting, Slandering, and in idle, profane, obscene Discourse? Is the truth of our Religion discoverable this way, or rather do not we join with Persons of all Religions in Scandalous Practises? Since therefore, we profess ourselves Christians, let us resolve to be so in fact, let us endeavour to edify and convince all of the Truth of our Faith by a consistency of Behaviour; by these means, our Faith will become useful, and entitle us to the Reward promised in the next Life.

ARTICLE,

ARTICLE, I.

DISCOURSE, I.

I believe in God, the Father Almighty, Creator of Heaven and Earth.

To us there is but one God, the Father, of whom are all things. 1. *Cor. c.* viii. *v.* 6.

THE Sum of the Christian Faith is taught in the Apostles Creed, which I shall now begin to explain to you. Here, Dear Christians, you will find Sublime Truths concerning the Being, and Nature of God; concerning the high Mystery of God made Man; concerning the Mission of the Holy Ghost; The Establishment of a Church; The Sublime Truths of an other World; and the Mystery of Eternal Life. This short Sum of Christian Doctrine, without exaggeration, is more worth than all the Philosophers ever wrote; because

because it teaches that one Science, without which, all Science is nothing, and which no other Science teaches, viz. the Science of Eternal Life.

The Divis. The first Article of the Creed, is the Subject of this Discourse; but as this Article is too much for one Discourse, I shall therefore divide it in two parts, the first, viz. *I believe in God*, shall make up this Discourse, wherein, I will *first* explain to you what is meant by these words *I believe*, and *secondly* prove to you, that there is a God, from whom all things proceed, and that there is but *one* only God. and no more; lastly I shall inform you of the Nature and Attributes of God.

Now, as the Creed contains the principal points of our Faith, so the first Article, *I believe in God*, is the principal Point of the Creed, the first Foundation of Faith, and Ground of all Truth, all Religion, and Virtue. It is called the Apostles Creed, (*a*) because, according to the ancient Tradition of all past Ages, it was first composed by the twelve Apostles, at the time of their Dispersion, when, by a Persecution raised against them at Jerusalem, they seperated themselves in order to go and preach the Christian Faith throughout all Nations. Then they, by common agreement, made a Creed containing the Faith they were going to preach, that all, in different parts of the World, might teach *one* Faith, and all Christians have *one* Belief, as there is but *one* God, and *one* Faith, as St. Paul says. (*b*)

(*a*) vide Rub in. Exp.Sym. boli. St. Ambrose Serm. 38. et St Aug. Serm. 181 de temp. St. Irenæus L. 1. adverf. hære, Valenti, c. 2.

(*b* Ephes. c. 4. v. 5.

But, before I enter upon the Substance of this Article, it will be necessary to consider a little

little what is meant by the Words *I believe*, which have so much relation to the whole Creed in general; for altho' these words are mentioned no more than twice, yet they are understood in the several parts of it, and virtually to be expressed not only to every distinct Article, but even where an Article consists of several Parts, to each of those also: Thus as we say, we *believe* in God, we say also in Effect, we *believe in Jesus Christ;* we *believe* that he is the only Son of God; we *believe* that he is our Lord; we *believe* that he was conceived by the Holy Ghost, and so on.

To believe, is to assent to the Truth of any Proposition, either on the Authority of the Assertor, or on the probability of the Thing itself. You must observe, that Faith is divided into *Human* and *Divine*: *Human* Faith, is an assent to any Proposition on the Testimony of Man; *Divine* Faith is an assent on the Testimony of God, founded upon Divine Authority; so that in matters of Divine Faith, when a Christian says, I *believe*, he does not mean *I think so, I judge so*, or *I am of such an Opinion*, but I am fully persuaded, and do really and firmly assent to the Truth of such and such Propositions, through a full reliance on the Veracity, Testimony, and Revelation of God, and the Declaration of his Church; and this is absolutely necessary in the Case before us; *for Flesh and Blood hath not revealed* (c) *unto us those Truths* to which we give our solemn Assent in the Creed; *neither received we it of Man, neither were we taught it, but by the Revelation of Jesus Christ.* (d) The first Point of this Creed is to believe, that

(c) Mat. c. xvi. v. 17.

(d) Gal. c. i. v. 12.

there

P. I. there is a God, by which Term, we underſtand, one eternal. independent, ſelf exiſtent Being; who was without Beginning, and will be without End; from whom proceed all things.

This is the Foundation of Faith, according to the Maxim of St. Paul, that *he who thinks to approach God, muſt firſt believe that he is, and that he is the rewarder of thoſe who ſeek him.* (e) To deny the being of a God, was never a prevailing Error, it is ſo very abſurd, that of all Paradoxes, that could be advanced, it is the moſt contradictory to the common Notions of Senſe, and Reaſon to imagine, that this World, and all things therein, and every Man himſelf, came here by Chance. Let a man but conſult his Senſes, let him liſten to them, and they will all combine to evince, and illuſtrate this great, and ſolemn Truth of the Exiſtence of a Deity; The Light proclaims it to the Eye, Thunder to the Ear, Heat and Cold ſpeak it to the Touch, Food to the Palate, and Odours to the Noſtril, in a Word, every thing we ſee, hear, feel, taſte, or ſmell, is full of God. (f) If we turn our Eyes upwards, and behold the vaſt, and beautiful Frame of the Heavens, and the ſhining Orbs therein daily rolling on in an orderly and undiſturbed Courſe, this alone demonſtrates to us a Supreme Being, who made, rules, and governs thoſe different Bodies; for as holy David ſays; *The Heavens ſhew forth the glory of God, and the Firmament declareth the work of his Hands,* (g)

Return your Eyes to the Earth, and behold her covered with an endleſs variety of Herbs, Fruits, and Flowers; obſerve the birth and progreſs

(e) Heb. c. xi. v. 6

(f) Rom. c. i. v. 20

(g) Pſ. 18. v. 1.

progefs of the vegetable World ; follow the rifing and defcending Sap, and mark the opening Leaf and Bud; afk who cloathed the Lilly with a beauty, which all the fplendor of Solomon could not equal; behold a beautiful Difplay of every thing upon her extenfive Surface, and ftill each individual appropriated to it's Ufe; *Grafs for the Cattle, and herb for the Service of Men. Corn for the Support, and Grapes, and Wine for the joy and Comfort of his Life*. (*h*) (*h*)Ps. ciii. v. 4. 5.

Confider next the Animal World ; behold, how you yourfelf are made, trace Life through all her fecret fprings, follow the circulating Blood along the Veins, and liften to your beating Heart ; watch the Starts and Sallies of your Imagination, and meditate with wonder on the Operation of your Soul, then fay, why are all thefe things thus? Whence do they proceed? To pretend to fay that they come by *Chance, Neceffity,* or *Atoms,* is a Refource unworthy any, but, the weak, and wicked Wretch; who would perfuade himfelf into the Belief of fuch a Syftem, as is beft fuited to his own apprehenfions. Hence then, we muft naturally refer to one only, firft, and fupreme Caufe, and that is God; *in whom, and through whom all things do live, move, and have their Being*. (*i*) None ever denied the Being of a God, but Libertines, Profligates, and Fugitives of human Laws, as well as of Divine Providence, whofe Crimes had fo vifibly prejudiced them againft God, that all plainly faw, it was the juft Fear of his Judgments, and no other Argument, made them deny his Being. (*i*)Acts c. xvii. v. 28.

As to the Heathens, the moft Idolatrous, and moft Superftitious, even whilft they worfhiped falfe false Gods without number, never lost the Notion of the true one; a Notion so deeply imprinted, that Superstition itself could not wear it out, for whenever a Man fell under a great distress, which no false God could relieve, their Hands were still lifted up to Heaven crying out, God help me. Their wise Men (called the Ancient Philosophers) by the help of Philosophy alone, carried the Notion of a God as high, as Reason could go, and wrote nothing low, or degenerate of the Divine Nature, and Attributes, but they knew so much of the true God, as to ascribe to that Blessed Nature, all that was Wise, Good, Great, or Happy; calling him Author of Wisdom, Author of Truth, Merciful, Kind, and Beneficient to Men: True, and worthy names of God: But these Men, tho' they knew God, did not Glorify him as God. And certain it is, that Men and Nations, were once so blind, as to adore Stocks and Stones, the Sun, Moon, and Stars, dead Men, and other Deities not worth mentioning; never worshiping him from whom all good is derived, living strangers to God, or as St. Paul has it, *without a God in this World;* (*k*) for he, that lives without the true God, is truly without a God, and what is Man without God? Man without God, is not even Man, for without God, all is either Nothing, or Misery; for Happiness, is a contradiction in Nature without God. This was the misfortune of many great and powerful Nations, and is still so to some; But in their Misfortune, let us Dear Christians, know our own Happiness, who not only know God, but know him by clear Revelation, and miraculous

(*k*) Eph. c. ii. v. 12.

lous Works, and visible Effects of his Power; who know him by signal Marks of Favour and Grace; which Knowledge is worth all other Knowledge besides; for from this, all our good begins, from this first, and greatest Blessing, and which, if thoroughly improved, is Eternal Life; only take heed of that Sin of the Ancient Philosophers, left knowing God, you should not Glorify him as God.

Now from what has been said, it plainly appears that there is a God, or Supreme Being, who rules and governs us and all Things; this Nature alone tells us, the Pagan Philosophers themselves confessed and acknowledged it, and it is a Thing so manifest, that the Scripture tells us that *none but Fools deny it.* (*l*)   [*l*] Pſ. 13 or 14. v. 1 P. II.

I come now to my Second Point, which concerns the Unity of God. By this Article of the Creed, we do not only believe the existence of a God, but we also profess, that there is but *one* God; for we do not say, *I believe in Gods*, but *in God*, the Singular Number, which signifies *Unity* or *one* God.* That there is, or can be, but one God, who is the Sovereign Lord of all Things *visible*, and *invisible*; who gave all

---

* The Pagans and Heathens, and some blasphemous Hereticks, denied the Unity of God; In the *Greek*, and Ancient *Latin* Creeds, we read, *I believe in One God:* in opposition to the *Valentinians, Cordonians, Marcionites*, &c. Who introduced a plurality of Gods, and St. *Irenæus*, assures us, they were the Disciples and Successors of that first grand Heretick Simon Magus,—*Omnes Simonis Samaritani Magi Discipuli et Successores Sunt. Lib.* 1. *C.* 30. ——Some of them asserted two coeval and coexistant Principles,

Things their Birth, and on whom they entirely depend, is evident, and appears in the very firſt Thought, or Conception of the Deity ; for it being the eſſential *Property*, I may ſay, the *Specifick* Attribute of God, to include in Himſelf the whole *Plenitude of Being*, and all manner of Perfection as in it's native Center: It is plain that nothing can be, but as an emanation of this eſſential Being, nor ſhare in the leaſt Perfection, but as communicated from this original ſource: So that to conceive any Object remote, and independent, or to imagine an Equal really divided, or in Nature diſtinct, would be to annihilate the Notion of a Deity, and no'leſs a contradiction, than to conceive an irrational Man, or a rational Brute; beſides, if he was not the only one, he would not be the Sovereign of all, his Empire would not be abſolute, nor his Dominion Univerſal, ſince a Competitor would have a right to diſpute with him, if not the Superiority, or the Preheminence,

Principles, *viz. God* and *Matter ;* from which Syſtem as *Tertullian* very juſtly obſerves, they really made two Gods. The reaſon which induced *Hermogenes* to embrace this Opinion, was that puzzling Queſtion, ſo famous in the primitive Church Πόθεν τὸ κακὸν, that is, from whence was Evil? For he being unwilling to make God the Author of Evil, and withal imagining it to be a Subſtantial Nature, and to have an Original Cauſe ſuitable thereunto, therefore in order that he might throw the Source and Origin of it upon another, he affirmed *Matter to be a natural Evil Principle*, coeternal with God, who was contrary thereunto, from whence all other Evil had its Riſe, and Origin; ſo that they believed there were two Gods, the one, *a good God*, the other, an *evil God*, who was the Creator of the World, the Giver of the Law, and the Cauſe and Author of all Evil.

at

at least, an Equality and Independence, and if we conceive them as different Beings, this difference would be either in Something, or in Nothing, if in Nothing, they would be the same; if in Something, the other would not be infinite; but want the different Quality. Hence, *Tertullian* says, that a Multiplicity of Gods is the destruction of them, that is to say, destroys the very Notion of a God; and again, if God is not *one*, he is not God. For seeing that under the Notion of a God, we necessarily include the Supreme and Sovereign Good, which is the source and Fountain of all created Beings; it follows, that he is essentially *one*, because no more than one absolutely Supreme. no more than one independent prime Author of Things, on whom all Things depend, in Nature can be. For what is absolutely Supreme, can admit of no Rival; and what entirely depends on *One*, is necessarily independent of any other, in the same way of dependence, that is, whatever depends on God, as the first or total Cause of his Being, cannot depend on another Cause of the same Rank; and the reason is, because then it would owe it's Subsistence equally and totally to both, which implies a Contradiction. Besides what is divided in many, is imperfect in all; neither can there be an equality in one, without a lessening in the other, because Equality speaks an Independency, and where there is a thing independent of the original Supreme Sovereign Being, its Power and extensive Dominion is restrained, and consequently it ceases to be what it is supposed to be, that is, absolutely Supreme, Infinite, All-sustaining, and

Tertull.
L.1.adver
Marcionem.

E 2 in

in a Word, Indivisible, Incommunicable, and Inimitable.

This natural Truth of the Unity of God is confirmed by the Authority of holy Writ, which, almost in every Page, makes mention of one God, the Supreme Ruler of Heaven and Earth; hence, Moses says, *hear O Israel, the Lord our God is one*.(*d*) And David thus says, *thou art God alone*, (*e*) And in the Book of Wisdom we read thus, *For there is no other God but thou.* (*f*) *who hast care of all.* And St. Paul says, *that there is no God but one.* (*g*) And in his Epistle to the Ephesians, he says, there is but *one God, one Faith, one Baptism.* (*h*) For this Reason, it is set down as a first Principle of Religion, and as the Basis of all Moral Virtue. *Thou shalt not have strange Gods before me*, that is, thou shalt have no other Gods but me.(*i*) Before I close this Point, it will not be improper to put you in mind of the Wording of this Article; for by saying, *I believe in God*, we do not thereby only own His Existence, and credit the Truth of his Words; but we moreover signify, that we put our Trust in him, and that we love, and seek Him, as our chiefest Good and last End.

(*d*) Deut. c. vi. v. 4.
(*e*) Pf. lxxxv. 10.
(*f*) Sap. c. xii. v. 13.
(*g*) 1 Cor. c. viii v. 4
(*h*) Eph. c. iv. v. 5.

(*i*) Exod. c. xx. v. 3

P. III. It will not suffice, that we believe a God, but we must also believe rightly of Him, we must entertain reverent and worthy Conceptions of Him; ascribing to him, and to him alone, certain Powers and Prerogatives, Incommunicable to, and Incompatible with every other Nature, which therefore, we call the Divine Attributes. These are high Matters for Reason and Discourse, but I design to confine them

them within the Holy Scriptures, for no Man should prefume to know any farther of God, than what he has been pleafed to reveal of himfelf, either in his Words, or his Works.

St. Jerome takes notice, that God is called by many different Names in the Hebrew text of Scripture, which different Names exprefs each a Divine Perfection. One of thefe Hebrew Names call Him the *Strong,* another *Providence,* another *God of Sabboth,* or *Lord of Hofts,* another abfolute *Lord,* another *moſt high,* another *moſt munificent,* but the greateſt Name of all is this; *I am who am,* (*k*) this was the Name, God gave himfelf, when he fent Mofes to lead the Ifraelites out of Captivity.

(*k*) Exod. c. iii. v. 14.

To begin therefore on this Matter, the firſt Attribute of God, and which expreſſes moſt of the Divine Nature, is the Name, God gave Himfelf, when he faid, *I am who am,* the other Divine Attributes, which we know from Scripture, are as follows. *Omnipotent, Provident, Merciful, Good, Kind,* and *Beneficent* to Men, *Juſt, All-Seeing,* the *Moſt-Holy, Immutable, Immenſe, Infinite,* and *Eternal.*

Firſt, the Name which God gave himfelf, *I am who am,* fignifies, that God is a Being, the Being of Beings; being independent, cauſed by no other, and Caufe of all others, a Being of Beings, is all that can be expreſſed, all Good, all Happy, all Joy, all Comfort, all Sweetnefs, all Pleafure, all Delight, all that is Wife, Happy, Great, Good, Juſt, Powerful, *above all that is, or can be conceived, and all that is not conceivable,* all that is defirable, and all that fatisfies defire, all that is admired, and all that

that is admirable, all that Truth can tell, all that Wifdom can know. It is evident, that the Being of Beings, is all this, and infinitely more. But here I am quite loft, and Words lofe their Signification when we fpeak of God ; it is enough for us to know, that God is abfolutely all; and this one Thought of God, has more of Comfort, than all Creatures together can afford, nor would I part with this one Thought of God for all this World : This is the Folly of Men, to divide their Hearts among fo many Creatures, and leave Him, who is abfolutely all; and by one mortal Sin to lofe this *all*, and that forever.

Next, God is *Omnipotent*, that is, all Powerful, or an unlimitted Power of effecting every thing according to his own Will and Pleafure. Again we confider God as *Providence*. The Providence of God, is his all feeing Knowledge, and all difpofing Wifdom, and all executing Will and Power, by which He governs the World ; but with a particular regard to human Affairs, allotting to all Men their Portion of Adverfity and Profperity, their Portion of Health and Sicknefs, of Comforts and Sorrows, of the Goods and Evils of this Life. This Providence of God brings all good to pafs, and permits all Evil, but does none, it turns all Evil either to the good of Juftice, or Mercy; fo that this Divine Providence in human Affairs is double, one Providence of *Juftice*, and another of *Mercy ;* all thofe, who are obedient to its Commands and co-operate with its Will, and Defigns, are under the Providence of *Mercy*, that Providence which is good

to

to Men, which preserves from Harms, both of Soul and Body, and makes all turn and co-operate to their Good; but all those, who are rebellious and Fugitives of the *good Providence*, viz. all the Wicked, are under the Providence of *Justice*, which either punishes, or forsakes, and frowns upon them. All Men are under one of these Providences, and it is impossible for any one to escape, for if he falls out of one Hand of Providence, he drops into the other. *Providence* again, has a double design, one to bring all to the End of Nature, and to keep on the Government of the World: Another to direct Things to the good of Religion and Supernatural Ends; acting with high designs, which is one Cause, that makes so many deep Secrets in Providence, and its ways unsearchable. There is a *Providence* even in the Direction of Brutes; a *Providence* over the World, a *Providence* over every Man, and a great *Providence* over States and Kingdoms; but the greatest of all over the *just*. It is by this *Providence*, Families rise, and Men manage wisely, and succeed, Harm is kept off, and every Man's Life, which has a Thousand Dependences, is preserved by a Thousand Providences. In a word, there are deep Secrets in Providence, as well as in Nature, it's Mazes are intricate, and full of windings, and all within the Circle of Goodness, Justice, and Equity. But why do the *wicked* often prosper, and the *just* suffer; some Reasons for this are plain. First, it is the nature of Goodness to make His Sun shine upon the Bad, as well as the Good: Secondly, some Tempers are won to Virtue by Sweetness, and
the

the greatness of God's Blessings. Thirdly, one Wicked Man is permitted to prosper, in order to punish another; and one Kingdom to flourish, to punish the Sins of another; and another to rise in it's turn to pull down that; God often makes the Wicked execute Judgment on the Wicked. Fourthly, God is like an indulgent Father, he trains up his Children the Just, by all the Arts of suffering, to make them hard and proof for Labour and heroick Deeds; to kill the Seeds of corrupt Nature, to perfect Patience, and work an Eternal Weight of Glory, all their sufferings turning into Virtue; and so the scourge turns into a Blessing; these are Reasons we know, but there are many other we do not.

Moreover, God is *just* in distributing Rewards and Punishments; just in making all Men suffer, what others have suffered by them. *Justice* in God, is a Will to repair the order of *Justice*, prejudiced by our Sins; This Justice, is sometimes called Anger, but, properly speaking, there is no Passion in God, but all is a calm Tranquility, for God, is so high above Creatures and their Injuries, that whatever passion he seems to put on, he still preserves his Enemies, and our Sins neither afflict, or tire him; his Anger is nothing but Justice. Now the Nature of Justice, is first, to leave no Sin unpunished, which *Mercy* has not pardoned; Secondly, to patronise all the Just; Thirdly, not to be swayed, or ever turn from the right. Such is the great Attribute of Justice, in whose Scale we are all to be weighed; but remember Dear Christians, that those, who both offend against

against *Justice*, and despise or neglect *Mercy* offered, will at last sustain the Punishment both of angry *Justice* and injured *Mercy*.

Again, God is *allseeing* or *omniscient*, that is, knows all Things; He is all Eye and Light even in Darkness, and sees the very secrets of Men's Hearts, which is often the greatest kind of Darkness, He foreknows and sees Men's wills, tho' never so disagreeing, the past and future are present to him; and all our Sins, tho' past, and future, are as present to God as they were the very moment we committed them; for properly speaking, God cannot be said to remember or forget; only one thing, God is said to forget, viz. Men's Sins that are repented of.

Next, God is *most high*; first, He is high in his Nature, secondly, in his Knowledge, thirdly, He is high in Majesty and Dominion; for all is His; lastly, He is high in Habitation, whose Throne is above all height.

Again, God is *all Holy*, Holy through all his Works, Holy in our Creation, Holy in our Redemption, Holy in our Justification, Holy in Heaven, and Holy upon Earth, and Holy even in Hell itself, Holy in the Womb, Holy in the Manger, and Holy on the Cross, Holy in His Mercies, and Holy in his Punishments, infine, he is all Holy.

Farther, God is *immense*, or *omnipresent*, that is, really and actually present at one and the same Time in all Places, and all Things, whose Substance, as well as Benefits, sustains all things in being; *in Him we live, move, and are*, as in an immense Sea, not of Waters, but of Blessings;

Blessings; and we depend more essentially on his Influence, than the Heat on the Fire. or the Ray on the Sun, or the Infant on the Womb. He is present in Hell, as a severe Judge, on Earth, as a mild Ruler; in Heaven, as a glorious King. Every where present to succour the Pious, every where present to judge the Wicked.

Moreover, God is *immutable* or *unchangeable*; The immutability of God, is a firm Possession of all Good, which can neither change to any thing Better, or Equal, or Worse. God is first, Unchangeable in Nature; secondly, in Councils; and thirdly, in His Judgment, ever hating *Wickedness*, and loving *Justice*, with the same Love and Hatred: not like Men in continual Change; changeable of Mind, of Will, of Counsel, of Desire, of Affection, in a perpetual hurry of change, and commonly from Good to Bad, from Bad to Worse; till at last they change from Life to Death, and from Earth to Hell.

Lastly, God is *infinite* or *Eternal*. It is hard to say what Eternity is, because we know not what Time is, only this we are sure of, that he was without Beginning, and will be without End: God alone is Lord of Eternity, and inhabits it; He is King of Ages, and is said to reign beyond Eternity, that is to say, beyond our Notion or Conception of Eternity. To thee O God the Eternal and Immortal, belongs the Age of Life; to us the Age of Death, thou seest all things die, and when they are once Dead, they will never return to the same Life.

Such Dear Christians are the Divine Attributes which we know, and what we do know,

is

is in God after a different manner from what we think; for when we call God good, that does not fully exprefs his Perfection, and if you call Him Goodnefs itfelf, that does not yet fufficiently exprefs it, for His Nature is incomprehenfible, and His manner of Exifting, different from that of all Creatures, He is a pure Spirit, in whom there is no Compofition of Accident, Quality, or Quantity, or Degrees of Perfection, but all in Him, is one Thing, and that Infinite.

We know at leaft enough of the Divine Nature, to praife, love, and admire Him; for tho', he is above all Praife, yet what we call our Praife, He calls his Glory, and this, is what He requires from us; who of all the Works of the vifible Creation, are alone capable to give Him Thanks. Wo be to that Chriftian then, who knowing God, neglects to adore, love and praife Him as fuch. The bare Belief of a God, and the Knowledge of his Nature and Attributes will avail us nothing, unlefs we endeavour to ferve Him, and approach to Him. Would you then Dear Chriftians, know the way to approach to Him, it is in a few words this; The firft degree, or ftep, is to retire from his *oppofite* the Devil, for the farther you retire from one oppofite, the nearer you approach to the other; the fecond, is *Humility*, becaufe to the humble God ftoops; The third degree, is *Love*, for it is the nature of Love to unite; Laftly, the way to approach to Him, is by *Prayer;* and all the Advancements and Acts of Virtue, are the fteps and degrees by which you may approach

proach the Divine Nature, and poſſeſs Him, who in one Word, is all we can deſire, hope, or wiſh for, &c.

ARTICLE, I.
DISCOURSE. II.

I believe in God, the Father Almighty, Creator of Heaven and Earth.

The Father of whom are all Things. 1. Cor. c. viii. v. 6.

THE firſt Part of this Article, viz. *I believe in God*, I explained in the laſt Diſcourſe, wherein I proved to you the Exiſtence of a God, as alſo, that there is but one God; I likewiſe laid before you in part, the Nature and Attributes of God. What therefore I now intend, is to explain to you the ſecond part of this Article, which is; *The Father Almighty, Creator of Heaven and Earth.* This exhibits to us other Attributes of God. But for the proper illuſtration of this ſubject, it will be requiſite that we conſider what is meant by thoſe Terms, of *Father Almighty, Creator of Heaven and Earth.* In this Article, God is particularly Diſtinguiſhed by the Title, or Character of *Father*, but in what ſenſe or for what Reaſon, I proceed to conſider.*

The Di-
vil.

In

---

* The Title of *Father* denotes God to be the Origin of all Beings, in contradiction to the *Gnoſticks*, and ſome other Hereticks of the firſt Ages, who denied God's Paternity

In the first place, God has undoubtedly a most equitable Right to this application, as being the first Fountain, from which we received our Being; so that God is our Father by *Creation*, which seems to imply a better Right to the Title of Father, than *Generation*; for those, whom we call our Fathers, are no other, than second Causes or Instruments in the Hand of Almighty God our first Father, who as St. Peter says, has *given us all things which appertain to Life*, who encreases, nourishes, and preserves this Life, so that Men are but improperly Fathers in comparison of God; again, Man is particularly called the *Offspring of God*, even in the Language of Heathens, as St. Paul testifies of them, in the Acts of the Apostles. And the Prophet Malachi plainly asserts, that *Creation* constitutes a right of Paternity, *For have we not all one Father*, says he, *hath not one God created us*. This Notion of God's Paternity (founded on *Creation*) is universal, and as ancient, as Creation itself.

P. I.

2. Ep:
Pet. c. i.
v. 3.

c. xvii.
v. 28.

Mal. c.
ii. v. 18.

Again, God's Claim to this Title, is founded on *Redemption*, for thus Moses said to the Isra-

Paternity in this respect, by disowning him to have been the Creator, and Producer of the World, and of all Creatures therein; and therefore refused to give him. that appellation, or title of *Father;* and thus acting therein far worse, than the very Heathens, who by the glimmering light of Nature alone, conceived God under this Notion, that he was the *Father Omnipotent*, and as such, they reverenced and adored him, as *Lactantius* assures us in these Words; *Omnem Deum,---necesse est inter solennes ritus et precationes Patrem nuncupari, non tantum honoris gratia, verum etiam rationis; quod et antiquior est homine et quod vitam, salutem, victum præstat, ut Pater. Instit. Lib. 4. C. 3.*

elites,

elites, is not he thy Father, that hath poſſeſſed thee, and made thee, and created thee? And thus the Prophet Iſaias cryed out doubtleſs, *thou art our Father, though Abraham hath not known us, and Iſrael hath been ignorant of us; thou O Lord, art our Father, our Redeemer.* But in order that his Title might be perfect, and without Flaw, altho' we are the Children of God, both by *Creation* and *Redemption*, yet He has been pleaſed to make Himſelf our Father by *Adoption;* For *you have received the Spirit of Adoption of Sons,* ſays St. Paul, *whereby we cry Abba,* (that is) *Father.* Therefore, *behold,* ſays the Apoſtle, *what manner of Charity the Father hath beſtowed upon us, that we ſhould be called the Sons of God*; ſo that God is in a particular manner, the Father of all the adopted, that is, of thoſe to whom He has given his Spirit, in whom the Holy Ghoſt reſides; of theſe, God is properly Father, and theſe, are worthy to be called his Sons: All Chriſtians ought to be ſo, but ſome are degenerated, and by Sin are become Sons of the Devil. Some few there are, on whom God's Affections are placed, becauſe they do Actions worthy of the Name of the Sons of God, as Acts of Faith, Hope, Love, Obedience, &c. which prove them not to be degenerated Sons, but born of God, and Heirs to his Kingdom. Our Lives therefore ſhould in all things anſwer the Dignity of our Vocation, and as St. Paul ſays, *our Converſation ſhould be in Heaven,* (*l*) or at leaſt, not unworthy thoſe who aſpire to that heavenly Bliſs. Acknowledge O Chriſtians, your Dignity of being made the Sons of God by Baptiſm; do not by a wicked Life, and a degenerate Converſation

Deut. c. xxxii. v. 6

Iſai. c. lxiii. v. 16.

Rom. viii v. 15.

1. John. c. iii. v. 1

(*l*) *Phil. c iii. v. 20.*

verfation forfeit your Dignity. Remember of whofe Body, and under what Head, you are a Member, and how you were fnatched from the power of Darknefs, and transferred into Light.

Again, God is called Father of *Mercies*, but not Father of *Judgment*, becaufe *Mercy* is his own Offspring, but *Judgment* has it's rife from our Sins. *Mercy* in God, is a Will of relieving our Miferies: This Mercy fhews itfelf, firft, in patiently bearing with Offenders, in being flow to punifh, and inclined to pardon; fecondly, his *Mercy* is manifold, that is, God feldom grants one fingle Mercy, but many to the fame Perfon; thirdly, his *Mercy* is univerfal, He proclaims pardon to all, who will repent and turn to him; and even when he punifhes Sinners, His very fcourges are *Mercies*, for it is to be obferved, that Punifhments which are lefs than Death, and do not quite deftroy, are fo many Mercies to make Men repent: Thefe you will fay are harfh Remedies, but ftill let me tell you, they are Remedies, and even in thefe, *Mercy* has the Art to mix fweets with the bitter, and alleviate Sorrows with Comforts, and Pain with Refrefhments, fo that Mercy, even in Punifhment ftill fhines with all it's Rays of Divinity. Thus Gods *Mercy* is above all his Works; were it not for this Divine Attribute, we had all been confumed long fince, and nothing fhews the Magnanimity of God more than Mercy; when neither Multitude, nor Magnitude of Offences can move His Tranquility.

Secondly, the Title of Father is here added to the firft Perfon of the Bleffed Trinity, in order

der to distinguish him from the two other Persons, viz. the Son, and the Holy Ghost, who also *bear Testimony in Heaven.* (*m*) so that we are here obliged to believe, and adore a Trinity, or three distinct Divine Persons in a most perfect Unity of Nature.

(*m*) 1 John c. v. v. 7.

Thirdly, the most eminent Notion of God's Paternity, is with respect to the second Person of the Blessed Trinity, who is called His Son, and by way of Eminence his *only begotten* (*n*) and *beloved Son,* (*o*) as He is *the Father of our Lord Jesus Christ.* (*p*) He is called Father upon account of his begetting the second Person, by an Eternal Generation, and the second Person, viz. Jesus Christ, is called his Son, with respect to his *Relation* to the Father; now how, and in what manner this *Relation* subsists, will come more properly under consideration in the next Article: Let it suffice then for the present to say, it is greatly different from any resemblance of it with regard to ourselves, and it is chiefly in this Sense, that the Term *Father* seems to be added to God in the Creed.

(*n*) John c. i. v. 14
(*o*) Mat. c. iii. v. 17.
(*p*) 2 Cor. c. i. v. 3.

P. II. The next thing, which offers itself in this Article, is that great and glorious Attribute of God, by which He Rules, and Governs every thing with an unlimited and absolute Dominion, expressed by the Word *Almighty*.

The Apostles in order to confirm our Faith and Hope in God, and to raise in our Minds a more noble Idea of his Grandeur and Majesty, adjoin'd that glorious Epithet *Almighty*, that is, all Powerful: No Epithet is more frequently given to God in the Scripture, than this of *Omnipotent*. Which word implies a Power
of

of doing all things; not only what we can conceive, or imagine, but infinitely more, and whatever is not in itself inconsistent; a Power also, of using, and disposing of all Creatures according to His own good Pleasure; and that each of these high Prerogatives, both belong in the most eminent manner to God, is abundantly evident both from Scripture, and many other considerations.*

G   Nothing

---

* Contrary to that monstrous and blasphemous Heresy of the *Valentinians, Simonians, Menandians, Gnosticks*, &c. who affirmed, as I have already observed, that there were two Gods, the one *Good*, and the other *Bad;* and that *Matter* was co-eternal with God, from whence, the bad God proceeded, and out of which confused Heap, he produced the World, in the same order and regularity, wherein it now is; but some of the *Gnosticks*, did not allow *Matter* to be co-eval with the first, or good God, yet they affirmed it's co-existancy with, and even pre-existancy to the bad God, or inferior God, whom they believed to be the Creator of the World. These monstrous Hereticks, imagined a copulation of thirty *Aions*, or Sacred Beings, as they termed them; fifteen of whom were Male, and fifteen Female, begotten and generated one from another; and from whom proceeded the *Creator* himself, as also the *Matter*, out of which he made the World.--Now this ridiculous, and monstrous Opinion, was an impious Reflection on the Almighty Power of God, as tho' he had not sufficient Power to prepare, or create *Matter* for his Work of Creation.---Again, there were other Hereticks, who derogated from the *Almighty* Power of God, by ascribing the Creation of the World to Angels; as did the Followers of *Simon Magus*, viz. the *Saturninians, Basilidians, Carpocratians*, and others, who all combined in this Degradation of the Almighty, and the taking from him, the Honour and Glory of this first manifestation of his Divine Power, in creating and framing this stupendous Fabrick of the Universe; and all this quite contrary to the Christians Belief of the Almighty Power

Nothing Dear Christians, conduces more to the framing a just Notion of the Deity, than the consideration of His unlimited Power, and no word, more aptly expresses this Power, than that of *Almighty;* therefore, the Reason why the Apostles inserted this Attribute of *Omnipotence* in the first Article of the Creed, and not in the rest, was not only to excite an awe, and Respect for the Supreme Being, but chiefly, because it facilitates and opens a way towards the believing of the subsequent Articles; and indeed of all the Points of the Christian Doctrine. Because if we believe God to be *Almighty,* all Powerful, and able to do whatsoever he pleases, how can we question the Possibility of his Wonders, since nothing resists an Almighty Power? So that the Notion of *Omnipotency,* being once imbibed, this grounds all our Faith, and whatever is after proposed to be believed, tho' the Object, be never so obscure, or difficult to comprehend, or surpassing the Order of Nature, and limits of human understanding, yet we conclude, that nothing

er of God; who no ways stood in need of an eternal Substance, or *Matter* antecedent to the Creation of the World, from whence it should be formed or taken; neither stood he in any want of the help of Angels to effect so great a Work; since he was infinitely able of himself to create ten Thousand more Worlds, if it had pleased him so to do; for we believe him to be *Almighty,* and that he Created all Things both visible, and invisible out of Nothing, but by his only Word; and that he governs and rules all as he pleases; and that all Things are subject to him, and depend upon him.---But whosoever is willing or desirous, to examine farther into this gross and ridiculous System of those frantick Hereticks, I refer them to the first and second Book of St. *Irenæus.*

nothing is impossible to Him, who is Omnipotent; and therefore we stand in need of no other Argument, than the Testimony of His Word, to convince us of the Truth and posibility of the thing; without questioning with our modern Scepticks, how this, or that can be; for as his Word, is the Manifestation of his Will; so his Will, is the Manifestation of His Power. Hence we read in the Book of Esther, *O Lord, Almighty King, all things are in thy Power, and there is nothing that can resist thy Will.* (*q*)   (*q*) Estr. c. xiii. v. 9.

Besides, the Belief of an Almighty Power, does not only strengthen our Faith in regard to all revealed Points of Doctrine, but it also confirms our Hope, and Confidence in the Promises of God, tho' they seem never so great, and above human Nature; it likewise cures Despair, and prevents our being too much dejected; it supports us, who are frail and weak in the heroick Acts of Virtue; and animates us to undertake great things for the Glory of God; because he that is Almighty, is our strength; moreover, it teaches us to fear God, to respect Him, to dread Him, and *to work out our Salvation*, as St. Paul says, *with fear and trembling* (*r*). For who can offend with impunity an all powerful Being? Who can think to escape the justice of him who is Almighty? Therefore the Scripture Exhorts us to *Fear Him, who after he has killed, has Power to cast into Hell.* (*s*)   (*r*) Phil. c. ii. v. 12.

(*s*) Luc. c. xii. v. 5.

Let therefore, this be an established Principle, that God is *Almighty*, for so He says of Himself, *I am the Almighty God,* (*t*) it is also written in the Apocalypse or Book of Revelations, *The Lord God, who is, and who was, and who is to come*   (*t*) Gen. c. xvii. v. 1.

the

(*u*) Apoc. *the Almighty.* (*u*) The same is attested in many
c. i. v. 8. other places of the holy Scripture; Hence the
Angel said, to the Blessed Virgin, *no Word*
(*w*) Luc. *shall be impossible to God* (*w*) that is to say, there
c. i. v. 37. is nothing conceivable which God cannot Effect,
unless it be, what is inconsistent with the Divine
Perfection, as *Sin, Ignorance, Deceit, Death* &c;
for as St. Augustin well observes, if God could
die or *lie*, or either *deceive* or be deceived, or
Serm. ad act unjustly, He would not be Almighty; and
Cat de as He is infinitely Good, and just, so He can do
Symbol. nothing, but what is good and just.

But you must here observe, that tho' we ascribe the Title of *Almighty*, to God the Father, yet the same, is equally proper to the *Son*, and to the *Holy Ghost*, for as it is a positive Attribute essentially flowing from the Divine Nature, and the Divine Nature or Substance, being one and the same in all three Persons, so the Properties which follow from it must likewise be the same, and as " We say in St. Athanasius's
" Creed, that the Father is God, the Son is
" God, and the Holy Ghost is God, so we
" confess, the Father Almighty, the Son Al-
" mighty, and the Holy Ghost Almighty, and
" yet there are not three Almighties." The Reason why we attribute this Title more especially to the first Person of the blessed Trinity, that is to God the Father, is, because He is the Fountain of all Beginning, as not proceeding from any other.

P. III. I proceed now to the last particular of this Article, *Creator of Heaven and Earth;* the Sense of this is; in the beginning of all Time, God by infinite Power, made out of nothing Heaven and Earth,

and

and all things contained therein, whether spiritual or Corporal, visible or invisible. On the first Day, light was made an universal Good, an Expression of Divine Goodness itself, which shines both upon the Good and Bad. God wisely beginning the Ornament of the World from Light, without which all the work would have been vain, and useless, because unseen. The next Day, God made the Firmament, a Work of Strength and Power, which looks like Glory itself. The third Day, the Waters were divided from the Earth, and the vast weight of Waters received the Command of God for their Bounds, called the Sea, a Work prodigious for depth, length, breadth, and the Motion of it's Tide; the Earth by this means being left dry appeared the center of the World, a ponderous Weight in the midst of the air unmoved, cloathed with Greens and Herbs of all sorts (wholesome and innoxious, had not Man's Sin poisoned them, or rather deprived him of Prudence to discern between wholesome and unwholesome) bedecked also with Flowers, enriched with Seeds, and all it's Fruits, the Food of Life, and stored with Minerals in it's Bowels, which afford matter to so many rare pieces of Art, and Gold which governs the World. The fourth Day, God made the celestial Orbs, the Sun, the Eye of the World, a Work noble and admirble in it's Magnitude, in Height, in Situation, in Motion, in Influence, and in Heat; And the Moon the Eye of the Night, and the Stars in all their Magnitudes watching in their Courses like the Armies of God, Images of the Saints, who shine in Heaven like Stars in the

Firmament,

Firmament. The fifth Day, God made Birds and Fish, next, he formed the several sorts of Animals, and all other living Creatures, each in it's Element, and each with a Blessing, made to rejoice and to feed on the Stores of nature, and to be a proof of a Providence; Works wonderful in two things, first, in Structure and Arrayment of their Bodies; and secondly, in their Instincts and Properties, in changing their Food and medicinal Herbs, in changing their Climate, and the Seasons for Health, as also in their industry in using their arms offensive and defensive, in getting their prey, and strong Inclination to encrease and breed up their young; all these works were perfect and without defect, in all their vigour and youth of Nature. The Palace being so built and adorned with all things, either for use, Pleasure, or Science; Lastly, He made Man even *to his own Image* and likeness, as Moses testifies (from whom we have a genuine Description of the World's Creation) and constituted him Lord over all Creatures in this World, and endowed him with exquisite Senses and Appetites to taste of all the Goods provided, and to reflect upon his Pleasures: But these Appetites were all made subject to the superior Power of Reason, which was made to command Appetite, as well as Brutes; all Creatures were made subject to him, and the Goods of Providence given to serve the noble Ends of Nature and Virtue, and he endowed with Liberty and free choice, to use all well, or ill, that he might be capable of a reward in doing acts worthy of Praise: Man was made in the last place, as the Master-piece of Creation,

(x) Gen: c. i. v. 27

Creation, the End of Nature, for whom the World was made, to be his Palace; and he, made as were, it to behold and admire all the Scenes of Divine Perfections in His Works, as being alone capable to reflect, and know, Love and Serve God, to admire His Works, and to return Thanks, and make a right ufe of all things given to him. You fee now, Dear Chriftians, for what End all was made, and for what End Man was made, all Creatures for Man, and Man for God; he who anfwers not this End, in vain was he made, and better had it been for that Man never to have had a Being.

I fhall not here, enter into Arguments againft the Principles of fome fort of People, who pretend that the World was eternal and never had a beginning: Others there are, who would perfuade us, that it owes it's Birth to fome ftrange unintelligible Caufe; which they call *the fortuitous Concourfe of Atoms*, that is, that there were from all Eternity, certain fmall Particles of Matter, fluctuating backwards and forwards in the Void of Space, but at laft, fome how or other, they jumbled themfelves together into that beautiful and regular Form, in which, we have feen them ever fince; Man himfelf according to them had no better original, than to be the Spawn of Chance. Now, what can be more contrary to human Senfe and Reafon, then thefe fenfelefs Suppofitions? The very Heathens themfelves have already confuted, and expofed them. For my part, till I fee a Number of Letters fhaken together into an ingenious, and accurate Poem or Tract of Philofophy, I fhall think we ought juftly to withhold

hold our assent from such a whimsical, and unnatural System.

The last thing to be considered in this Article, is, the means which God used in this Work of Creation; which was neither manual Operation with respect to Himself, as some have impiously and absurdly fancied, nor the Ministry of Angels, as others have supposed, which Opinion is held by the generality of the Turks even to this Day: But the sole and entire Instrument was the Divine *Fiat*, that is the efficacious *Word* of God; He had only to say, let such a thing be, and immediately it was so; Thus *the Heavens and the Earth were finished, and all their Ornaments*. (*y*)

(*y*)Gen.c. ii. v. 1.

I shall now conclude this Article, with a brief Recapitulation of what I have said upon the whole, that the Mind may behold at one glance, what hitherto she has contemplated at several Views. When therefore we say, *I believe in God the Father Almighty, Creator of Heaven and Earth*, we profess that there is a God, and only one, who was from all Eternity, and will be without End, self-existent, independent, and of a spiritual Subsistence, infinite in Power, infinite in Wisdom, infinite in Goodness, infinite in Duration, and infinite in all Perfections; and in whom we put our whole hope, trust, and confidence. We consider this Being in quality of a *Father*, as he is the Universal Parent of all Creatures, in as much as all of them derive their Being from Him; but more particularly of all good Christians, who have received the Spirit of Adoption, by which they call him *Father*, as St. Paul says (*z*) But in a more particular manner

(*z*) Rom. c.viii v15

Art. I. *Disc.* II.

ner we acknowledge His right to this Appellation, as being by Nature the *Father* of his Eternal Son, the second Person of the Blessed Trinity; not that there is the least inequality, between the Father, Son, and Holy Ghost, who are all one and the very self same Eternal God; but we call the Father the first Person, because He proceeds from no other; the Son the second Person, because He proceeds from the Father only; and the Holy Ghost the third Person, because He proceeds both from the Father and the Son: We likewise call him *Father*, to distinguish Him from the other two Persons in the Sacred Trinity: Besides Creation is appropriated to him as being a Work of Power, (tho' not so as to exclude the Son and the Holy Ghost,) and therefore we acknowledge him to be the true Author of Creation, both visible and invisible, that the Heavens and the Earth were by the free and voluntary Act of His Divine Will produced out of *Nothing*, in obedience to His bare Word, and that, at a certain determinate Time, agreeable to his own good Pleasure: And in this full Latitude we believe and assent to this first Article of the Christian Faith.

Let us then who believe these Truths, praise and bless our merciful God, who has called us to the Knowledge of them: But be sure take care that your Lives are conformable to your Belief, that in the End you may receive the Reward, His Goodness has prepared for those who truly believe in Him, and serve Him as they ought.

ARTICLE, II.
DISCOURSE. I.

And in Jesus Christ, his only Son our Lord.

I believe that Jesus Christ is the Son of God. Acts. c. viii. v. 37.

HAVING, Dear Christians, in the former Article treated of the Belief of one God *Father Almighty*, who made us and all Things, I come now to the Second Article of the Creed, which relates to our belief or Faith *in Jesus Christ*, the second Person of the Blessed Trinity, who was made Man for our Redemption.

The connection of this Article with the foregoing is observed to be very just; that as in the Divinity there is nothing intervening between the Father and the Son, so that immediate Union might be perpetually expressed by a constant Conjunction in our Christian Confession.

The Division. P. I.

What therefore I intend in this Discourse is first to enquire whether there ever was such a Person as *Jesus Christ*, and secondly what we are to believe of Him with regard to the Names, Titles, or Office He bore.

That there was such a Person as *Jesus Christ*, is manifest beyond all dispute, for we have not only the Authentick Testimony of the Evangelists as Vouchers of this Truth; but the general consent of almost all Nations, and of all

such

such Writers, as have touched on the Transactions of those Times, with regard to the Jewish Common Wealth: And there is such a plain and undeniable Tradition of this Fact, handed down through all Ages, that to deny it, would be to cancel all manner of Authority, and to row against the stream of all Antiquity; I dare say there is scarce any Nation (unless perhaps among the wild Indians) but what is so far Christians as to allow of the Reality of His having existed, tho' they will not subscribe to all, that true Christians affirm concerning Him. Both Jews and Turks agree, that He was a Man powerful in Works, tho' they deny Him to be the Son of God, or the Messiah promised in the Law; But to believe both is the distinguished Character of a Christian. I shall not trouble myself here to quote many profane Authors who might be alledged in Confirmation of this Truth; let it suffice to instance this one Passage of *Josephus the Jew*, taken from his Book of the Jewish Antiquities. *Lib.* 18. c. 4. wherein he declares, " That at that Time, there was a wise Man,
" named *Jesus* (if it be so, we may call him a
" Man, for he wrought many Miracles, and
" taught the Truth, to those who received
" it with joy) who had a great number of Dis-
" ciples, as well among the Jews, as the Gen-
" tiles; that he was the Christ; and that being
" accused by the Chief of his Nation he was
" crucified by Pilate's Order. That neverthe-
" less he was not abandoned by those who lov-
" ed him; to whom he appeared alive on the
" third Day, as was foretold by the Prophets,
and

"and that he was the Author of the sect of the Christians which remain to this Day."

This Testimony of *Josephus* is produced by *Eusebius*, St. *Jerome*, and several others after them, as a Record very important for the establishing the Christian Faith; but we shall ground our Narrative upon the Testimony of the Evangelists. This JESUS was born in *Bethlehem of Juda* in the Country of *Palestine*, under the Reign of *Augustus* the Emperor about 1771 Years ago, according to the Usual Computation; in or about the Year 4000 after the World's Creation. His Life and Conversation was obscure in Nazareth of Galilee (the Place of His abode) till he was about thirty Years of Age, when He began His preaching. Afterwards, the whole Country of Palestine, but chiefly the Cities of Carpharnaum and Jerusalem were the Theatre of His preaching and Miracles, till the time of his Death, which happened about three Years after. When being wrongfully accused by the Jews, He was Sentenced to be crucified, by that wicked President Pontius Pilate, and died upon a Cross between two Thieves.* Having thus proved to you that there was such a Person as *Jesus Christ*,

and

---

* It is observed that in the *Nicene*, and ancient Greek Creeds, we read that we believe in *one* Jesus Christ, *in unum Dominum Jesum Christum*, which was designed against those blasphemous and horrid Imaginations of the *Gnosticks*, *Cerinthians*, and others, who by dividing *Jesus* from *Christ* affirming him to be two different and distinct Persons, and not *one Jesus Christ*, as the Creed declares. Against which Error of *Cerinthus*; St *Irenæus* "assures us, that St. John levelled his Gospel, persuad- "ing them, that it was not they said, viz. that there
"was

and given you a short abridgment of his Life and Death, I proceed now to the Explanation of His Name.

With respect to His appellation, though He is promiscuously spoken of in the holy Scriptures, sometimes by the Name of *Jesus*, and sometimes by that of *Christ*, yet it appears that the former only was His proper Name, the latter an expressive Epithet denoting His Character. The Name of *Jesus* as St. Luke observes was expresly given Him and appointed by the Angel, even before He was conceived in His Mother's Womb; for when the Angel appeared to the Blessed Virgin to announce unto her the

P. II.

" was one *Jesus* the Son of the Creator, and another " *Christ*, who came from the *Pleroma*, who remaining " impassible, descended into the foresaid *Jesus* the Son " of the Creator, and afterwards returned back to the " *Pleroma* again." Lib. iii. c. 11. and in another place he says, If these invented stories should be admitted, it would necessarily follow that there are two Christs ; for if one suffers, whilst the other is incapable thereof, and one is born, whilst the other descends into him so born, and afterwards leaves him, it is most certain that they are not one, but two. *Si enim alter quidem passus est, alter autem impassibilis mansit, et alter quidem natus est, alter vero in eum qui natus est descendit, et rursus reliquit eum, non unus, Sed duo monstrantur.* Lib. iii c. 18. which division and Seperation of our Saviour's Person, is a most intolerable Blasphemy.---But, tho' the Eastern Creeds did read in *one* Jesus Christ, in the West, where the Churches were not so much infested by the *Gnosticks*, the Creed, as our present one doth, expressed this Article without the addition of the Term *one*, saying, *and in Jesus Christ his only Son our Lord*, &c. In which Words, our Faith is declared in the Son of God, wherein we have him first described by his Name *Jesus* and then by his Office that he is *Christ*, and afterwards by his Natures both divine and human, the happy Tidings of the *Incarnation* of the Son of God, and her Election to be the Mother of God, he said to her; *Behold thou shalt conceive in thy Womb, and shalt bring forth a Son; and thou shalt call his Name Jesus.* (*a*) The Reason whereof is expressed in St. Matthew, for *he shall save his People from their Sins.* (*b*) And this Name was accordingly conferred on him on the Day of his Circumcission. (*c*)

This Name of *Jesus* had been born by several others before our Saviour, as by *Jeoshua* or *Joshua*, which originally comes from the Hebrew Word *Oshea*, which Signifies a *Saviour*, and as a Proof that they are the same, the name *Jesus* is given to the Son of Nun, as we read in the Acts of the Apostles, (*d*) and by St. Paul in his Epistle to the Hebrews. (*e*) However, though this Name or Epithet was given to others, yet it is certain, that in its true Sense, it belongs only to the Person of *Jesus Christ*, in whose adorable Name alone, we have Salvation properly so called: For Jesus Christ has purchased Salvation for us all, and that by the costly price of His most precious Blood; He redeemed us from Sin and Hell, the greatest of all Slaveries, and in which all Mankind were involved, through the Disobedience of our first Parent Adam in eating the forbidden Fruit, by which, we were all condemned to eternal Death, and which we must unavoidably have undergone, had not this our Blessed Saviour, through His infinite Mercy and Goodness bought us off, as I said before, with the price of his most precious Blood (in such a manner, and by such means as we will hereafter consider) and so delivered us

(*a*) Luc. c. i. v. 31
(*b*) c. i. v. 21.
(*c*) Luc. c. ii. v. 21.
(*d*) C. vii v. 45.
(*e*) C. iv. v. 8.

us from that eternal Curſe; and reconciled us to God, and obtained for us a Title to the eternal Happineſs of the Kingdom of Heaven. In a word, ſo emphatically does the Term *Saviour* belong to Him, that *there is no Salvation in any other, neither is there any other Name under Heaven given among Men, whereby we can be ſaved.* (*f*)   (*f*) Acts c. iv. v. 12.

From hence, we are to underſtand, that all Grace and the whole Œconomy of Man's Salvation is put into the Hands of *Jeſus*, ſo that He is our Saviour in this Senſe; that we can be ſaved by no other; and as he has Power to ſave all, ſo he has Goodneſs to refuſe none; and that there is no Caſe tho' never ſo deſperate that is to Him incurable; and therefore the only reſource of all Men, whether juſt or Sinners, whether weak or ſtrong, is ſtill to have recourſe to *Jeſus Chriſt*. All Men are in a continual dependance on Him, but nothing can be better for us than that dependance. From this there follows a certain Truth, which Men little reflect on, which is this, that if *Jeſus*, is a Saviour, and declared to be the general Deliverer of Mankind, who has a Power to deliver all, and Goodneſs to refuſe none, which is a certain Truth, then it follows, that no Man can be miſerable, that has a recourſe to *Jeſus*; ſecondly, whoſoever has recourſe to Him, will be delivered from his Sins; this is a Truth of Salvation, from hence I infer, that the Reaſon why ſo many Chriſtians ſtill groan under the load of their Sins and Miſery, is not purely the Violence of Temptation, or a frailty of Nature, or the Malice of the Devil as they would make us believe, but the unqueſtionable Cauſe is, they

have

have not had recourse to *Jesus*. Neglect not therefore in all your Afflictions, Troubles, and Temptations to call upon the Name of *Jesus*, and beseech Him to be your Comfort and Support; this Sacred Name, is of unspeakable Comfort to the Saints, and of Terror to the Devils, it puts us in Mind of the Incarnation of the Son of God, and Man's Redemption; wherein the Power, Wisdom, Goodness, and inexpressible Love of God, appears more conspicuous, than in any other Instance of his Providence.

I proceed now, to examine why, and in what Sense *Jesus* is called *Christ* or the *Messiah*, as we find, He is promiscuously so stiled in the Sacred Writings, which in effect signifies the same, *Messiah* is an Hebrew Word, and *Christ* comes from the Greek Word χρίσος the Signification of each in our Language is *Anointed*, but we adhere to the Greek, and every where upon this Occasion, instead of saying, *Jesus the Anointed*, we say *Jesus the Christ*, or *Jesus Christ*.

This Name or Title, is applied to *Jesus*, as a Mark of those Eminent Characters or high Offices, to which He was ordained by God, and set a part thereto, as King, Priest, and Prophet, and such were anointed in their Inauguration (as an Emblem of Grace) as we read in the Old Testament, (*g*) and consecrated to the Divine service. And this Solemn Ceremony is performed to this very Day among Catholicks, upon their Kings and Priests. Now Jesus Christ is both *Prophet*, *Priest*, and *King*, and He was anointed, not by Men, but by God, not with Oil, but with the fullness of all Spiritual

(*g*) Levit. c. viii. v. 10 &c. Exod. c. xxviii v. 41. et c. xxix v. 7. See also the book of kings. 1 kings. c. x. 3 kings c. xix.

ritual Graces which superabounded in Him, in whom says St. Paul, *the whole plenitude of the Divinity dwelleth corporally* (h) whence the Psalmist says; *that God anointed him with the Oil of Gladness, beyond all those who were partakers with him.* (i)

(h)Col.c. ii. v. 9.

(i)Pf.xliv. v. 8.

As to the first of his being a Prophet, he was promised as such in the Law, where Almighty God thus speaking to Moses says; *I will raise them up a Prophet out of the midst of their Brethren like to thee: And I will put my Words in his Mouth, and he shall speak all that I shall command him.* (k) Whence this Opinion of his being a Prophet was current among the Jews his Cotemporaries, as we read in St. Matthew; *The people said; this is Jesus the Prophet, from Nazareth of Galilee.* (l) By this Title or Office, He is prophetically characterised by the Prophet Isaias thus; *The Spirit of the Lord is upon me, because the Lord hath anointed me, he hath sent me to preach to the meek, &c.* (m) as is evident from our Saviour's applying those Words to Himself, citing them as spoken of Him, and declaring them to be fulfilled in his Person, which he openly did in the Synagogue at Nazareth, as St. Luke relates. (n) He constantly speaks both to his Disciples, and the Multitude in the style and manner of a Lawgiver; *I say unto you,* see St. Matthew (o) His Declarations are peremptory; *he taught as one having Power, or Authority, and not by Glosses and Comments on the Law, as did the Scribes and Pharisees.* (p) And lastly, He adds this Assurance, that upon the Principles of his Law, we shall be judged at the last Day. The *Words*

(k) Deut. c. xviii. v. 18.

(l) Mat.c: xxi. v.11

(m) Isa. c. lxi. v. 1.

(n) Luc.c. iv. v. 21.

(o) c. 5:

(p) Mat.c. vii. v. 29

F

Words which I have spoken, the same shall judge him at the last Day. (q)

(q) Johnc. xii. v. 48.

Now the Prophetic Office, as applicable to *Jesus*, chiefly consists in this, viz. the Promulgation, and Establishments of the Gospel; as also to declare to us the joyful Tidings of Salvation, and [in as much as the Word Prophet imports a Lawgiver] to give to Mankind that Law which is to be the Rule of their Actions; and in this Sense, never was Prophet so Solemnly anointed, as He was: The fulness of the Holy Ghost is his Oil, and His Character and Authority are openly declared by the Voice of the Almighty Father, as we read in St. Matthew. (r) Never was Mission so strongly attested as his, His whole Life being one continued Scene of Miracles; His very Enemies being oftentimes obliged to confess, that the Finger of God was with Him; Angels, Men, and Devils bearing Him Witness, and the astonished Multitude declaring, that *the like had never been seen in Israel*. (s) Besides, the Narration of the Evangelists bears Testimony of His several Prophecies concerning the manner of his Death, his Resurrection, and the Destruction of Jerusalem; the Reprobation of the Jews; the calling of the Gentiles; the Persecution of the Apostles; the Establishment of His Church, &c. so that we acknowledge Him for our Prophet.

(r) Mat. c. iii. v. 17.

(s) Mat. c. ix. v. 33.

In conjunction with the Prophetic, our Blessed Saviour was also anointed to the Sacerdotal or priestly Office, by which He became an *high Priest according to the order of Melchisedech*. (t) Now the grand Business of the high Priest, was by an *expiatory Sacrifice*, to make an Atonement for

(t) Heb. c. v. v. 10.

for the Sins of the People (*u*) And never was this Bufinefs fo compleatly executed, as by this our high Prieft; who devoting Himfelf to Death for the Sins of His People, offered his moft facred Blood as a *Sacrifice of Expiation* for Sin, to atone by His innocent Sufferings the injured Juftice of Heaven. Whence St. Paul thus writes to the Hebrews. Chrift, fays he, acting as *high Prieft of the good things to come,* by *a more ample and perfect Tabernacle, not made with hands, that is, not of this Creation, neither by the Blood of Calves, nor of Goats, but by his own Blood, entered once into the holy Place, having obtained eternal Redemption for us: For if the Blood of Goats and Oxen, and the Afhes of an Heifer being Sprinkled Sanctify fuch as are defiled, to the purifying of the Flefh; how much more will the Blood of Chrift, who by the Holy Ghoft offered himfelf unfpotted to God, cleanfe our Confcience from dead Works to ferve the living God.* (*w*) *Chrift therefore was Prieft of the new Teftament.* Being chofen by Him who faid unto Him, *thou art my Son, to Day I have begotten thee.*(*x*)

But here it may be natural to enquire after the Perfon, and Prieft-hood of Melchifedech, of whom fo honourable mention is made in holy Scripture. This Melchifedech as St. Paul teaches (*y*) was King of Salem, and Prieft of the moft High: He was in feveral refpects a manifeft Type of our Saviour, as may be fhewn from His Name, which is interpreted *King of Juftice;* as likewife from the Place of which he was King, viz. *Salem,* which Signifies *Peace.* And our Bleffed Saviour is called by the Prophet Ifaias, *Prince of Peace;* (*z*) And

(*u*) See Levit. c. 4.

(*w*) Heb. c. 9.

(*x*) Acts c. xiii. v. 33.

(*y*) Heb. c. vii. v. 1. 2.

(*z*) Ifa. c. ix. v.

of

of whose coming the Royal Psalmist thus speaks; *Mercy and truth have met each other: Justice and Peace have kissed.* v. 11. *Truth is Sprung out of the Earth: And justice hath looked down from Heaven.*

(a) Ps. lxxxiv.

12. (a). Again the Apostle remarks, that *Melchisedech* is discribed, *without Father or Mother, or Genealogy;* no mention being made; either of *the Beginning or End of his Life;* but likened unto the Son of God, he continueth a Priest for ever, (b) Finally his offering was bread and Wine (c) The same which Christ made use of, in that mystical Oblation at his last Supper; when taking Bread, He blessed it, broke it: And gave it to his Disciples, saying take and eat for *this is my Body,* and taking likewise the Wine saying, *this is my Blood of the New Testament.* (d) But Jesus Christ is both Priest and Victim, having entered once into the Sanctuary, for Man's Redemption, not with the Blood of Beasts, but with his own most precious Blood, which He ceases not to offer daily, by the Ministry of the Priest, under the Mystical Forms of Bread and Wine; being called by God, *a Priest for ever according to the order of Melchisedech* (e)

(b) Heb. c.vii.v.3.
(c) Gen. c. xiv. v. 18.

(d) Mat.c. xxvi. v. 26.

(e) Heb. c. vii. v. 17.

Another part of the High-Priest's Office was to make *Intercession;* which Jesus Christ does for us in the most prevalent manner: On this Foundation the Apostle builds that Persuasion, that *he is able to save for ever those who come to God by him, always living to make* (as Man) *Intercession for us.* (f)

(f) Heb. c. vii. v. 25.

Another Privilege peculiar to the Character was that of *Blessing,* or *Sanctifying.* This also was in a peculiar manner exercised by *Jesus*

Several

Several times. and in a very Solemn manner; his Power and Right appearing in that, His Blessing was always effectual and beneficial, as always conveying some miraculous Benefit to the Object, and to His Disciples even the Holy Ghost, and Supernatural Power. *(g)* In a word, so extensive was this Power in Him, that as the Apostle teaches, *God having raised up his Son hath sent him to bless you, that every one may convert himself from his Wickedness (h).* From what has been said, it evidently appears that *Jesus Christ* is most truly, and in the most eminent manner our Priest.

(g) John. c. xx. v. 22.

(h) Acts c. iii. v. 26.

The third Office belonging to the *Messiah*, and to which *Jesus* was anointed, is the *regal*, or Office of a King; as is evident both from the ancient Prophecies, and Traditions. The Prophets who Speak of Him under this Character are numerous, witness the Royal Prophet, Ps. c. ii. v. 6. The Prophet Isaias. c. xxxii. v. 1. The Prophet Jeremias. c. xxiii. v.5. and the rest. *(i)* And that they do speak of him, is evident from the unerring application of them, by the Angel Gabriel, in his Salutation to the Blessed Virgin. *The Lord shall give unto him* (says he) *the Throne of his Father David, and he shall reign in the House of Jacob for ever, and of his Kingdom there shall be no End.* *(k)* A Circumstance which had been often promised by the Prophets, and sometimes expressly by God Himself *(l)* with which Promises the Expectations of the Jews were so big, that they seldom spoke of the *Messiah* without the addition of the regal Title; as may be seen in the Writings of the Rabbins, and Commentators.

(i) See Dan c. vii. v. 14. 27. and see Mich. c. iv. v. 7,

(k) Luc: c. i. v.32. 33.

(l) See Isa c. ix. v. 6. 7. Num. c. xxiv. v. 17 Ps. cxxxii v. 11. Acts c. 2. v. 30

The

The Jews ever did, and do to this Day in the Perfon of their *Meffiah* expect a King; but their grand miftake, is in the nature of his Kingdom: Being an ambitious and earthly minded People, they fondly flattered themfelves, that He was to be a temporal Prince and Deliverer; that He was to reftore and aggrandize their Nation, and to make his appearance, with all the Pomp of an Earthly Monarch. They never confidered the difference between thofe paffages, which relate to his firft appearance, and thofe, which contained the Account of His Triumphant Return, or Second coming. He acknowledged that he was a King, but at the fame time declared that his Kingdom was *not of this World*. (*m*) that is, not to take place under the prefent Order and Œconomy of things, nor was He ever found to affect any thing of Royalty, in the Eyes of the World; but on the contrary, *when the Multitude would have made him their King, he fled away and concealed himfelf in the Mountain*, as St. John relates (*n*). His Sovereignty is Spiritual, and of a higher Nature, than that of the Kings of the Earth, for tho' He governs the World without Controul, and nothing refifts his abfolute Will; yet he reigns in a more particular manner, *by his Grace*, in the Hearts of the *juft*, who are perfectly Subject to his Will, and throughly obedient to His Commands; He rules, protects, and rewards the Faithful; He has given them pofitive Laws, and by his Sole Right and Authority enforces thofe Laws, with the promife of Rewards to all that fhall keep them

(*m*) John c. xviii. v 36.

(*n*) John c. vi. v. 15.

them; and Threats of Punishments to those who shall break them, for they *who obey not the Gospel, shall Suffer eternal punishment.* (*o*) And to say truth, the regal Title cannot belong so *justly*, to any one as to Him, who reigns in the Hearts of his faithful Subjects; or so extensively as to that Prince, whose Dominion reaches over the whole Circuit of Creation; *for all Power*, says he, *is given to me, in Heaven and Earth.* (*p*)

(*o*) 2 Thes. c. i. v. 8.

(*p*) Mat. c. xxviii. v. 18.

But at His Second coming, when he shall have put down all principality, and Power; and subdued all his Enemies under his Feet, (*q*), Then shall truly commence that Reign which is to endure for ever, and that Dominion to which there shall be no End.

(*q*) 1 Cor. c. xv. v. 24. 25.

But I have said enough of his Name; the Dignity of His Person is more to be regarded; It is that which renders Him, not unequal to the Father; and it is that which constitutes Him Mediator between God and Man; and it is that which claims our Respect, our Adoration, and Worship; and it is what I shall explain to you in the next Discourse: And so conclude this with the Words of the first Epistle of St. John, where he says, that *we have seen and do testify, that the Father hath sent his Son to be the Saviour of the World,* so that, *whosoever shall confess that Jesus is the Son of God, God abideth in him, and he in God.* (*r*)

(*r*) 1 John c. iv. v. 14. 15.

✳✳✳✳
✳✳✳
✳✳
✳

ARTICLE

ARTICLE, II.
DISCOURSE. II.
And in Jesus Christ, his only Son our Lord.

I believe that Jesus Christ is the Son of God. Acts. c.viii. v. 37.

IN the last Discourse I laid before you the Grounds, and Authority we have for believing that there really was such a Person as Jesus Christ; as also the Reasons why He was so called, and what we are to believe of Him, as to his Name, &c.

The Divis.

What then I intend in this, is first to prove that Jesus Christ the Son of the Blessed Virgin Mary, was the true Messiah, promised to the Patriarchs, and foretold by the Prophets; this will appear from the Prophecies concerning him, and the Miracles which he wrought. Secondly, that he is the *only* Son of God. And lastly, that he is our Lord, which three Points shall make up the subject of this Discourse.

It may perhaps seem unnecessary to prove that Jesus Christ is the true *Messiah*, since we have a firm Faith of this already from the Authority of the Evangelists: But as there are many in this Age of Infidelity, who look upon them as Impostors, and laugh at all Christianity as a human Invention and mere Romance; I will therefore [for the honour of Jesus Christ; the Dignity of the Christian Faith,

Faith, and the Salvation of my Neighbour) shew to every Understanding that is not wilfully blinded, this great Truth, promised in the Law and the Prophets.

If Jesus had not come in the manner He did, P. I. and if he had not done what he hath done, it would have been no crime not to have known and acknowledged Him; but coming with all the Marks and Signs which the Scripture gives of the *Messiah*; and having done such wonderful Works, the incredulity of Men cannot be palliated with excuses, since these very Things prove *Jesus Christ* to be the true *Messiah*, or Redeemer of the World, as I shall make appear by the Consideration of them.

In the first place the Prophets who were sent by God, according to the Belief of our greatest Enemies, and who worked so many miracles for the Proof of their Mission, who signed with their Blood the Truth of their Prophesies, which have been found true and faithful, by the event of what they foretold; whose writings could never be falsified, nor altered the least by Christians, since they were always in the Hands of the Jews: These Prophets, I say, foretell particularly and distinctly, the Mysteries of *Jesus Christ*; the Time of his coming; the Place of his Birth; the Virginity of his Mother; the Quality of his Person; the kind of Life he would lead; The Miracles he would work; his Passion, Death, Burial, and Resurrection, with all their Circumstances; as also the Conversion of the Gentiles; the Reprobation of the Jews; and the Establishment of the Christian Church throughout the Universe.

Jacob foretold the time of his coming, where he says that, *The Scepter shall not be taken away from Juda, nor a Ruler from his Thigh; till he comes that is to be sent, and he shall be the Expectation of Nations* (*f*) Here we see an illustrious Prophecy of what could not be foretold but by the Spirit of him who pierces future Ages, and disposes of Kingdoms. He foretells that the Sovereignty and royal Authority should enter into the Tribe of Juda, and that it should remain there till the coming of the *Messiah*: He foresaw that which was to be effected after a Thousand Years; he foresaw what was to come contrary to all human Appearance; for *Rubin, Simeon,* and *Levi* were all elder brothers to *Juda*, and by Right of Seniority were to be preferred. Nevertheless the Royalty enter'd into the Tribe of *Juda* in the Person of David, and was there established, and continued till the coming of the *Messiah*, notwithstanding the Murmuring of the other ten Tribes, the revolt of Israel, and the Captivity of Babylon. The Prophet Daniel also foretold the time of our Saviours coming. (*t*)

(*f*) Gen. c. xlix. v. 10.

(*t*) Dan. c. ix.

As to the Place of his *Birth*, it was foretold by the Prophet *Micheas* that it should be *Bethlehem*, and so it was, *Thou Bethlehem Ephrata art a little one among the Thousands of Juda, out of thee shall He come forth unto me, that is to be Ruler in Israel* (*u*).

(*u*) Mich: c. v. v. 2.
(*w*) Isa. c. ix. v. 7.
(*x*) Jer. c. xxiii. v. 5. 6.

The Prophet *Isaias* (*w*) and *Jeremias* (*x*) foretold that He should issue out of the Race of *David*; and it is so clear and evident, that Jesus Christ

Chrift iffued from thence, that he was commonly called the Son of David; and it is proved from his Genealogy in St. Matthew and St. Luke.

The Prophet Ifaias foretold that he fhould be conceived and born of a Virgin and he was fo; *Behold a Virgin fhall conceive, and bear a Son, and his name fhall be called Emmanuel.* (*y*) that is to fay, *God with us*. *(y)* Ifa. c. vii. v 14.

The Prophet *Balaam* foretold that a ftar fhould appear at his Birth (*z*) and fo it did. The Royal Pfalmift foretold the Kings of the Eaft fhould make Him prefents, (*a*) and they did fo. The Prophet *Malachias* foretold that a Meffenger fhould go before Him to prepare his ways (*b*) and St. John Baptift did fo. *Ifaias* prophefied, that He fhould be carried into Egypt, that He fhould be meek, merciful, peaceable; That He fhould reftore light to the Blind, hearing to the Deaf, and fpeech to the Dumb; That He fhould be defpifed, humbled, and afflicted, and put to Death with the wicked for the Sins of Men. (*c*) And holy David wrote almoft every particular Circumftance of his Death and Paffion; he foretold that His Body fhould not corrupt in the Sepulchre, and that he fhould rife again, (*d*) all which was verified in Him, and agrees fo plainly to our Bleffed Redeemer Jefus Chrift, that there needs no application.

(z) Numb c. xxiv. v 17.
(a) Pf. lxxi. v. 10.
(b) Mal. c. iii. v. 1
(c) Ifa. c. xxxv. et 42. et 53. fee alfo O fee. c. xi. v. 1.
(d) Pf xv. xxii. xl. lxxxviii.

The Prophet *Zacharias* foretold, that he fhould enter into Jerufalem riding upon an Afs (*e*) and that he fhould be fold for thirty Pieces of Silver with which the Potters Field fhould be bought (*f*) the Prophet *Jeremias* foretold

(e) Zac. c. ix. v. 9
(f) c. xi. v. 12.

told that he should establish a new Law, and a new Covenant (*g*). That he should abolish the Priest-hood, and Sacrifices of the old Law, and be the Author of a new Priest-hood, and a new Sacrifice was foretold by the Prophet *Malachias* (*h*). And the Prophet *Isaias* foretold, that the Jews should be cast off, for not receiving the *Messiah*, and His Law. (*i*) And that the Gentiles should become the People of God, is foretold by almost all the Prophets. (*k*). The Prophets announced that the Messiah would come. But St. John Baptist proclaimed that he was come, and pointing to Him with his Finger said, *behold him*. His Testimony cannot be refused by any reasonable Man ; for he led a most innocent and irreprehensible Life, even from his infancy ; he was a disinterested Man, who contemned Honours, Riches, and the Delights of the World ; The Perfection and Sanctity of his Life was, so eminent that they took him for the Messiah ; insomuch that the Synagouge sent to him Priests and Levites to be informed of him, whether he was the *Christ* or not ; if he had but answered he was, they would have believed him, tho' he had given Testimony of himself ; with how much more reason then ought we to believe him, when he gives Testimony of another. (*m*)

But if the Predictions of the Prophets, and the Testimony of the Precursor should not be judged sufficient to prove the Mission of *Jesus Christ*, at least the Miracles which he wrought, evidently shew, that He was sent by God. When a Person gives Testimony of himself of having an extraordinary Mission from God, if he

(g) Jere. c. xxxi. v. 31. 32.

(h) Mal. c. 1.

(i) Isa. c. 1. v. 1. 2.

(k) See Ps. ii. et 22. Isa. c. ii. c. xi. c. xlii. c. xlix. c. lx and lxvi.

(m) St. John. c. 1. v. 27.

he has a mind that Men should believe him, he ought to give proof by some Sign or Miracle that he is so sent: And if he does work evident, palpable, and uncontestable Miracles, we ought then to believe that he is sent by God, and so give credit to his Doctrine: For it is impossible that God should work a Miracle in Confirmation of Falsehood. Now *Jesus Christ* shewed clearly and effectually, that He was sent by God, and that He himself was God; since He has worked so many Miracles in Confirmation of his Mission and Doctrine. He has made his Power appear in all the orders of the Universe, by the Miraculous Works He has wrought; in giving Health to the Sick, Sight to the Blind, Hearing to the Deaf, Speech to the Dumb, and Life to the Dead: And He confirmed the Miracles of his whole Life by his glorious Resurrection, after He was Dead: Now who ever heard the like to this? But more of this hereafter in it's proper place.

Now there are many powerful Reasons more than sufficient, to convince any Man, that has but common sense, that such Miracles were really performed by *Jesus Christ*, and not impostures: But this shall suffice at present, that the Evangelists frequently name the Persons, the Circumstances of Place, and manner, in which the Miracles were wrought; They also give an Account of the Miracles that were performed by themselves in publick, and in the Presence of many Witnesses: If then these accounts had not been evidently true, there would have been Thousands and Thousands ready to have given them the lie; and so have

have ruined their Credit, and that of their Gospels. They inform us, that *Jesus* fed four Thousand Persons with Seven Loaves only at one time, and at another, Five Thousand Persons with Five Loaves; They tell us that *Jesus* raised Lazarus from the Dead in *Bethania* near Jerusalem; as also the Son of the Widow in *Naim* at the Gates of the City, as they were going to bury him, in the sight of Numbers of People; that they brought into Jerusalem the infirm of the Neighbouring Towns; and that by the Shadow of St. Peter passing upon them they were all cured. If then these accounts were false, the Apostles would certainly have had as many Witnesses against them, when they preached and published the Gospel, as there were Persons in *Naim*, in *Jerusalem*, and in the Neighbouring Towns.

The Evangelists relate, that at the Crucifixion and Death of *Jesus Christ*, the Sun was eclipsed, and that Darkness covered the whole face of the Earth; that the Earth trembled; the Sepulchres opened, the Veil of the Temple was rent, and that all this happened in the Feast of the Pasche, at which time there were in the City of Jerusalem above Eleven Hundred Thousand Persons, according to the History of *Josephus*, who came to the Feast from all those parts of the World, where the Jews were then dispersed, as may be seen in *Philo*, *Tacitus*, and *Josephus*, and from thence they returned to their respective Homes. Now, if these Miracles had not been true, there would have been Persons in every place, who could have deposed against the Apostles, and the Gospel which they preached,

preached, by declaring that they were at that very Time in Jerusalem, and that they neither saw, or heard any such thing, but this they could not do; For these Miracles were so evident, so notorious, and acknowledged by all, that the Apostles who preached them were received by all the World. The Gospels which contain them being published, not one of the Pharisees, who were enraged with spite against *Jesus Christ*, and His Religion, ever dared to contradict the Narration of those Miracles, in any of the Books which they composed; but on the contrary, all the Enemies of the Christian Religion, even Jews, and Gentiles, have acknowledged these miraculous Works.

As to the Miracles of the Apostles, and primitive Christians which they wrought in the Name of *Jesus*, they were so evident, that the Pagans not being able to refute them by any Artifice, attributed them to Magick, as may be seen in St. Augustin. *(l)* But to attribute them to Magick, is a Malice as black, and diabolical, as the Art itself; and indeed nothing can be more ridiculous, for Magick has no Power but by the help and concurrence of the Devil, and can any one think that the Devil would assist the Apostles to do Miracles, to destroy his own Kingdom, since the Apostles by these very Miracles abolished the Worship of the Devil; and made the true God, the God of Israel, who was not known but in Palestine, and to a few in other parts of the Earth, to be known and adored by all the World.

Let us then with joy, cry out with St. Philip, we have found the *Messiah, of whom Moses and the Prophets*

(l) L. 1. c. 10. de consen Evang.

(n) John. c. i. v. 45. *Prophets wrote*, (n) we know him by his wonderful Works. But alas! what will it avail us Dear Christians, to know him and believe him to be our merciful Redeemer, if we do not follow his Example, and practise what he taught, for instead of being a good and amiable Redeemer to us; we make him our terrible and severe Judge: It will be no advantage to us, to bear the Name and Character of Christians, unless we be truly good and virtuous. All Christians therefore, ought to look upon the Doctrine of *Jesus Christ*, as a Law that obliges them; as a Rule to which they must conform their Lives; as a Covenant that God hath made with them, which contains Conditions, which being complied with, He promises us an eternal Reward in the Kingdom of Heaven, but not otherwise.

P. II. Having thus given you an Abridgment of the Prophesies concerning *Jesus Christ*, and the Miracles which He wrought; there needs but little more to be said in proof of his Divinity, or his being truly the *Son of God*: For you cannot but see that the *Messiah* promised to the holy Patriarchs, and to our Forefathers in the Law, is described in such Characters, as plainly shew him to be more than Man, that is, to be the Son of God, not by *Adoption only*, which is common to all Christians, but by a real *Communication* of the Divine Nature, and consequently of all the Attributes which are the necessary Perfections of the God head.*

Now

* Contrary to this Truth, of the Catholick Belief, *Arius* broached this Error in the beginning of the fourth Century

Art. II. *Disc.* II.

Now *Jesus Christ* has a Right several ways to this Appellation of being called the *only Son* of the eternal Father, or as it is expressed in this Article, *his only Son;* but for brevity sake, I shall
L   only

Century; he affirmed that Jesus Christ, was not Equal to the *Father*, as not having the same Nature or Essence; that there was a time when he was not; that he was created, &c. that he was only the adopted Son of God; all which is quite contrary to what the Scripture asserts of him. In the first place, the Scripture declares, that God alone is to be worshiped, and the same Scripture asserts, that our Saviour is to be worshiped and adored; and therefore he must be God: Thus St. Stephen adored him with divine Worship, when he cried out, *Lord Jesus receive my Spirit;* And again to him is ascribed, *Glory, and Praise, and Dominion, even forever and ever;* for St. John expressly tells us, that he heard, every Creature in Heaven, and Earth, and under the Earth, saying, *Blessing, and Honour, and Glory, and Power be unto him that sitteth upon the Throne, and unto the Lamb forever and ever* Rev. c. v. v. 13. Here we see the same Honour and Adoration is jointly paid to both the Father and the Son.

Besides, it is certain that he who made all things is God, and it is affirmed, that all things were made by the *Word*, viz. by Jesus Christ; for St. John assures us, that without him was nothing made, that is made. c. i. v. 3. from whence we may infer, that Christ the Creator is God.---Add to this that he is called *God, Blessed above all forever.* Rom. c. ix, v. 5. Again he is called *the first and last, Alpha and Omega, which is, which was, and which is to come, the Lord God Almighty.* Rev. c. i. v. 8. 17.

If it be said that the Word God, is a *relative* Term, and that our Saviour is stiled God in respect of his Office, and the Relation he bears to us, but not in respect to his *Nature;* I answer, he is stiled God, before any thing was made by him, for *in the beginning was the Word, and the Word was with God, and the Word was God: All things were made by him.* 1 Ep. John c. i. v. 3.

Now it is certain, he could not have any Relation to his Creatures *before* they were made, nor any *Office* or
                                                                    Authority

only confider two ways; The firſt is founded on his Birth or entrance upon human Life, which was not in the common way, or after the ordinary means of Generation, but by the immediate

Authority over them; he muſt therefore be God *Abſo-lutely* and not *relatively*, but God by *Nature*, and not by Virtue of his *Office* or *Authority*, but ſuppoſing the Word God to be *relative ;* the Term *Jehovah*, which is often apſplied to the Son, is of *abſolute* Signification, and implies unchangeable neceſſary exiſtence, the incommunicable Property of the Supreme Deity, whoſe Name only is *Jehovah*. Thus the Prophet Zachariah introduces God ſpeaking, *they ſhall look on me*, viz. *Jehovah*, as appears from what goes before, *whom they have pierced.* c. xii. v. 10. And St. John makes uſe of the ſame Words. c. xix. v. 37. It would be needleſs to cite all the Paſſages, in which the Name of *Jehovah* is given to our Bleſſed Saviour.

Whoſoever then is obſtinate in the diſbelief of our Saviour's Divinity or God-head, muſt be ſtrongly tempted to rejeƈt the Scriptures, as a Book full of Blaſphemy; ſince every Idea *diſtinƈtive* of God from his Creatures, is there aſcribed to our Saviour; unleſs *Paternity*, a mere Relation of Order, be the *diſtinƈtive* Idea of God, which is ſo far from implying any *Inferiority*, that it proves the very *reverſe*, for unleſs *only Son*, and *only Begotten*, ſignifies the *only Created*, It muſt follow, that he is uncreated, and therefore of the ſame divine nature with his Father, and of courſe, equal in all things to him, unleſs we ſpeak, of his *human nature*.

To ſay, that when creative and providential Powers are aſcribed to the Son, theſe are the Attributes and Power's of the Father only, but communicated *to*, exerciſed *in*, and manifeſted by the Son, is the utmoſt abſurdity. For how can there be a Communication of the divine Eſſence? Since whatever Attributes are communicated, muſt be proportioned to the capacity of the receiver: and if the Son be not infinite, what is finite, cannot be ſuſceptive of infinite Attributes.

But what chiefly deſtroys the whole Frame of the *Arain* Principles is, that they have made two Gods, viz. a *Supreme God*, and an *inferior God*, in direƈt oppoſition to the firſt Commandment; *thou ſhalt have no other Gods*

immediate Spirit and Power of God. For his Mother (without any carnal Knowledge of her Husband, or any Man whatsoever, as herself affirms that she knew not Man *(o)* conceived him by the *Holy Ghost*.

(o) Luc. c. i. v. 34. 35 See Mat. c. i. v. 18

But there is yet a nobler and more exalted Sense, in which we are to understand this Relation between Jesus Christ and the Almighty Father, for he did not then at his Incarnation first commence to be the *Son of God*, but he was so, long before the Foundations of the World were laid, even from all Eternity. It seems to have been the principal Design of St. John's Writings, to confirm and illustrate this mysterious Truth: (And with good Reason indeed, is it so often and so strongly urged by the Sacred Writers, since it is the main Hinge, on which turns the whole scheme of Christianity) for he begins his Gospel with acquainting us, that the *Logos* or *Word* (a Term often used to express the second Person of the Blessed Trinity) *was in the beginning* (or from all Eternity) *with God;* and that this *Logos* or *Word* was moreover Himself *God*, and expresly the Author of Creation, (which

See John c. i.

L 2   is

Gods but me; no other *Elohim*, a Word expressive not only of supreme, but also of inferior God, so that the plain Sense of the Commandment is this: *Thou shalt have no other Gods*, whether supreme or inferior, but the one *Jehovah*.

But some may say, that there are several texts of Scripture, which seem to imply the Son to be inferior to the Father; to which I answer, that they are to be understood, as spoken of his *human nature*, as for Example, when he said, *the Father is greater than I.* John c. x. v. 30. And in another place, speaking of the time of the Day of Judgment he says, *no Man knoweth, nor the Son, but the Father.* Mark. c. xiii. v. 32.

is also positively ascribed to him by St. Paul,) For *all things were made by him: And without him was made nothing, that was made.* The same Apostle else where declares it to be the express command of God, *that we should believe in the Name of his Son Jesus Christ,* he also declares that the Reason why he wrote was, that *we should believe in the Name of the Son of God.* St. Paul tells us, that being (before his Incarnation) *in the Form of God, he thought it no robbery to be equal with God.* And our Blessed Saviour himself, so far from declining the Title of *Son of God*, confirms and vindicates it against those who charged it as Blasphemy upon him. He openly asserts the Father and Himself to be one, and declares, that *whosoever hath seen him, hath seen the Father.* Nay he even required of some of those Persons who applied to him to be healed of their Distempers, that they should subscribe to this Article, viz. that they *believe* in Jesus Christ *the Son of God.* Again, when St. Peter had made a solemn Profession of this Truth of the Divinity of Christ, by declaring Him to be *the Son of the living God.* Our Saviour in recompence of this Faith and Profession, declared to him the Dignity to which he was pleased to raise him, viz. to be *the Rock on which he would build his Church.* *

(q) Eph. c. i. v. 9.
Col. c. i. v. 16. 17.
Heb. c. i. v. 2.
(r) John. c. i. v. 3.
(s) 1. Ep. of St. John c. iii. v. 23.
(t) 1. Ep. John c. v. v. 13.
(u) Phil. c. ii. v. 6.
(w) St. John c. x. v. 36.
(x) John c. xiv. v. 9.
(y) John c. ix. v. 35.
(z) Mat. c. xvi. v. 16.
(a) Mat. c. xvi. v. 18.

* Again it is remarkable that amongst the Jews at the time of our Saviour's appearance, *Messiah,* or the *Son of God,* were convertible Terms, designing the same Person, as is evident from several Passages in the new Testament, Nathaniel said to Jesus, *Rabbi, thou art the Son of God, thou art the King of Israel.* and again Martha said,

(a) John c. i. v. 49.

From

From all which it is evident, that Jesus Christ is no created and subordinate Being, and by Consequence, of the same Nature; Power, and

said, *I believe thou art the Christ the Son of the living God*. (b) and we read in St. Matthew, that two Men possessed with Devils cried out, *what have we to do with thee, Jesus, thou Son of God?* (c)

Now *Christ* is called in Scripture on several respects, *the Son of God*, he is so called on the account of his temporal Generation, being conceived in an extraordinary manner, in the Womb of the blessed Virgin, by the Power of the Holy Ghost; whence the Angel told the Blessed Virgin Mary, He should be called the Son of God. (d) And he is so called by reason of his great Dignity and Authority, being next in Order to the Father, and sat down on the right hand of the Majesty on High, whereby he hath the actual possession as Heir of all. *God hath in these latter Days Spoken unto us by his Son, whom he hath constituted Heir of all things, by whom he also made the World, who being the Splendor of his Glory, and the figure of his Substance.* (e) and again, *thou art my Son, this Day have I begotten thee*. (f)

But it is to be observed, that tho' others may be called the Sons of God, yet *Jesus Christ*, is called in the Scriptures, *the only Son of God*, and that in such a particular Way and Manner, as never any other was, is, or can be; for St. John assures us, that *God so loved the World, that he hath given his only begotten Son; that every one, who believeth in him, should not perish, but have everlasting Life* (g) And in another place he says, that *God sent his only begotten Son into the World, that we might live through him.* (h)

The *Valentinians*, and *Gnosticks*, imagined that our Saviour proceeded from his Father by *Emission*, that is, by sending him forth like a Tree that produces, or sendeth forth it's Branches; consequently by Division and Section from that Nature or Being, from whence he was emitted. Wherefore *St. Athanasius* in one of his Creeds, expressly opposeth the Generation of the Son, " to this Emission of the Gnosticks. We believe says " he, in one only begotten Word, born of the Father " without beginning of time; from all Eternity, being
" not

(b) John c. xi. v. 27.
(c) c. viii. v. 29.

(d) Luck. c. i. v. 35

(e) Heb. c. i. v. 2. 3.
(f) ibidem. v. 5.

(g) c. iii. v. 16.
(h) Eph. c. iv. v. 9

and Duration, or (as the Athanafian Creed has it) *Con-fubftantial, Co-eternal and Co-equal with the Father:* And this appears more fully from the confideration to which He Himfelf appeals, (*b*) viz. That many of his daily works were fuch, as were plainly an over-match for any thing lefs than the Divinity; efpecially that Power abiding in Him, which was never communicated-even unto the Apoftles themfelves, viz. the Power of fearching into the very Hearts of Men, and becoming acquainted with their moft dark and hidden Thoughts, the very Moment they conceived them; as you may fee in St. Matthew, St. Luke, and St. John (*c*) This I fay, we no where find to have been exercifed by any Man, either Prophet or Apoftle, and therefore it appears to be not only an Attribute, (as is univerfally acknowledged) but an *incommunicable* Attribute of the Divinity: For wherever there is the appearance of this Knowledge or Power in any other Perfon, it is by *Re-*

(*b*) Mat. c.xi. v. 4 5.John c. xiv. v. 11 12.

(*c*) Mat. c. ix. v. 4. Luck c v. v. 22. John c. xvi. v. 19

" not a Divifion from the impaffible Nature, or an Emi-
" ffion, but a perfect natural Son."(*i*)
    As for the manner of the Fathers eternal begetting of the Son, I fhall not pretend to enquire into this incomprehenfible Myftery. For which reafon, great caution is to be ufed in our Searches therein, and Expreffions thereof, that we do not with too great nicety and curioufnefs dive into his profound and incomprehenfible Secret. This is the advice of the famous and pious *Alexander* Bifhop of Alexandria; for if, " Says he, the
    " knowledge of many other things far inferior to this,
    " exceed the reach of human underftanding, how then
    " fhall any one without Madnefs pretend curioufly to
    " fearch into the Effence of the Divine Word? Of
    " whom the Holy Ghoft by the Prophet fays, who fhall
    " declare his Generation? (*k*)

(*i*) Expofi. fid. Tom. i.

(*k*) Epift. ad Alex. Conftantinopl. apud Theodorit. Ecles. Hift.

velation,

velation, but in Jesus Christ it was absolutely *from Himself.* He knew or perceived *in his Spirit*, or by his Spirit, what they thought, says St. Mark (*d*). And St. John assures us that, He needed not that any should give testimony of Man, for he knew what was in Man (*e*)

(*d*) Mark. c. ii. v. 8
(*e*) John c. ii. v. 25

To these Testimonies from the sacred Scriptures, I shall subjoin a Passage or two from the Writings of the first Posessors of Christianity after the Apostles, which may serve for instances of the general sense of the primitive Church on this important Article. The *Logos*, or *Word* (says St. Justin Martyr) *being the first begotten of God, is God.* (*f*) *Know ye* (says St. Irenæus) *that Jesus, who* Suffered for us, and who took up his abode among us, that same Jesus is the *Word of God.* (*g*) *Let our Accusers know* (says Origin) *that he whom we Esteem, and believe to be from the Beginning God, and the Son of God, is his own Word.* (*h*) *we say* (saith Tertullian) *that he proceeds from God, and therefore is called the Son, and God by reason of the Unity of Substance.* (*i*) From these Considerations it appears, that the true Reason of Christ being called the *Son of God*, is on account of his having one and the same nature with the Father, and being Himself the very same eternal God.

(*f*) St. Just. Apol

(*g*) Adv Hæres. L. 1. c. 1

(*h*) Contra Celsum. L. 3.

(*i*) Adv. Gent. xxi See also Theodoret Hist. Eccles. l. ii. c. viii. et l. i. c. ii et. 4.

There remains still one Character of Jesus Christ to be considered in this Article, which is that of *Lord of us*, or as it is expressed in the Creed *our Lord*.

Now it clearly appears, that Christ by Virtue of his divine Nature, has a just and indisputable Right of Dominion over us, especially as we are his Creatures, since from Him we

received

received our very Life and Being, for as St. Paul fays, it was *by Him God made the World.* (*k*) (*k*)Heb. c. i. v. 2. But this Appellation is in a more particular manner due to him, in as much as he has *redeemed* and *purchafed* us at the Price of his moft precious Blood, that we fhould thenceforth become his; and we know that purchafe conveys a moft equitable Right of *Dominion*. Well therefore, may we call him our *Lord*, who paid fuch a Price for us; and with joy ought we to lift under fuch a Mafter, who hath delivered us from the Hands of that cruel Mafter the Devil, and the intollerable Bondage of Sin, and Mifery. For thefe Reafons it is, that we call Jefus, *our Lord*. Having therefore given you a fufficient Account of this Article; I fhall now conclude it with a fhort Review of the whole; from which it appears, that to fay, *I believe in Jefus Chrift, his only Son our Lord;* is in effect to fay thus;

I believe that there was once on Earth fuch a Perfon as *Jefus Chrift*, who was fent by God to procure and declare to us the Terms of Salvation; and that he was the very *Meffiah* promifed by the Father, and foretold by the Prophets, and that he was, as his Name imports, truly the *Saviour* or Redeemer of all Mankind. I believe alfo, that the fame Jefus, who affumed human Nature, had another Nature, viz. that of God, in as much, as he was truly and perfectly God, as having the Nature of God, by communication from the Father; for which Reafon, we call him *his only Son*. Laftly, we acknowledge Him to be *our Lord;* not only upon account of his being God; but alfo by Virtue of of that Price which he paid for our Redemption, Namely his Blood, by which alone, he has an undoubted right of Dominion over us. Let us then always believe and profess these certain Truths, that we may partake of the eternal Life, which is promised to those, who truly believe in Him.

ARTICLE, III.

DISCOURSE. I.

Who was conceived by the Holy Ghost, born of the Virgin Mary.

When his Mother Mary, was espoused to Joseph, before they came together, she was found with Child of (or by) the Holy Ghost. Mat. c. i. v. 18.

IN the former Article, I treated concerning the *Divinity* of Christ; in this, I shall speak of his *Humanity*, or Incarnation.---This great Mystery of God made Man, transcends the Understanding both of Men and Angels: However the Truths of it are certain and undoubted, and upon these Truths, all our hopes of Salvation are grounded. There is a method to partake effectually of the Mystery of God made Man, and there is an effectual way never to partake of it.

My

The CREED EXPLAINED.

The Divis. My design in this Discourse shall be so to instruct you in the Truths of this Mystery, that you may know by what means, you may partake of it; and by what means, Men are excluded from the participation of it.

P. I. Almighty God seeing the fall of our first Parents in Paradise, and in what a sad and miserable Condition they had involved themselves, and all their Posterity; He thereupon out of the Bowels of his infinite Mercy and Goodness promised to repair it, by *the Seed of the Woman*, (*l*) which should *bruise the Serpent's Head*. (*l*) But how was this to be brought about, since Reason tells us, that no one of *human* Race, was likely to make sufficient Satisfaction and Atonement for the Sins of a whole World? Now to accomplish this, the Eternal Son of God condescended to take our Nature upon Him, and to become Man, that in his human Flesh, he might Suffer the Punishments due to our Sins; and in Virtue of His Divinity, cancel the whole Debt of our Offences: The frailty of his human Nature, rendered him passible and obnoxious to Suffering; and the Dignity of his Person, enhanced the Merit of every Action of his Life, to an infinite degree, so as to render his Atonement abundantly satisfactory to the injured Justice of Heaven. Yet although it was necessary to these purposes, that Christ should take the human Nature upon Him, it was not absolutely necessary that he should put himself entirely, and in all respects upon a level with His Creatures: The Dignity of his Person and Character, demanded some distinction; and we accordingly find, that there were several very remarkable

(*l*) Gen. c. iii. v. 15

remarkable and miraculous ones made; viz; firſt, He came not into the World by the ordinary means of Generation, but was conceived in a miraculous manner by the immediate Power and Virtue of the *Holy Ghoſt*. Secondly, his Body was formed and perfected in an Inſtant, and immediately inſpired with a Soul. Thirdly, at the ſame Inſtant, the Divine Perſon was united both to Body and Soul. Fourthly, from the ſame Inſtant, the Soul was endowed with a perfect uſe of Reaſon.

But we muſt obſerve, that although this Myſtery of the Incarnation be here attributed to the *Holy Ghoſt*, yet we are not to think that it was by Him alone, without the concurrence of the *Father* and the *Son*. For this is a Rule, without exception in the Myſtery of the Bleſſed Trinity, that all the external Works of God are done indiviſibly by all the three Perſons of the Bleſſed Trinity, becauſe their Power is all one indiviſible Power in them, and ſo the Conception of our Saviour being the Effect of one and the ſame Divine Power, it belongs to the *Father* and the *Son* as much as to the *Holy Ghoſt;* Therefore, when we ſay that Chriſt was conceived by the *Holy Ghoſt*, it is the ſame as to ſay, that his Conception was by the Power and ſpecial Gift of God, after a ſupernatural and not natural manner like other Men. Now the Reaſon why the Conception is here in a particular manner attributed to the Holy Ghoſt is, *firſt*, becauſe it was a Work of Goodneſs and Love, and the Holy Ghoſt proceeding from the mutual Love of the *Father* and the *Son*, Works of that kind are aſcribed to Him. *Secondly,*

condly, becaufe it was a Work of Grace, without any Merits of Man, and the Holy Ghoft being the Fountain of Grace, therefore this extraordinary Work of Grace is attributed to him: For the holy Scriptures particularly attribute *Power* to the Father, *Wifdom* to the Son, and *Love* and *Grace* to the Holy Ghoft. And as the Conception of Jefus Chrift, (by which *the Word was made Flefh*) is a moft fingular Proof of God's immenfe *Love* towards Man, fo it is therefore afcribed particularly to the *Holy Ghoft*.

However though Chrift did not become incarnate by human generation, yet he did verily and indeed become Man in all refpects like one of us, Sin only excepted, of a rational Soul and human Body: He entered into a Body, which was prepared for him (*m*) in the Womb of the Bleffed Virgin, with this Body he was born, thisBody was nourifhed, and encreafed in the fame way as thofe of other Children, confifting of Flefh, Blood, Bones &c. like the Bodies of other Men. And as his walking on the Waters (*n*), entering into a Houfe where the Doors were all fhut, (*o*) and other fuch like Circumftances were evident proofs of his *Divinity*, fo were his Sufferings, his Scourging at a Pillar, his Crucifixion &c. proofs of his perfect *Humanity*, at leaft with refpect to the corporal part; and certainly if he would fo far condefcend, as to be endued with this groffer, and lefs worthy, he would not omit the nobler and more excellent part of the human Compofition, viz. the rational and intellectual Soul,

(*m*) Heb. c. x. v. v.

(*n*) Mat. c. xiv.
(*o*) John. c. xx. v. 19

without

without which also, he could not be a perfect and compleat Man. *

This I mention as well against the Errors of *Appollinaris* and his Followers, who maintained or held that Christ had not a human Soul compleat;

* Tho' the Son of God out of his infinite Goodness and compassion to us, became Man, that he might accomplish his gracious Design of redeeming the World; yet such is the degenerate and corrupted Nature of Mankind, that several of them, even in the beginning of Christianity, as well as in these latter Days, have disbelieved in the Incarnation of the Son of God, and looked upon it as a mere Dream or Fancy. As for example, the *Ebionites*, *Cerinthians* in the first Age; and *Carpocrates*, *Marcionites*, *Barbesianists* and others in the second Age; who all affirmed, that. Christ was conceived and born in the same way and manner, as all other Men are, in the ordinary way of Generation by the Conjunction of Joseph and Mary; and thus of course, that *Jesus Christ* was not God, but a mere Man: Some indeed held that his Body was framed in Heaven, and so passed through the Blessed Virgin Mary, as Water through a Pipe, without receiving any thing of his Body from her, which notion was also espoused by *Basilides*.

Now against all these Hereticks, *St. Irenæus*, who lived in the second Century, wrote five Books, in which he excellently well proves the Verity and necessity of Christ's assuming a real and bodily Substance from the Flesh of the Blessed Virgin; and in the fortieth Chapter of his third Book, he tells us, that all the various Blasphemies of these divers Hereticks, were rejected and Condemned by the Church, and the contrary Truth preserved, in the Apostles Creed, as a precious Depositum and most Sacred Treasure; so that the Catholick Belief is, that the Body of *Christ*, was a real, true, and material Body; for if *Christ* had been incarnated, and suffered only in shew and appearance, he had been the greatest Deceiver and Liar that ever was in the World, and of course, could not possibly have been the Saviour, and Redeemer of Mankind.

pleat; as against the Errors of *Valentinus*, and *Apelles* who maintained that Jesus had only a fantastical, or aerial Body, contrary to the Epistles of St. Paul to the Hebrews and Romans, where Christ is said to be from the seed of *Abraham* and *David* (*q*) Now the Incarnation was an union of the two Natures, not a Confusion, half human, and half divine, for each of them was entire, and perfect in itself (which the human Nature, cannot be without a Soul.) Then as a common Man is compounded of two Principles which are almost as discordant as Divinity and humanity, so the two compleat Natures of God and Man, by an union something like (but more astonishing) than, that of the Soul and Body, became one Christ.

(*q*) Heb.
c. ii. v. 16
Rom. c.
iv. v. 3.

Thus *the Word was made Flesh*, (*r*) in such a manner however, as not to lose his former Nature, and have that wholly absorpt and buried in Humanity, but continuing still so distinct from it, as to be virtually seperated: For that the Divine Nature could suffer, and die for us, were an absurdity too gross and palpable for the most clouded Imagination to conceive.

(*r*) John
c. i. v. 14

But let us now see, how this great Mystery of the *Incarnation* was executed. The Evangelist tells us that the Angel Gabriel was sent by God to a City of Gallilee, called Nazareth, to a Virgin espoused to a Man, whose Name was Joseph, of the House of David, and the Virgin's Name was Mary (*f*) Here we may observe that the Scripture very justly remarks two things; the first is, that she was a *Virgin*, to shew us her purity from all carnal Commixtion; the second, that she was *espoused to Joseph*, to put

(*f*) Luck.
c. i. v. 26.
27.

put us in mind that he was to be a fupport to her and her divine Babe, and fcreen her from the imputation of any criminal Commerce, and penalty of the Law, which commanded Perfons of a difhoneft Character, that is to fay, who were found guilty of Adultery to be ftoned to Death. However, though this was a fecurity to the Bleffed Virgin againft the penalty of the Law, yet as her Pregnancy began to fhew itfelf even before they came together, that is, before the Confummation of the Nuptials. *(t)* This caufed great fears and difquiets in *Jofeph* her fpoufe, in fo much that he had thoughts of putting her away privately, till he was informed of the Myftery by the Angel, who faid to him, *Jofeph Son of David fear not to take unto thee Mary thy Wife, for that which is conceived in her is of the Holy Ghoft.* (*u*)

But that we may omit nothing of the feries of this Myftery, let us hearken to the Voice of the Angel: For as St. Luke relates; *the Angel being come in, faid unto her; Hail full of Grace, the Lord is with thee: Bleffed art thou among Women,* (*w*) at which Salutation, the Bleffed Virgin was furprifed; but the Angel foon difperfed her fears, by this Familiar and encouraging Speech: *Fear not Mary, for you have found Grace with God.* And forthwith, he denounced the future Event of his Embaffy. *Behold you fhall conceive in your womb, and fhall bring forth a Son and you fhall call his Name Jefus. He fhall be great and be called the Son of the moft High, and the Lord God will give him the Throne of his Father David; and he fhall reign in the Houfe of Jacob for ever, and of his Kingdom there fhall be no End,* (*v*) This promife

(*t*) Mat. c. i. v. 18

(*u*) Mat. c. i. v. 20

(*w*) Luc. c. i. v. 28

v. 30.

(*v*) Luc. c. i. v. 31 32. 33.

promise appeared very mysterious to the Virgin, who was conscious, not only of her present, but future Virginity; Upon which the Blessed Virgin made Answer, as St. Luke says; *How shall this be done, since I know not Man,* (x) (*x*) v. 34. wherepon the Angel unfolded the whole Mystery, saying; *The Holy Ghost shall come upon thee, and the power of the most High shall overshadow thee; and therefore also the Holy which shall be born of thee, shall be called the Son of God.* (y) (*y*) v. 35. And in order to confirm her in the Truth of this Promise, the Angel told her, that her Cousin Elizabeth had conceived a Son in her old Age, and that she was Six Months gone, who was esteemed barren; to shew her, that nothing is impossible to God. (z) v. 36. (z) Then Mary replied, *Behold the Handmaid of our Lord, be it done unto me according to thy Word.* (a) v. 38. *(a)* And then the Angel left her; when the same Moment the Holy Ghost, after an extraordinary and miraculous manner framed a human Body of her Substance, within her chaste Womb, which being animated with a rational Soul, was instantly united to the Divine Nature in the Person of Jesus Christ, that is, the second Person of the most adorable Trinity.

This stupendous Work being effected by the Power and Efficacy of the holy Spirit, it is therefore said in this Article, that *he was conceived by the Holy Ghost,* that is to say, by means of the Holy Ghost, so that by this declaration all mankind are excluded from a Right of Paternity over *Jesus.* From hence arises a natural Question, since all mankind are excluded from a Right of Paternity over *Jesus,* how is He then the Son of *David* and *Abraham,* according to the Flesh?

Flesh? And how were the several Promises made good to those Patriarchs? Briefly thus; *Jesus Christ* entered into the World among the descendants of both those Patriarchs, and therefore by those who allowed Him only a natural Generation, could not be denied to be the Son both of *Abraham* and *David*, being as was supposed *the Son of Joseph*, (*b*) who was lineally descended from them both, as appears from his Pedigree given us at large by two Evangelists, viz. St. Matthew, and St. Luke. (*c*) This Honour, it is true, was only imaginary with regard to Joseph, who was no more than his reputed Father; but the same cannot be said with regard to Mary, for she was his real Mother, and he received of her Substance in the Womb, as other Children do, so that Christ was descended from the Loins of *David*, as was promised in this respect, for his Mother was also a descendant of that House, and of the same Family with her Husband, and as it was always the Custom of the Jews to inter-marry with those of their own Tribe, this being I say their constant Custom, it therefore sufficeth that we have the Pedigree of *Joseph*, though but his supposed Father, for this proves the Blessed *Virgin Mary* to have been of the same Tribe and Family, who was his real Mother.

(*b*) Luc. c. iii. v. 23.

(*c*) Mat. c. i. Luc. c. iii

The Blessed Virgin was now far gone in her Pregnancy, when an Edict came out from *Augustus* the Emperor, commanding all his subjects of the Roman Empire to repair to the City or Place they belonged to, in order to be enrolled (*d*) among the rest, says the Evangelist, *Joseph went up from Galilee into Judea to the City*

(*d*) Luc. c. ii. v. 4. 5. 6. 7.

City of David called Bethlehem, as being of the House and Family of David, to be enrolled there with Mary his espoused Wife who was then big with Child. And it came to pass, that when they were there, the time of her delivery was expired, and she brought forth her first born Son, and wrapped him up in Swadling Clothes and laid him in a Manger, because there was no room for them in the Inn.

Thus, Dear Christians, was the Mystery of God made Man accomplished, a Mystery, as St. Paul says, which was hid from Ages and Generations, but at last revealed to Angels, and made manifest to Men, (*e*) God in the Flesh, the Saviour of the World born, the Messiah come in all the Circumstances foretold by the Prophets. Ah Christians! did we but truly reflect and consider on this wonderful Goodness of God towards Man, this alone would teach us the great Obligation we have of Loving God with all our Hearts, and with all our Souls; for what could God do more for us than he has here done? Consider well this great Mystery: You say you believe it, but have you ever seriously reflected upon what you believe? Have you ever thought how infinite must the Love of God be, in sending his only son to become Man, to expose him to such poverty and want, and all that is here contemptible, and after cruel Torments to die upon a Cross, and all this, that Man might be saved, that sinful dust and ashes might be exalted to Glory? And is there not in this something wonderful and worthy of Love? Blush then and be confounded at all your past ingratitude
and

(*e*) Colos. c. i. v. 26.

and infenfibility, who having fo much reafon to love God, yet love Him fo little.

But let us now fee further what profitable inftructions we may here learn from this Myftery; firft there is nothing fo proper as this Myftery to raife our *Devotion* towards God; nothing could give us fo great an Idea of his Majefty, as to behold fo great a Perfon as *Jefus Chrift* made a *Sacrifice* to Him; nothing could give a truer notion of his *Power*, which was able to return a greater Honour to himfelf by Jefus Chrift, than the Sins of Men could take from Him; nothing gives us a truer notion of his *Wifdom*, which found out fo Sovereign a remedy for the moft incurable of all Evils; nothing better fhews his *juftice*, than to fee him exact fo great a Ranfom for Sin; and nothing better fhews his *Mercy*, than to fee Him charge Man's Sins, rather upon his own Eternal Son, than upon His own Creatures who offended; again, there is nothing more proper to raife the *Hopes* of Sinners to Heaven, than to fee God come from thence to fave them; nothing more proper to prevent that *Defpair*, which our mortal and finful Condition would infpire, than to fee God fo much Love and value human Nature as to exalt it to fo high a pitch; nothing fo proper to fhew us the greatnefs of our *Crime* and *Ruin*, as to fee the greatnefs of the remedy; and nothing more proper to convince us how great was the *Paradife* we loft, and the *Heaven* we hope for, than to fee God Himfelf do fuch aftonifhing Actions to regain it. Such are the Inftructions of this great Myftery.

The Fruits and Benefits of it are thefe. *Firſt*, Remiſſion of Sin, and Redemption from Hell; for it is a certain truth, that we have all of us been redeemed from Hell and Eternal miſery by Jeſus Chriſt. *Secondly*, vocation to Grace, adoption among the Sons of God, Reſurrection to Life, Society with Angels, Inheritance with Chriſt in his eternal Kingdom of Glory. But tho' there is nothing more effectual than thefe Benefits of Redemption, yet it is a certain Truth that all partake not of thefe Benefits; for though Almighty God could not love us more than what He has done, by giving us his only Son to be our Redeemer, which in effect is giving himſelf; yet there is ſomething required on our part, without which the whole Benefit is utterly overturned. It is therefore of the greateſt importance to know what it is, that makes us effectually partake, of the Myſtery of God made Man, left we ſhould be found to have no part in the Merits of Jeſus Chriſt. I will tell you then, Dear Chriſtians, what it is that makes void the whole Benefit of our Redemption; it is a ſinful Life, and this I will ſhew you in ſuch plain Terms that no one can be ignorant of it.

P. II. The end of Chriſt coming into this World, was as I ſaid before to redeem loſt Man; now this Redemption is twofold; *firſt*, Redemption from Sin, and *ſecondly*, Redemption of the Sinner from Hell. Take notice of this, and obſerve well the Œconomy of God's Grace, and the order by which Chriſt wrought our Redemption; there muſt be a Redemption from Sin before there could be a Redemption from Hell, for it is improbable, nay impoſſible, that any Man could be Redeemed from the
ſlavery

flavery of the Devil, and from Hell, before he is fet free from his Sins: Therefore do the Prophets every where cry out concerning the Meſſiah, that he ſhould deliver his People from their Sins ; that Sin was going to be deſtroyed ; it is in this ſenſe, that he is the Saviour of Men, that by ſetting them free from the Slavery of Vice and their Paſſions, they might ſo regain a perfect Liberty ; and ſo be ſet free from the Slavery of the Devil, be redeemed from Hell, be reconciled to God, and recover the right to the Inheritance of his Kingdom, and ſo be put in poſſeſſion of that Inheritance. It is in this ſenſe, that Chriſt is the Saviour of Man, nor can it be in any other ; for thoſe who continue in Sin are in no ſenſe ſaved ; for as they are ſlaves to vice, ſo are they alſo to the Devil, and therefore will have no part in the Redemption of Jeſus Chriſt. From whence it is evident, that a wicked and ſinful Life overturns all the Benefits of Redemption, and therefore thoſe who continue in Sin, do not partake of the Myſtery of God made Man.

There is nothing then, that ought to give a Chriſtian a greater abhorrence of a ſinful Life, than this Myſtery ; and on the other hand it is the greateſt inducement to virtue and ſanctity; whether we conſider the Myſtery in the perfection of the Law he has given, or the greatneſs of the Example who is Jeſus Chriſt, or the greatneſs of the Grace, or the greatneſs of the Dignity, or the Reward we are called to. Thoſe who have quitted their Sins, and lead a ſober, juſt, and pious Life like Men redeemed from Hell, like Men who have quitted
the

the company of those who perish eternally; such as these I say are effectually made partakers of the Incarnation and Birth of Christ. In a Word to be saved through Jesus Christ, all must in the *first* place firmly believe every Article of our Creed, and all that Christ has taught; *secondly*, they must faithfully acquit themselves of the Duties of the state and calling they are in, and observe the Commandments of God and his Church.

But to compleat the Explication of this Article: It may be necessary to observe, that the Mother of Jesus, was not only a Virgin before her Conception, and immediately after her Parturition, but even for ever after, during the whole Term of her Life; for such as have held the contrary Opinion have been condemned by the Church; though there be no particular mention of this, either in the ancient or modern Creeds; yet the holy Fathers thought it strongly implied by several considerations; and therefore the Catholick Church has always stiled her, *the ever Virgin Mary*.

As to what may be objected, that *Joseph* is said, *not to have known her, till she brought forth her first born Son*, (f) by which expression, some would have it, that at least he knew her after; no more is intended by this Phrase, than absolutely to exclude the Co-operation of all *human* means in the Conception of *Jesus*, and to assert that Joseph knew her not, either before or during the time of her Pregnancy, that the whole of it might be ascribed to the Holy Ghost. And as to the Gospels making mention of the Brethren of Christ; this seems clear to be intended

(f) Mat. c. i. v. 25.

ed only in that general sense, in which the Jews
called all those of their own kindred by the
Name of Brethren. Thus *Abraham* called *Lot*
his *Brother*, (g) though he was only his Nephew, (g) Gen.
as being the Son of *Haran* Abraham's Brother, c. xiii. v.
and there is hardly a more common thing in 8.
the old Testament, than to find this Title given
to collateral Kindred. Hence it appears, that
there is no valid Objection against the Blessed
Virgin Mary's perpetual Virginity, as well after she brought forth the Redeemer of the
World, as before her Conception; and indeed
Decency seems to require it, and this Doctrine
is, what the ancient Fathers of the Church have
all been unanimous in Determining.

Let us now sum up in short, the Truth of
what has been said of this Article, we must
then first believe, that *Jesus Christ* the Son of
God, whose Divinity we before considered,
did become truly Man, by taking Flesh, not
by Creation, or from any foreign or separate substance; but from the real Flesh and Blood of
the Blessed Virgin Mary; so that he was really and truly conceived in the Womb of the
Virgin, not after the ordinary way, but entirely
miraculously and by the immediate virtue and
extraordinary effect of the Holy Ghost, and
that in consequence thereof, and of his being
the Son of God, the Virgin Mary is truly stiled
the Mother of God; and she is so called by St.
Elizabeth, as we read in St. Luke, (h) and the (h) c. i.
Church in the Council of *Ephesus*, which was v. 43.
held in the Year of our Lord 431 against the
Nestorians, has condemned those, who deny that she is the Mother of God. We must
also

also believe, that the whole Blessed Trinity indivisibly wrought this miraculous Conception, but the second Person only became actually incarnate, because the two Natures divine and human were united in his Person only. We likewise believe, that the Blessed Virgin Mary was a Descendant of the House of *David*, and espoused to St. Joseph of the same Tribe and Family; That she always remained a pure and immaculate Virgin, as well before, as after Child-birth, so that she became a Mother, without Detriment to her Virginal Integrity, by the aforementioned Power of the Holy Ghost; and why should this seem incredible, that the Blessed Virgin should bring forth a Son, and she still remain really and truly a Virgin? Since we read *that nothing* is impossible to God. (i) And thus much we assent to, when we say we believe *in Jesus Christ, who was conceived by the Holy Ghost, born of the Virgin Mary.*

(i) Luc. c. i. v. 37.

To conclude, let our Lives be conformable to the humble, innocent, and mortified Life of our Dear Jesus, who is established by the eternal Father as our Model, let our Life resemble His, let it be a Copy, and a representation of His, that we, by participating of his Virtues, Spirit, and Graces in this Life, may be partakers of his Glory in the next.

ARTICLE

ARTICLE, IV.
DISCOURSE. I.

Suffered under Pontius Pilate, was crucified dead and buried.

Pilate having scourged Jesus, he delivered him unto them to be crucified.---And he gave up the Ghost---And Joseph took the Body and laid it in a new Monument, (or Sepulchre.) Mat. c. xxvii. v. 26. 50. 60.

THE Apostles having in the two preceeding Articles, professed Jesus Christ in the Glory of his Divinity, as the eternal Son of God; and in the Mystery of his Conception, and joy of his Birth, as Man. They now in this Article, set Him before our Eyes, in his Passion and Death.

I shall therefore in this Discourse, *first*, examine into the import of the Word *suffered;* and *secondly,* lay before you in part, the Mystery of our Saviour's Passion, with some Reflections thereupon.

The Divis.

O It

P. I.

If we would trace the Sufferings of Chrift from their Beginning, we muft go back even to the very firft Inftant of his Birth, in the ftable of Bethlehem, where we fhall find him expofed to all the Wants and Inconveniences of Life: From hence, let us follow him through the whole courfe of his Life; we fhall find it one continued fcene of Poverty, Labour, Perfecution, Contempt, and Suffering.

From the firft hour almoft, that he enters on His Office, he has Enemies who lie in wait for his Life; one while, He is branded with the Title of Impoftor. (*k*) Another while, he is rejected as a Dæmoniac. (*l*) He is not only ftript of his *Divinity*, but even of his *Humanity*, and made a Partner and Confederate with Beelzebub the Prince of the Devils. (*m*) The moft inveterate Enemies are reconciled, the moft oppofite Factions united to contrive and effect His Deftruction. (*n*) To Day, he is affaulted by Pharifees. (*o*) To-morrow, by Saducees. (*p*) The next Day, by Herodians. (*q*) And fometimes by all in Conjunction; one ftrives to draw him into Blafphemy, another into Treafon; and when they cannot make his Actions liable to the penal ftatutes, they endeavour to bring thofe Laws by their Interpretation, to correfpond to his Actions. His Words are mif-interpreted, his Actions vilified; and an Odium thrown on the moft exalted Difpenfations of his Benevolence. This is, the uninterrupted Bufinefs of near Three Years, and but a Prelude to his laft forrows, which were as great, as diabolical Malice could inflict.

(*k*) Mat. c. xxvii, v. 63.
(*l*) John c. viii. v. 48.
(*m*) Mat. c. xii. v. 24.
(*n*) Luck c. xxiii.v. 12.
(*o*) Mat. c. xix. v. 3.
(*p*) Mat c. xvi. v. 1.
(*q*) Mat. c. xxii.v. 16.

Thefe

* These are ushered in by the blackest Perfidy and Ingratitude, for after our Saviour had eaten the Paschal Lamb with his Apostles, as he desired to do before he suffered, (r) to teach us a perfect Obedience to the Law of God: After he had, to the Astonishment of Men and Angels, humbled himself to that degree, as to wash the Feet of his Apostles, nay even the Feet of the Traitor Judas; to teach us, with what Humility, and Purity, we ought to approach to the Blessed Sacrament of the Altar, which he then was about to institute, in order to leave behind him a singular Memorial of

(r) Luck c. xxii. v. 15.

---

* Now it is to be observed, that several of the ancient Hereticks, as *Cerdon, Marcion, Saturninus,* and others held, that our Saviour Christ did not really suffer; since they affirmed, that he had no substantial Flesh, but that his body, was a mere Phantom, or Apparition. Contrary to all which, St. Ignatius Bishop of Antioch, in his Epistle to the Smyrnæans, gives thanks to God, that they firmly adhered to the immovable Faith, that *Christ truly suffered, and not as some Hereticks affirm, that he only Suffered reputatively, and according to outward appearance. Epist: ad Tralles:* And Origen, in one of his Creeds, declares the same, that Christ truly, and not imaginarily, suffered under *Pontius Pilate. Passus est in veritate, et non per imaginem. in Proœm. Lib.*---And we prove the same Doctrine from the Comment of St. Cyril Bishop of Jerusalem on this Article, where he says, *that Jesus suffered truly for all Men, for his Cross was not in Opinion, nor his Redemption in Opinion, nor his Death in Opinion. Catch.* 13. And indeed, the Passion of Christ, is so convincing an Argument of what he suffered, that one would think no Man could be so absurd and unreasonable, as to ascribe all he suffered and under went for love of us, to opinion and fancy; for if the Actions of *Caiphas, Herod,* and *Pilate,* relating to our Saviour's Passion, were true and substantial; how can a Man deny the Passion itself to be so, seeing it was equally attended with the same ocular and visible Demonstration?

his Love towards us, viz. his own most precious Body and *Blood*, (*f*) to manifest the desire he had of always remaining with us; for being now to depart out of this World, he would notwithstanding, leave *Himself*, after a Spiritual manner to abide with us forever. Then having said a Hymn in Thanksgiving; He went with his Disciples over the Brook Cedron, (*u*) and entered into a Garden, which was in the Village called Gethsemani near Jerusalem. (*w*) But Judas, one of the twelve Apostles, one of his chosen Friends, one of his Companions, was gone to accomplish his wicked Treason, and offered himself a voluntary Instrument to betray his Lord and Master into the Hands of his implacable Enemies, (*x*) who readily embraced the offer, and thereupon agreed to give him thirty Pieces of Silver. (*y*) There is no doubt, but that Christ, might many ways have been delivered up into the Hands of the Jews, but for the greater Ignominy, he chose to be sold, and that by his own Disciple, that we might learn to bear with false Brethren; and to teach us, that there is no place, or state of Life so holy, from which we are not in danger of falling. Ah Judas! to what height of Wickedness, has the Spirit of Avarice brought thee, to sell thy Soul, thy Master, and thy God, who is the Treasure of Heaven and Earth, at such a vile rate. O Christians, how dangerous and abominable is the Sin of Covetousness! and yet, how often have you sold the same Lord for less, when you have parted with Him, for some petty Delight, or rotten Pleasure, for some fleeting

---

(*f*) Mat. c. xxvi v. 26. see Mark c. xiv. v. 22 and Luck c. xxii. v. 19.
(*u*) John c. xviii. v. 1.
(*w*) Mat. c. xxvi. v. 36.
(*x*) Luck v. xxii. v. 4.
(*y*) Mat. c. xxvi. v 15.

ing Honour, some sinful Thought, for some detracting Word, or the like?

But before this, several things happened, among which, was his foretelling that St. Peter would that very Night thrice deny Him, and that all the Apostles would be shocked and scandalized in Him, and forsake Him. (z) This is, what the Prophet Zacharias had long before foretold; *strike the Pastor, and the Sheep shall be dispersed.* (a) Although all should be scandalized in thee, said St. Peter, *I never will,* (b) Jesus replied, *Amen I say to you, before the crowing of the Cock this very Night, you shall thrice deny me.* (c) You shall deny that you are my Disciple, that you have any thing to do with me, you shall even deny, that you so much as know me; no said St. Peter, though I were to die with you, I will never deny you. Alas! Dear Christians, how often do we say, Dearest Lord, I never will deny thee, no, if I were to die, by no means will I deny thee? Yet for all that, how often is Christ, not once, but a second, and third time denied? I am sorry, says a Penitent, that I have sinned, I will never do the like upon any Account, I am resolved on it, no sweet Jesus, I will sooner die than any more offend and forsake thee; yet very often does it happen, that notwithstanding these Resolutions and Protestations, Christ is thrice and thrice too, quite abandoned, and forsaken. It is good without doubt to make good Resolutions, but we must have a care of putting too great Confidence in them; for in God we must hope and trust, and therefore to our Resolutions, we must join in humble, fervent, and continual Prayer, and we

(z) Mat. c. xxvi. v. 31
(a) Zach. c. xiii. v. 7.
(b) Mat. c. xxvi. v. 33.
(c) v. 34.

we must be very watchful and careful, not only to avoid the Sin, but also the Temptations and Occasions of it; *watch,* says Jesus Christ, *and pray that you enter not into Temptation.* (*d*)

(*d*) Mat. c. xxvi. v. 41. P. II.

Our Blessed Redeemer, being entered into the Garden of Gethsemani to begin his bitter Passion, (that as in a Garden began our Ruin, so there also might begin our Reparation,) and leaving there the other Apostles at some distance, he took with him, Peter, James, and John, who had been before Eye-Witnesses of his glorious Transfiguration on Mount Thabor; he now discovers to them that mortal Anguish, Fear, and Sadness which oppressed his Heart; *My Soul* says he, *is sorrowful even unto Death, stay here and watch with me.* (*e*) *And having gone a little farther, he fell upon his Face, praying; my Father,* says he, *if it be possible, let this Chalice pass from me, nevertheless, not as I will, but as thou wilt.* (*f*)

(*e*) Mar. c. xiv. v. 34.

(*f*) Mat. c. xxvi. v. 39.

You see Christians, your Dear Redeemer oppressed with sorrow even unto Death, that is to say, a sorrow, which would immediately have put an End to his Life, had he not miraculously prolonged it, to suffer still more for Love of us. Oh! what a sudden storm is this, that oppresses our Saviour's Soul? Cannot that Soul, which enjoys the beatifical Vision of the Divinity, dissipate all these inward Troubles? Yes Christians, His ever enjoying the happy sight of his God-head, could not have been capable of this excessive Sadness and mortal Anguish, had he not, by a Miracle, stopt the Communication between the Superior and Inferior part of his Soul. He was pleased to abandon the Inferior part to all her natural

Fears

Art. IV. *Difc.* I.

Fears and Apprehenfions, to fuffer the more feelingly, for Love of us. He gave the Martyrs thofe Spiritual Confolations, which fupported their Weaknefs under the fharpeft Torments; but would not allow himfelf any other Portion, but to take the very Dregs of the bitter Chalice of Punifhment due to our Sins; fo that, during the whole courfe of his Paffion, you muft confider him fuffering, as if he had been *only* Man, of a tender and delicate Complexion of Body, and liable to all our Pains and Miferies, excepting Sin. Thus being defirous of Company, (a Thing natural to Sadnefs and Fear) he faid to his Apoftles, *ftay here and watch with me.* (g) O! what a furprize muft this have been to thofe three Apoftles, to hear this new Language from their Lord and Mafter, and to fee him reduced fo low, as to be forced to feek Comfort from them? Our Bleffed Saviour under this Anguifh and Sadnefs, betakes himfelf to Prayer, the only fure Refuge under all Afflictions and Difficulties, the only Shield in the Day of Battle; but obferve, with what *Reverence*, he prays to his eternal Father, proftrate on the very Ground, and with what *Fervour, with a loud cry and tears,* fays the Apoftle. (h) Learn therefore to imitate him. In this Prayer, he condefcended fo far, as to allow the inferior part to petition, that the Cup of his bitter Paffion might be removed from him, but then he immediately adds, *not my Will, but thine be done.* (i) To teach under all Trials and Croffes, a perfect Submiffion and Refignation to the Divine Will. Though our Saviour Chrift, was in this Diftrefs and Anguifh, and

(g) Mat. c. xxvi. v. 38.

(h) Heb. c. v. v. 7

(i) Mat. c. xxvi. v. 39.

in

in the midft of his Prayer, yet he made two Interruptions to vifit his Apoftles, but found them both times afleep. Ah! Chriftians, is it not our Cafe (like thefe Apoftles) to fleep, that is, to indulge ourfelves in a flothful fenfual way of Living? whereas, the whole Life of our Saviour was fpent in Labouring for our Salvation, and all that he fuffered, he fuffered for us: Our Bleffed Redeemer, being in this defolate ftate, there appeared to him an Angel (k) from Heaven to Comfort him, (k) who is the joy of Angels. Good God! what Humility! for the Lord of Heaven and Earth, to borrow Comfort from his own Creature, and what kind of Comfort, think you did this Angel bring? No other to be fure, but the reprefenting to him the Will of his eternal Father, the Neceffity of his Paffion, and the Glory and Honour, which the God-head would receive thereby; the Redemption of Mankind and the like, all which, he underftood better Himfelf, than the Angel, but he would not refufe the proffer of Comfort, though from his own Creature; to teach us, not to difdain to learn of our inferiors.

(k) Luc. c. xxii. v. 43

Now, to conceive fome of the inward Sufferings of our Dear Redeemer in the Garden of Gethfemani, we need but refleƈt a little on the Caufes and Effeƈts of his bloody agony: As to the caufes, there were three, which concurred to afflict his forrowful Heart. *Firft*, a perfect and lively Idea of all the pains and Torments prepared for him, which were fo diftinctly reprefented to him, that we may fay, he was inwardly Scourged, Spit upon, Buffeted ed, Crowned with Thorns, Reproached, Blaſphemed and Crucified: All theſe, he underwent succceſſively in the different ſcenes of his Paſſion; but in the Garden, he ſuffered them all at once, by a full Repreſentation of all their aggravating Circumſtances. A *Second* Cauſe, more powerful than the former, was, the Repreſentation of all the Sins of the whole World, now laid to his charge, to be cancelled with the laſt drop of his moſt precious Blood. If holy David, as he ſays of himſelf, fainted when he conſidered the ſins of Men againſt God, *(l)* what muſt we think of his Sorrow, whoſe Charity, and Zeal for God's Glory is without meaſure, who is the immaculate Lamb of God, and who alone has a true Notion of the Malice of Sin, when he beheld not only a part of Men's Sins, as David did, but had before him, the Crimes, and Abominations of all Ages, paſt, preſent and to come: In a Word Chriſtians, all your Sins, and mine were preſent to his View, and Augmented his Sorrow in proportion to his Zeal and Charity. But there was ſtill a *Third* Cauſe of our Saviour's Agony, which we muſt not omit, I mean the foreſight, or Knowledge of what little Fruit, Men by their own Faults, would reap from all his Sufferings: Suppoſe a tender and loving Parent, had ſpent his whole Life in toiling, and labouring, watching and Solicitude ; to provide for his Children a comfortable ſubſiſtance, that he even delivered himſelf to Torments and Slavery to reſcue them, what a heart breaking Thought would it be, if he was aſſured, that but one of them, would render all his

Pſ. cxviii v. 53.

his Pains and Labour fruitlefs, and even take an Occafion, from the means provided for his Happinefs, to plunge himfelf deeper into mifery and ruin? It is hard to conceive, what Grief and Sorrow, would over-whelm a Parent in thefe Circumftances: What an Ocean then of Grief, muft of Neceffity wound the tender Heart of Jefus, who loved all Men with a tender Affection, witnefs his laying down his Life for them all: He clearly faw, what little ufe fome would make of his Sufferings, nay, what abufe many would make by perverting the greateft Pledges of his Love into a mortal Poifon? What a melancholy Reflection, to confider that eternal lofs of fo many Millions of Souls, for whom he was to Die, and that the Number of thofe, who by the Fruit of his Paffion, would efcape eternal Mifery, were but very few, if compared with thofe, who would be irreparably loft. For Chrift Himfelf affures us, *that many are called, but few chofen.* (*m*)

(*m*) Mat. c.xx.v.16

Thefe were fome of the chief caufes, of that mortal Agony, which our Bleffed Redeemer fuffered in his Soul; and if we may judge of the inward Pangs and Anguifh of his Soul, not only from the Caufes, but alfo from the Effects, we fhould certainly be convinced, that our Saviour's inward Sufferings, were the greateft, that were ever undergone in this World; for in all our Grief and Fears, the Blood naturally recoils to the Heart, to fupport the center of Life and Motion, but our Dear Redeemer's Heart, was fo oppreffed with Anguifh, that it caft him into a Sweat of Blood, to fuch a degree

gree, as not only to wet his Face, his Body and Garments, but alſo the very Ground, on which he lay proſtrate, as St. Luke relates. *(n)* This outward Sweat, was a ſign and token of the inward Agony of his Soul; and as ſince the Creation of the World, we do not find there was ever ſuch another Sweat, (at leaſt to ſuch a degree) ſo we may juſtly conclude, there was never ſuch an Anguiſh and Sorrow. *(n c. xxii v. 44.)*

After our Saviour had finiſhed his Prayer, he came to his Diſciples a third Time, and ſaid to them, *ariſe, let us go, behold he approaches, who ſhall betray me,* and *while he was yet ſpeaking, behold Judas one of the Twelve came, and with him a great Multitude with Swords and Staves,* ſent from the Chief Prieſts and Elders of the People; Judas had given them this, as *a ſign that whomſoever he ſhould Kiſs, was the Perſon whom they were to apprehend,* he therefore ſtep'd up to our Bleſſed Saviour and ſaid, *Hail Rabbi, and kiſſed him.* (*o*) And our Saviour, with the greateſt meekneſs anſwered, *Friend what art thou come for,* (*p*) *is it with a Kiſs that thou betrayeſt the Son of Man?* (*q*) Who would not imagine, but that ſo mild a Behaviour, might have mollified the Heart of the moſt obdurate Sinner, but alas! what Remedy is ſufficient to cure an obſtinate and perverſe Mind, inveterate in Sin? Let us learn from our Saviour's Meekneſs, to place a firm Confidence in his Mercy, for he denies his Friendſhip to none, who even offered it to Judas. Let us deteſt this moſt impious Treaſon, and take care never to invite our Saviour in among his Enemies, by receiving him into a Soul defiled with mortal Sin. But particular- ly

(o) Mar. c. xiv. v. 42. 43. 44. 45.
(p) Mat. c. xxvi. v. 50.
(q) Luc. c. xxii. v. 48.

ly let us learn, to refift in the Beginning, all our diforderly Paffions and Inclinations to Sin. This Wretch's Paffion, was *Avarice*, which not refifted, brought him by degrees to Theft, for St. John declares, *he was a Thief*, (r) and now to gain a little Money, he has loft his Lord and Mafter, his Life, and Soul, nay, and Money too; a dreadful Example! let us be Wife by his Ruin.

(r) John c. xii. v. 6

But to proceed, our Bleffed Saviour went to meet *the Multitude, and faid to them, whom feek you,* *they anfwered him, Jefus of Nazareth,* (f) upon which, he made Anfwer, *I am he;* whereby, he caft the whole Multitude to the Ground, to give them a proof of his Divinity, and to fhew, that it was not in their Power to apprehend him, unlefs he pleafed. Then Jefus afked them a fecond time, *whom feek you?* and they faid, *Jefus of Nazareth, I have told you,* faid he *that I am the Man.* (t) *Then they came and laid hands on him,* upon which, *his Difciples fled.*(u) O Chriftians! let us with penfive Hearts, contemplate how thefe ravenous Wolves feize upon the innocent Lamb of God with incredible Fury, how they bind and fetter him. Ah! what a fubject of Grief and Sorrow muft this be, to fee our Dear Lord draged with much violence along the Ways and Streets, followed by the Shouts and Acclamations of the Rabble; how different was this Entrance into Jerufalem, from that, which he made fome few Days before, when they cried out, *Bleffed is he that comes in the Name of our Lord. Hofanna in the higheft.* (w) Hence, we may learn to contemn the inconftancy of Wordly Favours. They brought

(f) John c. xviii. v. 4. 5.

(t) John c. xviii. v. 7. 8.
(u) Mat. c. xxvi. v. 50. 56.

(w) Mat. c. xxi. v. 9.

brought him first to Annas, who was President of the Supreme Council, and Father-in-Law to Caiphas the High-Priest: Here you might see, an imperious, haughty, and arrogant old Man taking to task the Infinite Wisdom of God, and with an Air of Authority, he examined our Saviour about his Disciples, and his Doctrine, who answered, that he taught Men openly, and that by them, he might be informed. (x) Now, could any thing be more mild than this Answer, and yet here, a vile Servant of that wicked Man, had the Impudence to give our Dear Lord a Box on the Ear, saying, *is it thus you Answer the High-Priest;* though this, was a great Affront to our Blessed Redeemer, yet he only made this meek reply; *if I have spoken Ill, give Testimony of the Evil, but if Well : why strikest thou me ?* (y) Learn from hence Patience and Meekness, under whatsoever Provocations, you meet with from your Neighbours, since you see our Blessed Redeemer had Power, to cast that insolent Wretch, both Body and Soul, into the eternal Flames of Hell, yet he seeks no Revenge; which is a Lesson for us, how to behave in the like Circumstances. (x) John c.xviii.v. 20. et 21.

(y) John c.xviii.v. 22. 23.

Our Suffering Redeemer, is from hence by order of *Annas,* hurried to *Caiphas;* there was assembled the great Council of the Sanhedrin determined, right or wrong, to take away the innocent Life of Jesus; they therefore proceeded to the Trial, calling the false Witnesses to depose against him. (z) These Men, though lost to Honour and Conscience, yet could object nothing, even sufficient, to satisfy this malicious Court: (z)Mat.c. xxvi.v.59

The

The High-Priest seeing this project of false Witnesses failed, he rose up and conjured him by the living God, to tell him if he was Jesus Christ the Son of God, upon which, our Blessed Redeemer, (who had given an astonishing example of Patience under the greatest provocations, by calmly holding his Peace, while he saw not only his Reputation, but even his Life too, attacked by the blackest Calumnies) out of Reverence to the adorable Name of God, made this Answer, *thou hast said it,* (*a*) that is, *I am;* and then he put them in mind of the last and terrible Day of Judgment, that through Fear thereof, they might be moved to desist from their wicked Intentions; for *I say unto you, hereafter you shall see the Son of Man sitting at the Right-hand of the Power of God, and coming in the Clouds of Heaven.* (*b*) At which Words, the High-Priest rose up in a Fury, rent his Garments crying out Blasphemy, what is your Opinion? the whole Sanhedrin answered, *he is Guilty of Death.* (*c*) But their wicked rage stoped not here, for no sooner, was this wicked Sentence passed on our Innocent Lord, but many Persons fell upon him, with the most unnatural Barbarity; some of them spitting their filthy Phlegm upon his adorable Face, which the Angels behold with raptures of joy; others pluck him by the Cheeks, others buffet him and strike him, while he being bound, is not able to wipe his Face, or ward off a Blow; others again, with some dirty Rag cover his Face, and then, as if he had been some Impostor, or Mock Prophet, at every Blow they insult him with these Words, *Prophesy unto us,* O thou

(*a*) Mat. c. xxvi. v. 64.

(*b*) Mat. c. xxvi. v. 64.

(*c*) Idem. v. 66.

Art. IV. Disc. I.

thou pretended *Christ who it was that struck thee.*
(d) So that, here was truly fulfilled that which *(d)* Luc. c.
the Prophet Isaias foretold, *I have delivered my* xxii. v. 64
Body to those that struck me, and my Cheeks to those
that plucked them, I have not turned away my Face
from them, who rebuked and spit upon me. (e) Be- (e) Isa. c.
sides many other Affronts they gave him, ripping l. v. 64.
up their old Calumnies, calling him a Seducer,
a Blasphemer, possessed with the Devil and the
like; all which, he endured with an invincible
Patience: Here Christians, be ashamed and
confounded at your impatience, who can scarce
take the least word, or smallest affront from
your Neighbours, when your Dear Lord, for
your sakes, hath endured all sorts of Insults, and
Affronts, and that from the Hands, of the basest
and vilest sort of People.

What I have here already related of our Saviour's Sufferings in Caiphas's Palace, very well
deserves our Compassion, and yet there was
another thing, which troubled him more sensi-
bly, than all that outrage of his Enemies; for
St Peter, the Chief of the Apostles, who had
received the most signal Favours from him,
and that very day boasted, that though all the
rest of the Apostles should abandon him, he
would rather die than forsake him: Yet, O the
weakness and inconstancy of frail Man, 'at the
Voice of a silly Maid, who said to him, *thou*
also wast with Jesus of Nazareth, (f) he immedi- (f) Mar. c.
ately, not only once or twice, but thrice denied xiv. v. 67
his Master, and even confirmed his denial with
Oaths and Execrations, that he knew not the
Man. (g) This, was doubtless a great Affliction (g) Mat.
to our Blessed Saviour, to see so dangerous 74.

a fall

a fall of a Person so much favoured and beloved. But what could be the cause of so sudden a Change in this great Apostle? There seems to have been three. *First*, a secret Pride and Presumption in his own strength; *for though all*, says he, *should be scandalized in thee, yet I will not* (*h*). Secondly, the neglect of our Saviour's admonition, in sleeping, when he ought to have watched and Prayed. And *Thirdly*, his exposing himself to danger, by running into bad Company. Let us therefore beware of these causes, and if we have imitated St. Peter's denial, by consenting to mortal Sin, let us learn and follow his Example, in being true Penitents; for he had no sooner denied our Saviour, but *he went forth and wept bitterly*. (*i*) Learn from hence, not to delay to do Penance for your Sins; he continued his penitential Spirit the remainder of his Life; and it is related, that he wept as often as he heard the Cock crow, (*k*) learn to imitate his perseverance.

The Night being now far spent, the Sanhedrin retired to their Rest, leaving our Saviour to the insults and out-rages of the Rabble, who knew nothing could ingratiate them more to their wicked Ministers, than to treat him with the greatest inhumanity. St. Luke expresses their Behaviour in these Words; *and blaspheming many other things they said against him* (*l*). Thus from their Malice and Cruelty, we may infer, what a dismal Night our Blessed Saviour had among them. Early the next Morning, the great Council of the Jews met again, and ratified their former Condemnation of *Jesus Christ*, and then concluded, that the best way to put

(*h*) Mat. c. xxvi. v. 33.

(*i*) Mat. c. xxvi. v. 75.

(*k*) Theod. Hist.

(*l*) Luck c. xxii. v. 65.

put him to Death, was to do it by the Authority of *Pontius Pilate* the Roman Governor; accordingly, they went with our Saviour in a Body to *Pilate*, and there alledged several accusations against him, and although our Blessed Saviour had no other Advantage, but Innocence and silence, *Pilate* saw, that all their accusations were nothing but the Effects of Envy; he thereupon declared our Saviour innocent; then the Jews urged farther, saying, that he stired up the People all over the Country from *Galilee*, even to *Jerusalem*. (m) Pilate hearing them name *Galilee*, and in order to get free of their importunity, he took an occasion to send him to *Herod*, who was then in Jerusalem, as one belonging to his Jurisdiction: This Wretch was overjoyed at the sight of *Jesus*, hoping, that he might prevail with him, to do some Miracle in his Presence, but finding, that ourSaviour would not gratify his idle Curiosity; He put on our Lord a white Garment in Scorn and Contempt, and thus exposed him to the Derision of his rude Guard, and in this fool's Livery sent him back to *Pilate* (n) Thus was our Saviour posted from Tribunal to Tribunal, first to *Annas*, then to *Caiphas*, then to *Pilate*, and from thence to *Herod*, and from him back again to *Pilate*, and in all these Translations entertained with new Scorn, Derision, and Contempt, the Streets ecchoing with the Insults of the Mob, wheresoever he passed. Here, Dear Christians, was verified to the full, what *Jeremias* had prophesied of him, *all that passed by the way, have clapped their Hands upon thee, they have hissed and wagged their Heads.* (o)

Pilate seeing himself disappointed, and that our Saviour was brought back again to his Tribunal

(m) Luck. c. xxiii. v. 5.

(n) Luck c.xxiii.v 11.

(o)Lamen c.ii.v.15

bunal, began to think with himself how to save his innocent Life, and to give as little Offence, as he possibly could to the chief Priest and Elders; he had now a second Time declared, that he found him Innocent, and that Herod was of the same Opinion; *(p)* but this, would not satisfy the Jews Malice; he therefore, proposes to himself two Schemes to save his Life, both extremely injurious to our Saviour Christ, but one, most inhumanly barbarous. It was the Custom of the Jews at the Paschal Solemnity then celebrated, to have one Person released to them, whom the People should choose: Now Pilate had at that time in custody one Barabbas, a notorious Malefactor, an Author of Sedition, and a Murderer; he made no doubt, but that the People would prefer the innocent Lamb of God to this infamous Wretch, detested by all good Men, he therefore goes out, and puts the Question to them, *whom will you that I release to you Barabbas or Jesus?* *(q)* The People, at the Instigation of the Priests and Elders, cried out, *dispatch Jesus and release to us Barabbas.* *(r)* Good God! was there ever such hatred, indignity, and obstinacy, as this of the Jews? Pilate, no doubt, put an outrageous Affront on our Innocent Lord, by setting Him on a level with Barabbas; but the Jews a much greater, by giving the Preference to such a notorious Malefactor. Now this Project of Pilate's having miscarried, he entered upon his *second* scheme, I mean the scourging of our Blessed Saviour at the Pillar. *(ſ)* This Flagellation, our Saviour always mentioned, when he told his Disciples of his Future Passion, as being a very afflicting and painful part of his Sufferings,

(p) Luc. c. xxiii. v. 15.

(q) Mat. c. xxvii. v. 17.
(r) Luc. c. xxiii. v. 18.

(ſ) John c. xix. v. 1

Art. IV. *Disc.* I.

Sufferings, and it was a Punishment the most ignominious (witness the Roman Law, which prohibited the scourging of any of their Citizens, upon any account whatsoever) so it was inflicted on our Saviour with the greatest Cruelty. The Number of Stripes are not set down by the Evangelists, but they are partly expressed by the Number of Executioners, for St. Mark relates, that they assembled a whole Band of Soldiers, whereas the Law of Moses allowed not quite forty Stripes (*t*) for any Malefactor; but the scourging of our Saviour was so cruel and bloody, that they made him but one wound from Head to Foot, as the Prophet Isaias foretold. (*u*)

Here Christians, raise your mournful Attention, and behold how these Monsters of Cruelty seize upon our Dear Lord, strip off his Garments, bind him to Pillar, that he might not be able to avoid one single Stroke, see how they cut and tear his most tender Flesh, adding Scourge to Scourge, Wound to Wound, Sore to Sore, with a most barbarous Cruelty. Contemplate now with compassion his most precious Blood, gushing out of every part of his Body. This bloody Scene, is the Effect of our Sins, we are the Guilty, he the Sufferer, our Sins had deserved the Flames of Hell, and He is scourged to rescue us from it. But the Soldiers Cruelty stopped not here, they dragged him into the Pretorium, (*w*) and there threw a purple Garment about his Shoulders, (*x*) twisted a Crown of Thorns, pressed it upon his Head, put a Reed into his Hand instead of a Sceptre, and in Derision and Scorn, they bent their

(*t*) Deut. c. xxv. v. 3.

(*u*) Isai. c. i. v. 6

(*w*) Mat. c. xv. v. 16.
(*x*) John c. xix. v. 2.

their Knees before him with this Salutation, *Hail King of the Jews.* (y) This done, they Spit in his Face, and buffeted him, (z) snatched the Reed out of his Hand, and struck him on the Head, (a) thus beating the Thorns deeper into his Temples. Pilate hoped now at least, that the Jews would be satisfied, and that their Fury would be turned into Compassion, at the sight of so piteous an object, as he then appeared, and therefore lead him forth in this miserable Condition to their View, saying, *behold the Man,* (b) but they still cried out, *Crucify him, Crucify him.* Then Pilate gave Testimony a third time of our Saviour's Innocence and the Jews perceiving he persisted in his Inclinations of setting him at Liberty, *cried out saying, if thou let this Man go, thou art no Friend to Cæsar.* (c) This moved Pilate more than all the other importunities; he was afraid, that some Information would be made against him at Court, and these human Respects prevailed upon him contrary to Truth and Justice, and his own Conscience, to pronounce Sentence on the *World's Redeemer;* and he condemned him to Death, nay even to the most Ignominious Death of the Cross; but first, he called for some *Water and washed his Hands,* saying, *I am innocent of the Blood of this just Man, look you to it,* then the Jews cried out, *let his Blood be upon us and upon our Children.* (d)

(y) Mat. c. xxvii. v. 29.
(z) John c. xix. v. 3.
(a) Mat. c. xxvii. v. 3
(b) John c. xix. v. 5. 6.
(c) John c. xix. v. 12.
(d) Mat. c. xxvii. v. 24. 25.

Ah Christians! how detestable must Sin be, since it has cost our merciful Redeemer so much to cancel it? It was Sin, that made Jesus bleed in the Garden, it was Sin, that scourged him at a Pillar, crowned him with Thorns, and condemned

demned him to Death: How then can we sufficiently blame our paſt Miſery in having conſented to Sin? I importune you to repent, to deteſt, and be ſorry for your Sins, without which Diſpoſitions you cannot reap the Fruits of our Redeemer's Sufferings. O! how great muſt have been the Love, our Bleſſed Saviour had for us, to cauſe him to ſuffer ſo much for our Redemption? The Angels were aſtoniſhed at this exceſs of Love, to ſee the King of Kings, and Lord of Lords, pierced with Sorrows, crowned with Thorns, and condemned to Death for us poor Worms of the Earth, of whom he had no need. O what Tranſports! what exceſs of Love is here! and after a Love ſo exceſſive, and ſo undeſerved, ſhall we not return him Love for Love? If the leaſt ſlave had but undergone half ſo much for us, he would certainly be the Maſter of our Hearts; and ſince it is our Lord and our God, that has done and ſuffered ſo much for us, ſhall we refuſe, to let him reign and govern therein; No, no, let us Love him in Truth, and in Deed, that is, in doing and ſuffering for him, let us ſerve, adore, and praiſe him here, that we may love, adore, praiſe, and bleſs him hereafter in the Kingdom of his Glory, Amen.

ARTICLE

ARTICLE, IV.
DISCOURSE. II.

Suffered under Pontius Pilate, was crucified dead and buried.

✻✦✻✧✻✦✻✧✻❀;✧✻;✧✻✦✻;✧✻✧✻

Pilate *having scourged Jesus*, he *delivered him unto them to be crucified.---And he gave up the Ghost.---And Joseph took the Body and laid it in a new Monument,* (or Sepulchre.) Mat. c.xxvii. v. 26. 50. 59. 60.

✻✦✻✧✻✦✻✧✻❀;✧✻;✧✻✦✻;✧✻✧✻

The Divif.

IN the last Discourse, I explained to you in part, the Mystery of our Saviour's Passion. What therefore I intend in this, is, to explain to you the Crucifixion, Death, and Burial, of our Blessed Redeemer Jesus Christ.

But, before I proceed to enter upon the Subject of this Discourse, it may be proper, first, to consider, why the Creed is thus particular, in specifying the determinate Time of our Saviour's Passion or Sufferings under *Pontius Pilate*, that is, during the Time, that *Pontius Pilate* was Governor of Judea.

Now

Now, for being thus particular, there were very good Reasons: For firſt, it tends much to the Eſtabliſhment of the Fact; a thing, ſo minutely and circumſtantially related, not being half ſo much expoſed to Cavil and Diſpute, as an Event related at random, and barely ſaid to have happened, without ſpecifying the Time, Place, or Circumſtances: And we have not wanted Opportunities, to make us ſenſible of the Uſefulneſs, and Neceſſity of ſuch Particularity; for many of the Jews, finding their firſt attack, which was to eſtabliſh the Fact and Truth of our Saviour's Sufferings, in which they triumphed, thinking they could not caſt a greater Odium upon our Religion, than by twitting us with the ignominious Death of it's Founder, they finding, I ſay, this proved unſucceſsful, in ſo much, that the Croſs of Chriſt was to us rather a matter of Glory and Triumph, than Shame and Confuſion; they thereupon altered their ſcheme, and endeavoured to deſtroy a Fact, which they had juſt before, been as induſtrious in endeavouring to eſtabliſh; accordingly, ſome who pretend to give us the Hiſtory, have dated it eleven, others ſeventy, and others near ninety Years further back, than the common Account; as thinking, if they could once unhinge the Circumſtances, the Fact itſelf might one Time or other, come to admit of a Diſpute; but ſuch an Artifice, is foreſtalled by the Introduction of *Pilate's* Name into our Creed; and therefore, even this part of the Article, is highly neceſſary, and a proper ſubject of every Chriſtian's Belief.

Secondly,

Secondly, it may be also observed, that this mention of *Pilate*, is necessary; because he himself, is said to have borne ample Witness to the Fact, and to some remarkable Circumstances attending it, viz. the apparent Malice of the Jewish Priests and Rulers; and the unblemished Innocency of our Dear Redeemer. *(e)*

(e) Euseb. Eccles. Hist. L. 2, C. 2

And thirdly, because by his means, it came to pass, that Christ suffered in the manner he did, a Punishment, which the Jewish Law was a stranger to, yet, such as had been preordained and signified, both by Types and Prophecies. *(f)* Crucifixion, was purely a *Roman* Custom: Under *Pilate*, the Jews themselves acknowledge, that they had lost the Power of Life and Death, *(g)* and by these means, it came to pass, that Jesus was crucified. *

(f) John c. iii. v. 14;

(g) John c. xviii. v. 31.

To

* Now with regard to the Passion of our Saviour, the Creed makes mention of the particular manner of his Death, viz. that he was *Crucified*, that is to say, that he was lifted upon a Cross, and nailed thereunto, where all the Spectators might behold him, without any delusion of their Senses, and see that he was a Man, and that he was that very Man, who was commonly known by the Name of *Jesus of Nazareth*, and not *Simon the Cyrenean*, as *Basilides* and his followers, blasphemously imagined; concerning whom, the primitive Records, as we learn from Theodoret, have left us this Account; " that " they affirmed, *Christ did not suffer at all;* but that Si- " mon of Cyrene, the bearer of the Cross, being taken " by the Jews for him, suffered in his stead, whilst he " stood by, and laughed at their folly and mistake; from " whence they farther affirmed, that we must not be- " lieve in him, who was really crucified; but in him, who " seemed so to be. Theodo. Epist. Hær. Fab. Lib. in " Hæres. Basilid." which horrid Opinion, was an evident Subversion of the Gospel, and a total destruction of the very Foundation of Christianity.

St.

Art. IV. Disc. II.

To enter now upon the Crucifixion or Death P. I.
of our Saviour upon the Cross, which is, the
most material part of Christ's sufferings, and
which is particularly taken notice of in this Article   Pilate had no sooner past sentence of
Death on the World's Redeemer, but the Jews
laid hold on him, stripped him of his purple
Garment, and cloathed him with his own; (*h*) (*h*) Mar. c.
they let the Crown of Thorns remain on his xv. v. 20.
Head, that he might not be without Torment;
then they loaded him with the heavy load of
the Cross, (*i*) and set out for Mount Calvary, (*i*) John
the place of Execution, with two Thieves, who c. xix. v.
were appointed to accompany our Saviour and 17.
to be executed with him; to verify what Isaias,
had long before prophesied of him, that *with*
the Wicked he was reputed. (*k*) Here Christians, (*k*) Isac:
contemplate, and take a view with Eyes of liii. v. 12.
Compassion of your Dear Lord and Suffering
Redeemer, in this, his last Progress or Proces-
sion. A Cryer leads the way through the
streets of Jerusalem, publishing aloud the pretended Crimes and Causes of his Death; then
followed the Soldiers and Executioners with
Ropes, Hammers, Nails, Ladders, and other
such like Instruments; after whom, goes along
our Blessed Saviour, all bruised and bloody,
with a Thief on each side of him, and the Cross
on his wounded Shoulders, dragging it forwards
step by step; followed and surrounded by the
Priests, the Scribes, and whole Mob of the

St. *Ignatius* thus expresses this Article in his Creed,
that *Jesus Christ was truly crucified*. *Epist. ad Tralles*. And
St. *Epiphanius*, in his explication of the Creed, gives this
sense of the present Article, *that he Suffered in truth upon*
the Cross. *Advers. Hæres. Lib. iii. in compend. Fid. Cathol.*

R   People,

People, reviling and scoffing at him. Oh what an unheard of piece of Cruelty is this, but all, is too little to serve their Barbarity. Ah Christians, let us now at least, take pity on our Saviour's Sufferings, and let us not add to his Load, by our Sins and offences.

Our Saviour having for some time, with unspeakable Labour and Torment carried the heavy Load of his Cross, which oppressed his wearied Body, wounded in every part, and exhausted by the Loss of so much Blood, at last, fell down and fainted under the Burthen, being unable, to carry it any farther, they compelled one *Simon* of *Cyrene* to carry it the rest of the Way. (*l*)

(*l*) Luck c. xxiii, v 26.

Being come to the Place of Execution, they violently strip off his Garments, which were congealed in his Blood, and thus renewed all his Wounds. Behold him Christians, bleeding a fresh all over his Body; but that moves not the Executioners to the least Compassion. It was costomary to mix a portion of Wine and Myrrh, to comfort the dying Criminal, but instead of this, they presented him with Wine mixt with Gall. (*m*) See how these hard hearted Executioners command him to lie down on the Cross, and with what Meekness, he obeys their cruel Orders; which being done, one of the Executioners comes with a large Nail or Spike, and fixes the Point on the Palm of our Lord's Hand, forces it's way with incredible Torment through the Sinews and Muscles, and drives it into the hard Wood of the Cross, and without delay, they seize upon the other Hand, stretch it out to the utmost extent, and so nail it fast;

(*m*) Mat. c. c. xxvii. v 34,

fast; the same inhumanity, they used in regard to his Feet; insomuch, that they disjointed all his Bones, as it was foretold by the Prophet; *They have dug my Hands and Feet, they have numbered all my Bones.* (n) O what Torments, what inconceiveable Sufferings are these! the Nerves and Sinews are the Instruments of Sensation, and these are no where more frequent, than in the Hands and Feet. It is a great pain to have even an Arm or Leg out of joint, yet our Saviour's Body was extended so barbarously on the Cross, that you might see, and count the separation of his Bones. In that Condition, they raised him up in the Air, and then let the Foot of the Cross into a hole, prepared for that purpose. O! with what Shouts, with what Blasphemies, (o) did the Jews insult over our Saviour now raised aloft, and hanging upon the cruel Cross, how did they Triumph in his Torments; who would not think, that human Nature was uncapable of seeing such Terrour, without being moved with Sentiments of Compassion, yet the savage Malice of the Jews, looked on with all the Pleasure imaginable, mocking at him, and saying, *he saved others,* but *himself he cannot save,* (p) *if he be the King of Israel, let him now come down from the Cross, and we will believe in him.* (q) While they were thus abusing him, he offered himself a bleeding Victim for our Sins, and those of the whole World, and prayed his Eternal Father to pardon them, *Father,* said he, *forgive them for they know not what they do.* (r) What Christian, after such an Example, dares so much, as think of resenting Injuries, how provoking soever. Our Saviour could not excuse their Fault, but he

(n) Ps. xxi. v. 18.

(o) Mat. c. xxvii. v. 39.

(p) Mar. c. xv. v. 31.

(q) Mat. c. xxvii. v. 42.

(r) Luck. c. xxiii. v. 34.

he reprefents it, as little odious as he can, by alledging their Ignorance. Let us learn from hence, to put always, the moſt favourable Conſtructions on our Neighbours Actions, 'tis but what Juſtice and charity oblige us to, and what, our Bleſſed Redeemer preaches to us from the Pulpit of the Croſs.

But to return to his Sufferings, we cannot confider one fingle Circumſtance in our Saviour's Crucifixion, but what is either exceeding ignominious, or painful. The manner of his Death is fhameful, as being upon a Croſs, which in thofe Times, was the Puniſhment of Thieves; the Place was ignominious, being noted for the common Execution of notorious Malefactors; the Companions of his Death, were Thieves, and he in the Middle of them, as the moſt guilty; the time rendered his Paſſion more reproachful, being the Solemn Feſtival of the Paſſover, when a prodigious Multitude, reforted to Jeruſalem from all Parts. Now, as to the painfulneſs of his Crucifixion, the whole weight of his Body, is ſupported by the Nails driven through his Hands and Feet; his Head, though wearied and racked with incredible Torment, has no other Place to reſt on, but the hard Wood of the Croſs, and even this cannot be done, without driving the Thorns deeper into his facred Fleſh, and fo increaſed his Sufferings; if he endeavours to eafe the Wound of one Hand, he muſt widen the Wound of the other; if he looks up to his heavenly Father, the God of all Confolation, he is refolved not to mitigate his Sufferings, but to execute on him his only Son, with the utmoſt
Rigour

Rigour, the Punishments due to the Sins of Mankind; if he looks upon those who are present, some are mocking, and others blaspheming him; his most afflicted Mother indeed, and some other devout Friends are pierced to the Heart, and truly compassionate his Sufferings.

See now, if ever Sufferings in this vale of Tears and Misery, equalled those of Jesus Christ; it was doubtless, in this doleful Condition, that the Prophet Isaias considered him, when he stiled him *a Man of Sorrows*. (f) In this painful Condition, he says, *I thirst*, (t) and they gave him *Vinegar to Drink*. (u) Ah barbarous Jews, is Vinegar, a Cordial for a dying Man; and more cruel we, if we neglect to satisfy his spiritual Thirst, by not labouring for our Salvation. When he had taken *the Vinegar, he said, it is consummated.* (w) And then, *crying out with a loud Voice, said, Father into thy hands I commend my Spirit,* (x) And *bowing down his Head* (in perfect submission to his Father's Will, and perfect Charity to us poor Sinners, to whom, in this posture he offered as it were the Kiss of Peace,) *he gave up the Ghost,* (y) and thus ended his mortal Life, which, from the very first Moment, till his Death, had been nothing else, but a series of Sufferings, endured for us.

(f) Isa. c. liii: v. 3.
(t) John xix. v. 28.
(u) Mat. c. xxvii. v. 48.
(w) John c. xix. v. 30.
(x) Luc. c. xxiii. v. 46.
(y) John c. xix, v. 30.

Let us now, if you please, recapitulate, or sum up in brief, the principle Heads of our Saviour's Sufferings, which he endured for us, from his entrance into the Garden of Gethsemani, till his Expiring on the Cross. He is betrayed by one of his own Disciples, who even conducted the Enemies of his Lord and Master to the Place of his Retirement, where they

they seized him in a most rude manner, as the vilest of Traitors and Murderers. After being forsaken by all his Disciples, and by one of them solemnly denied, he is hurried from one Court of Judicature to another; From *Annas* to *Caiphas*, from *Caiphas* to *Pilate*, from *Pilate* to *Herod*, from *Herod* back to *Pilate* again. His Torments were varied, as often as his Judges; one reviles him, another buffets him, false Evidences are suborned to accuse him of capital Offences, and in a Word, they were so resolutely bent on his Death, that with, or without Law, they were determined to effect it; a Wretch of the most infamous Character, was preferred before him; and in short, after a most shameful Taunting, Buffeting, Scourging, &c; He is at length led out and Crucified; put to a Death, at once the most painful and ignominious, and even the most inhuman methods were tried, to heighten if possible, his Agonies. Such were the Sufferings of our Blessed Saviour, previous to, and attendant on his Crucifixion; and thus much, we are required by the Words of this Article, to believe.

O Christians, consider well with yourselves, who it is that suffers all this! It is the eternal Son of God; equal and con-substantial to his Father; the great Lord and Maker of Heaven and Earth, infinite in Power, infinite in Wisdom, infinite in all Perfections: But for whom does he suffer all this? For poor Man, a wretched Worm of the Earth; for those very Jews who crucified him; for us ungrateful mortals, who for the most part, were never likely to thank him, or even, so much as think of his Sufferings.

Sufferings. O unspeakable Mystery! It is here, we discover the infinite Goodness and Charity of God, in thus wonderfully communicating himself to us, and laying down his Life for us. It is here, we discover his unparalleled Mercy, in taking upon himself our Miseries, and enduring the Stripes due to our Sins. Here, we learn to fear his Justice, which fell heavy upon his own eternal Son, who had but cloathed himself in the resemblance of a Sinner, in order to make Atonement for our Sins. O! what must the Guilty themselves one Day expect at his Hands, if they do not prevent the Terrors of his Justice, by laying hold of his present Mercy. Let us now repent, detest, and be sorry for our past Sins and Offences, against so good a God; and resolve never to be so ungrateful, as to Crucify him again by mortal Sin; Let us admire, give Thanks, compassionate, and endeavour to excite in our Hearts, all those sentiments of Piety, which must naturally arise, from the Contemplation of so moving an object.

The great instruction, we are to learn from this Mystery, is this, to make a right use of our Sufferings. The Law of God, since the Death of Christ, is, that none shall be glorified with him, who do not suffer with him. Now it is decreed, that all Men shall suffer in this World; and the Sufferings of Jesus Christ, are the Comfort of all who suffer, either justly or unjustly; but it is to be observed, though all Men suffer, yet, all Men do not suffer with Christ, for some suffer for their Crimes, and some for Truth and Justice sake; this latter,

is

is properly the Suffering of a Chriſtian, and there are none ſo dear to God, as theſe. Rejoice then Dear Chriſtians, rejoice when ſuch Sufferings befall you, it is juſt, then you are conformable to Jeſus Chriſt crucified, and are effectually partakers of the Myſtery of the Croſs. It is better to ſuffer for innocence, than for Crimes. In a word, there are two Croſſes, the Croſs of the Damned, which all wicked Men carry; and the Croſs of Chriſt; take your choice, whether you will carry the heavy Croſs of your Sins and unmortified Paſſions, or your Croſs in mortifying them; whether you will bear theſe Sufferings, which by Patience work an eternal weight of Glory, or thoſe, which by Impatience, will work an eternal weight of Miſery; all Men muſt bear one of theſe Croſſes, can you then demur upon the choice?

P. II. The next thing, which the Apoſtles propoſe to our Belief in this Article, after the Crucifixion of our Saviour Chriſt, is his *Death* * ſo that it is requiſite

---

* There were certain ancient Hereticks, who oppoſed this great truth of our Saviour's Death; by aſſerting that his Incarnation was not real, but fantaſtical and imaginary, and of courſe, that he did not die; now if ſo, how could he by magick, or any other way deceive the ſenſes of the Jews? And eſpecially ſo, as they themſelves, without any hindrance, might freely examine and ſearch into the certainty of his bodily ſubſtance, and thus eaſily diſcover the Deluſion, or Cheat, if there had been any. St. *Ignatius* aſſerts, that *he truly died; the heavenly, earthly, and infernal Inhabitants beheld it,* ſays he, *Epiſt. ad Tralles*. And *Origen*, declares, that Chriſt truly died our common Death. *Communem hanc mortem vere mortuus eſt Proœm. L.* And *Tertullian* well obſerves in his third Book againſt the *Marcionites*, that if Chriſt did not die,
(which

Art. IV. *Disc.* II.

requisite that we believe, that Jesus Christ truly and really died, that is, that his Soul was separated from his Body, so by consequence, he must be to all intents and purposes really dead, for Death is nothing else, but the departure or separation of the Soul from the Body; this was necessary to be specified, in order to confound such Hereticks, who should deny his Death, as some have done, who held his Crucifixion was only in appearance, and by consequence, that Jesus Christ did not really die, which was an Error of some primitive Hereticks, viz. the *Basilides*, and afterwards of the *Manichees*, contrary to this Article of our Creed, and all the four Evangelists, who affirm, that *he gave up the Ghost.* (z) That his Sufferings were to be carried to this Height, and not stop short of Death, was agreeable to both Types and Prophecies, and also requisite, or at least expedient on several Considerations. In the first place, to fix a certain and distinguishing Mark or Characterestick on him, by the exact Conformity of those Types and Prophecies. The grand Type of the *Messiah*, was the *Paschal Lamb*, which

(z) Mat. c. xxvii. v. 50. Mar. c. xv. v. 37. Luck. c. xxiii. v. 46. John. c. xix. v. 30.

(which could not be, if he had not had real and substantial Flesh) then says he, the whole work of God is overturned, the entire weight and fruit of Christianity, even the Death of Christ is denied, which the Apostle, so expresly asserts to be true, constituting it the chief Foundation of the Gospel, of our Salvation and his Preaching. *Everfum est totum Dei opus, totum Christiani nominis et pondus et fructus, mors Christi negatur, quam tam impresse Apostolus demandat, utique verum, summum eam fundamentum evangelii constituens et salutis nostræ et prædicationis suæ.*

S   was

was slain by a positive Ordinance; and Christ is called by St. John, *the Lamb which was slain,* (a) *from the beginning of the World;* (a) that is to say, in the fore-knowledge of God; and in as much, as all Mercy and Grace, from the beginning, was given in view of his Death and Passion. Again, Jesus Christ being the Author and Founder of a *New Testament,* it was necessary he should die; because as St. Paul says, *where there is a Testament; the Death of the Testator must of necessity come in.* (b) This in short, was the seal of his Doctrine, and the Ratification of his Promises. Again, as Christ *lived,* to give us the noblest Lessons, so he *died,* to leave us the brightest Example of Virtue and Piety; his Life, was Love, Patience, Meekness, Charity, and Humility; his Death, the most exalted Expression, both of these, and every other Perfection: His Death was also an undeniable Proof of his Humanity; his Actions proved him God, his Sufferings proved him Man; and in Conjunction, they are indelible Marks of the most stupendous Mystery of a Deity Incarnate.

Here Dear Christians, we ought to consider a little, how far, all this affected our Blessed Redeemer: Far be it from us, to suppose that God can die in his own Nature, that Immutability itself can suffer so great a Transmutation; or that *Immortality*, (c) could become mortal: The mortal part alone, that is to say, his human Nature, suffered the Laws of Mortality; the Divine, was still impassible, immutable, and immortal; yet by the hypostatical Union, the Divine Person, was firmly and indissolvably united

(a) Rev. c.xiii.v.8
(b) Heb. c. ix.v.16
(c) Tim. c.vi.v.16.

united to the Humanity, even when the Soul
and Body were *separated.* *

On the Death of Chrift, follows his Burial;
a Circumftance, both more material to be undergone, and to be fpecified in the Creed,
than may appear to us at firft View: By the
Circumftances attendant on his Crucifixion,
Chrift had begun to compleat the Words of
the Prophet Ifaias, where he fays, he fhall give
the impious for his Burial, and the Rich for

P. III.

---

* As for the *Burial* of our Saviour's Body, that, as
well as the precedent Claufe of his *Death,* was impugned
by thofe Hereticks, who denied, that he had a real and
fubftantial Body; but his *Burial,* was a moft fenfible and
undeniable demonftration, that he had a material Body,
feeing that, what was Buried, was real and certain, and
that it could be no other, than a true Body of Flefh,
which was committed to the Grave; and thus *Theodoret,*
well obferves againft thofe Hereticks, that *the Burial of
our Saviour was a fufficient confutation of them; for it was
neither his Soul, nor his Godhead, which the Grave received, but
his Body; for Graves, fays he, are only prepared for Bodies.*
Dialog. 3. And thus *St. Epiphanius* writes, *that we are
obliged to believe, that his Body was buried in truth, remaining without a Soul part of three Days, void of Breath and
Motion, wrapted in a linen Cloth, laid in a Tomb, and fecur-
ed by a Stone, and the Seals of thofe, who, rolled it on Anacephal.*
And *St. Peter Chryfologus,* to the fame purpofe fays, that
the Confeffion of the Burial of our Saviour proves, that
he affumed true Flefh, and that he really died. *Sepultum
dicis, ut veram carnem Chrifti, mortemque non perfunctoriam
probet confeffio Sepulturæ. in Symbol. Serm.* 60.

So that after our Saviour's expiration on the Crofs,
that he might in every thing become like unto us, (Sin
only excepted) and by his perfonal endurance fanctify
every State and Condition to all his Members, he permitted his Body, like unto ours, to be buried in a
Grave, and committed to the Earth, whilft his bleffed
Soul, fled to the invifible Receptacle of feparated Souls;

his

(d) Isa. c.liii.v.9. his Death, (d) that is to say, he was buried, where the Wicked were commonly punished, viz. on Mount Calvary; but by a special Appointment, he *made* it with the *Rich*, being interred honourably by *Joseph* of Arimathea, a Man of the first Rank in the Jewish State, in a Monument, which he had hewed out in a Rock,
(e) Mat. c. xxvii. v. 59. 60. for his own Family. (e) This Circumstance of Christ's *Burial*, is also a confirmation of his *Death;* and was likewise, a necessary Prelude to the ensuing Miracle of his Resurrection: For had his Body been left to putrify on the Cross, or thrown by in a negligent manner, as that of a common Malefactor, then the story, which the Jews raised of his Disciples stealing it away, might have been plausible enough, because then they would have had sufficient Opportunity; but this, is excluded by his Sepulchre: His Followers at that Period were weak, and few in Number, and the Body was secured, not only by the natural and artificial strength of the Monument, (as being excavated or hewn out of a Rock,) but by such a Guard or Watch, as the Jewish Rulers thought sufficient for their purpose. Now as the Circumstance of his Burial was predicted, and in itself so material, we are therefore required to believe, that as Christ *suffered,* was *crucified,* and *dead,* so also was he *buried.*

To conclude, our Lord being buried, his Blessed Mother and the rest of his Friends retired, for they were not permitted by the Keepers or Guard, to remain at the Sepulchre. We may easily conceive, that the Blessed Virgin and other devout Persons, were in great
Grief

Grief and Solicitude, and thereupon, gave themselves wholly to prayer, *expecting the blessed hope and coming of the Glory of the great God, our Saviour Jesus Christ.* (*f*) His blessed Mother, no doubt, comforted herself with that of the Psalmist! *In the evening weeping shall have place, and in the Morning gladness* (*g*). Let us in time of Grief, Sorrow, or Desolation, imitate them, by having recourse to prayer, and putting our Trust and Confidence in God; who will support and comfort us here, and eternally reward us hereafter in the Kingdom of his Glory.

(*f*) Tit. c. ii. v. 13.

(*g*) Pf. xxix. v. 6.

ARTICLE

ARTICLE, V.
DISCOURSE. I.

He descended into Hell, the third Day he rose again from the Dead.

He decended into the lower parts of the Earth. Ephes. c. iv. v. 9.--- *And he rose again the third Day.* 1. Cor. c. xv. v. 4.

THE Apostles having in the former Article professed the Passion, Death and Burial of our Saviour Christ; do now in this, declare his Victory and Triumph over them: so that, what is proposed to our Belief in this Article, is first, that the Soul of Christ after 'its departure by death, from his Body, did really and truly *descend* into Hell *; And secondly, that he raised

The Divis

---

* It is to be observed, that the meaning of the word *descended*, sometimes signifies only a simple removal from one place to another; but as it was the common Opinion, that Hell is in the Bowels or Heart of the Earth; from whence it was called by the *Latins, Infernum,*

raised himself from Death to Life on the third Day. These two Points, shall make up the subject of this Discourse.

P. I.

To enter upon this Subject, it will be first necessary to examine, what is meant by the word *Hell*. Now the word *Hell*, in the original Hebrew, is *Sheol*, that is, an inferior and low Place, the latin word is, *Inferi;* and therefore, both the Scriptures, and holy Fathers, and Doctors of the Church, use the word *Hell* upon several

num, and by the *Greeks*, *Hades*, and therefore in conformity to this common Notion, they termed the Passage thither, *a descent into Hell*, as in this Article of the Creed; by which they meant, that our Saviour's Soul being separated from his Body, went by a local Motion to the hidden or unseen Habitation of departed Souls, where it remained, till the Day of his glorious Resurrection.

But we must here take notice, that several Ancient Hereticks, viz. the *Arians*, or at least some of them, with the *Apollinarians*, and *Eunomians*, held that Christ's Body was void of a human or rational Soul, and that his Divinity supplied the place thereof, thus they assaulted the humanity of Christ, contrary to this Article of our Creed, were we believe, that his Soul descended into Hell; as *Origin*, St. *Athanasius*, St. *Ambrose*, St. *Jerom*, St. *Epiphanius*, with many others, who all apply this Action of our Saviour's, to his Soul alone. In proof whereof, they bring this Text of the Apostle, cited by him from the Psalmist; *Thou wilt not leave my Soul in Hell* &c. Acts. c. ii. v. 27. I shall now only cite, what *St. Fulgentius* says on this Point, that after the Death of the Son of God, his whole Humanity, was neither in the Grave, nor in Hell, but that he lay dead in the Grave with his Body, whilst he went into Hell with his Soul. *Humanitas vera Filii Dei nec tota in Sepulchro fuit, nec tota in inferno, sed in Sepulchro secundum veram carnem Christus mortuus jacuit, et secundum animam ad infernum Christus descendit. Ad Trasimund.* L. iii. c. 34. from all which, it is evident, that the *Descent into Hell*, relates only to the Soul of Christ, during it's Separation from the Body.

Occasions

Occasions, to signify divers inferior Places or States: As *first*, The Place and State of everlasting Damnation, which is properly called *Hell*, (*h*) as being the lowest, and remotest Place from Heaven. *Secondly*, Death, or the State of Man's Soul after it is separated from the Body. (*i*) *Thirdly*, the State or Place, where the Souls of those just Persons went, who died in God's Favour in the Law of Nature, and the Law of Moses, and who had duely satisfied for their offences before the Death of the Redeemer of the World, who was to open to them the Gates of the Kingdom of Heaven, by his Passion and Death; and by his Resurrection to introduce them into Heaven; this Place, is distinguished by St. Luke, by the Name of *Abraham's Bosom*. (*k*) *Fourthly*, the Place or State of Purgation, where the Souls of those are detained, who die in the Grace of God, but at the same time, under the Guilt of some less or venial Offences, or have not sufficiently satisfied the Divine Justice for former mortal or grievous Sins, for which, they are punished in this State; and therefore it is called *Purgatory* (*l*).

(*h*) Luc. c. xvi. v. 22. 23 24
(*i*) Gen. c. xxxvii. v. 35. et c. xlii v. 38.
(*k*) Luc. c. xvi. v. 22.
(*l*) 1 Cor. c. iii. v. 13. 14. 15 Mat. c. 5. v. 26.

It would be needless, and indeed endless, to trouble you, with all the whimsical and erroneous Interpretations, that have been put upon these Words of this Article, *He descended into Hell*, I shall therefore content myself. with only mentioning one or two of the most remarkable Errors; and so proceed to shew you, the true sense and meaning, which the Catholick Church has always understood it in.

In

In the first Place, by the Word *Hell* in this Article, cannot be understood the Place of the damned, because the Souls there, were out of the reach of Redemption, which was the design of Christ's descending; much less did Christ suffer the Pains of the Damned, as Calvin impiously maintains. (*m*) Nay it was impossible he should, as being never guilty of the least Sin, and therefore of course, could not suffer that perpetual Fire, and the never dying Worm, which jointly constitute those Torments; and seeing, that he was certainly to quit those Mansions of Despair in a very short Time, they could not be Mansions of Despair to him, and therefore, it could not be the *Hell*, where the damned Spirits are condemned to suffer everlasting Torments, in eternal Banishment from the Joys of God and Heaven. Besides, we may farther observe, that had the Soul of Christ been upon a descent into Hell in this Acceptation of the Term, he never would have promised the penitent Thief by way of Blessing, that he should attend him thither; that would have been more properly a Menace to the other Thief, who added to his former Crimes and Villanies by scoffing at him on the Cross, and therefore, was more likely to accompany him in such a descent, but to the penitent Thief, he said, *This day thou shalt be with me in Paradise* (*n*). Now we cannot suppose, that Paradise implies a Place of Misery and Torments; but whether perfect or imperfect, at least it implies a Place or State of Rest, and by our Lord's descending thither, it was then made by his Presence a Paradise, not only of Ease and Rest, but of Joy and Happiness.

(*m*) Instit. L. ii. c. 16 p. 10.

(*n*) Luke c. xxiii. v 43.

T There

There are others, who deny this Article of Christ's descent into Hell, meaning no more by the Signification of the Word *Hell*, than his Grave or Sepulchre; not considering, that his Burial or descending into the Sepulchre, was clearly expressed in the last Article, and therefore, there was no need of another to repeat it over again, especially in Terms more obscure. Besides, the Soul of Christ being separated from his Body by *Death*, and his Body laid in the Grave, the Soul therefore could not be in the Grave with the Body, but by Consequence, must be descended some where else. It is certain then, that by Hell in this Article, is not to be understood the Place of eternal Torments; nor the Grave. The true meaning therefore of the Word *Hell* is, that Christ descended into that Place, where the Souls of the just were preserved till he released them, called *Limbus Patrum* or *Abraham's Bosom*: In this Exposition, all the Fathers and Doctors of the Church agree; and it is without all dispute, the Place where the Soul of Christ retired at it's quitting the Body, in order to continue there, till the Time appointed for the Reunion of his Soul and Body, which was very shortly to take place, even within the space of forty eight Hours or there about. Now the Soul of Christ retired in this Place for a while, that he might conform to all the Laws of Humanity, and be in all things, as well in Death as Life made like unto us, *Sin only excepted:* But he did not descend as a Captive like others; but as a Conqueror like himself, Triumphant over the Devil, Sin, and Death, and *Free among the Dead,* (*o*) And seeing that it was necessary

(*o*) Pf. lxxxvii. v. 6.

Art. V. *Disc.* I.

necessary, that the Body of *Christ* should remain a while inanimate, to assure the World that he had really tasted of Death, agreeable to his own Predictions, and to lay a Foundation also for the Certainty and Greatness of the ensuing Miracle, viz. his Reanimation, the Soul must not only quit the Body, but also remain absent from it a while, in which while, it remained in that Place, where all those pious and faithful Souls, who had most heartily repented and fully satisfied for all their Sins, were detained, suffering nothing but the Tediousness of their Delay, and Doubtfulness how long it might last, before their great Deliverer would please to come and lead them out of Darkness into the eternal Light of Heaven, by which they hoped and longed to see the Face of God for ever. This was the Joy and happy Tidings, which he descended to bring them of their speedy Delivery, and Man's Redemption; to *tell those who were in Chains to be free, and those who were in Darkness to behold the Light.* (*p*) Thus says St. Peter, *was the Gospel preached to the Dead.* (*q*) And *Christ*, whose Soul could never die, *came preaching to those Spirits that were in Prison.* (*r*) so fulfilling that of Ecclesiasticus; *I will penetrate to the lower Parts of the Earth; and I will visit all that sleep; and I will enlighten all that hope in the Lord* (*s*) O! what Joy may we imagine filled the Souls of the just, when they beheld their Redeemer, for whose coming they had so long waited with Impatience, and ardent Desire of being set at Liberty; when they saw those obscure Recesses illustrated with the Splendor of his Divinity; what extasies of Love replenished their Hearts, whilst they embraced

(*p*) Isa. c. xlix v. 9.
(*q*) 1 Pet. c. iv. v. 6.
(*r*) 1 Pet 9 c. iii. v 1.
(*s*) Eccl. c. xxiv. v. 45.

T 2 the

the defired Object of their repeated Wifhes; and feemed already to grafp that eternal Happinefs, which they hoped to enjoy, in the clear Sight and Poffeffion of God. Then was fulfilled that of the Pfalmift, *And the Night fhall be my light in my Pleafures*. (t)

(t) Pf. cxxxviii. v.11.
P. II.

After our Bleffed Redeemer had remained with thefe pious Souls part of three Days, to comfort them with the welcome and joyful news of their Redemption, on the third Day after his Death, being *Sunday*, early in the Morning he united his bleffed Soul to his facred Body, and by the Power and Force of his Divinity he raifed it from Death to Life. *I have power* fays he, *to lay down my Life, and I have power to take it up again*. (u)

(u) John c. x. v. 18.

It may be here objected, that the Scripture teaches in many places, that God the *Father* raifed him up to Life: To which I anfwer, if we confider Chrift as barely Man, then in that Senfe, we may truly fay, that God the *Father* raifed him from the dead ; but if we confider him as God, then it is true to fay, that he raifed himfelf, as being Equal with the Father: It was the Cuftom of the Apoftles to afcribe Chrift's Refurrection to the *Father*, (w) yet certainly fo as not to exclude the *Son:* For as he had a Power to lay down his Life, fo he had alfo a Power to take it up again ; there is then no Contradiction, between Chrift and his Apoftles in their Account of the Refurrection ; For the Power, which each afcribes it to, is one and the fame, fince the *Father* and *He are one*. (x) To fay therefore, that Chrift was raifed up *by God*, is in effect no more, than to fay, that he was raifed

(w) Gal. c. i. v. 1.

(x) John c. x. v. 30.

raised up by the Energy or Power of the Divine Nature, which is common to all the three Persons of the Blessed Trinity. He is called in Scripture *the first born of the Dead.* (y) And St. Paul says, that *he is the first Fruits of them that Sleep,* (z) not only because he is the first and only Person, that raised himself to Life; but also, because he is the first that rose to Life eternal, and in such a manner, that neither the Malice of Men, nor the Power of Hell, nor the Tyranny of Death could exercise any farther power over him. For *Christ rising from the dead, now dies no more, Death shall no more have Dominion over him* (a) Then was fulfilled that of the Prophet Osee, as mentioned by St. Paul, where he says, that *Death is swallowed up in Victory. O Death where is thy Victory? O Death where is thy sting? The sting of Death is Sin. But Thanks be to God, who has given us Victory through our Lord Jesus Christ* (b)

  Now Dear Christians, although we have seen our Blessed Redeemer nailed to a Cross, wounded with a Lance, and to all intents and purposes as dead, as his greatest Enemies could have wished him, and actually deposited in a Sepulchre hewn out of a solid Rock, and the Entrance of the Sepulchre secured by a ponderous Stone, and guarded by a band of Soldiers: Yet we now find him again at Liberty, endued with Life and Motion, conversing, and performing all the animal Functions: Notwithstanding all the Malice of the *Jewish* Rulers, for all their Arts, all their Caution was too weak; nor were the bands of Death itself, strong enough to detain him, *as it was impossible that he should be holden by them.* (c)

(y) Col. c. i. v. 18
(z) 1 Cor. c. xv. v. 20.

(a) Rom. c vi. v. 9.

(b) 1 Cor. c. xv. v. 54. 55. 56 &c.

(c) Act. c. ii. v. 24.

But

But let us now look back a little and see, what Reason we have to expect a restored and rising, as well as a crucified and dying *Messiah*. Holy David plainly prophesied of the Resurrection of Christ, in these Words, *Thou wilt not leave my Soul in Hell, nor wilt thou suffer thy holy one to see corruption* (d) Now it is plain, that this is not applicable to the Prophets own Person, nor could he speak it of himself; for it is most certain, that he is both dead and buried, and it is as certain by the Confession of his Survivours, that his Body saw Corruption in its full Latitude to an evident Transmutation from Flesh and Bones, to Dust and Earth : we also conceive that his *Soul* was *left in Hell*, that is, (as I have explained before) in the State or Place of separate Existence allotted for those pious Souls, who died before the coming of our Redeemer. Now it is certain, that this Expression of the Psalmist, implies not such a Resurrection, as will hereafter be in common with us all, but a speedy and sudden one; such as was to take place shortly after the Dissolution, as if he had said " Thou shalt not suffer my Soul " to remain in a State of Separation from my " Body so long, as that my Body may see Cor- " ruption, but re-unite them in so short a Time, " as that my mortal part may not undergo " that common Law of Nature" Had this been true of *David* himself, we should have heard of it loud enough, either from Friends or Enemies ; and that it was not to be really verified in some Person or other, his Character forbids us to suppose. But since *David* himself is excluded, we must seek for this Person else where,

(d) Pf. xv. v. 10.

Art. V. *Disc.* I.

where, to whom we are plainly led by the very Terms of the Prophecy : It is *thy only one O God*; an Expression equivalent to the *Messiah: For David being a Prophet, and knowing that God had sworn to him with an Oath, that of the Fruit of his Loins,* according to the Flesh, he would raise up *one*, viz. Christ, *to sit upon his Throne, He foreseeing this spoke of the Resurrection of Christ ; for neither was his Soul left in Hell, nor did his Flesh see Corruption.* (*e*) And of him we do affirm it to be in all Respects true, for when about forty eight Hours had elapsed from the Time of his Death, (*f*) before the Worm had seized upon his mortal Part, the Divine Energy again united the mortal Part to the immortal, in Bands which shall never more be dissolved.

(*e*) Act. c. ii. v. 30. 31
(*f*) Mat. c. xxvii. v 46. et. c. xxviii. v. i. &c.

Thus Dear Christians are we prepared for, and led to this great Event above a Thousand Years before it's Accomplishment; but the less obscure, and more immediate Predictions of it, are so strong, and frequent, that unless Christ be risen, nay unless we do receive him as such, we throw on him the Imputation of Falsehood, and make him *a Liar like unto our selves*, (*g*) For it was his constant Practice to the Doctrine of his Sufferings, to subjoin that of his Resurrection : He taught his Disciples, *that he must suffer many things and be rejected by the Elders and chief Priests, and Scribes, and he killed, and after three Days rise again.* (*h*) He renewed the same admonition a little before his triumphant Entry into *Jerusalem*, (*i*) nor was this a Promise made only to his Disciples privately, but what he had publickly, and perhaps frequently asserted ; for the chief Priests made use of it as a Plea to *Pilate*

(*g*) John c. vii. v. 55.
(*h*)Mat. c. xx. v. 18. 19.
(*i*) Mark c. x. v. 34

late to procure a Guard to be set over the Sepulchre, saying, *Sir, we remember that, that Deceiver said, while he was yet alive, after three Days I will rise again.* (*k*) When he bid them *destroy this Temple, and in three Days I will raise it up again.* (*l,* But he spoke, says St. John, *of the Temple of his Body.* (*m*) And under the Type of *Jonas,* he always prefigured his own Death and Resurrection, as himself sometimes explains it. (*n*) We may then venture to alledge with St. Paul, that Christ must of necessity (that is, to fulfil the prefigured Character of the true Messiah) not only have *suffered*, but also have *risen again from the Dead.* (*o*)

(*k*) Mat. c. xxvii. v. 63.
(*l*) John c. ii. v. 19.
(*m*) c. ii. v. 21.
(*n*) Mat. c. xii. v. 40.
(*o*) Acts. c. xvii. v. 3.

What therefore we are required to believe by the second Part of this Article, is, that Jesus Christ who died upon the Cross on Friday about the Ninth Hour, (*p*) that is to say, about Three o'Clock in the Afternoon, (according to the Jewish manner of reckoning, who began their Day at Six in the Morning, which was the first Hour, according to their way of counting) rose again from Death to Life early on the Sunday Morning following. (*q*) This the Jews apprehended, since they required, that the Sepulchre might be made sure, *until the third Day*, at the expiration of which, they were sensible, that the Period they so much dreaded would expire; for say they, *the Deceiver said after three Days I will rise again.* (*r*) This Part of the fifth Article of our Creed, has held an undisputed Place in all the Creeds, from the earliest Infancy of Christianity, and is indeed one of it's most distinguishing Characteristicks. For the Belief of this Article, is of the greatest importance

(*p*) Mat. c. xxvii. v. 46. et 50.
(*q*) Mat. c. xxviii. v. 1. et 6.
(*r*) Mat. c. xxvii. v. 63. 64.

tance, and one of the principal Points of the Chriſtian Faith; it behoves us therefore to expoſe it in its cleareſt Light, and to conſider it as veſted, with all thoſe particular Circumſtances, which ſerve to render it more illuſtrious; becauſe the *Reſurrection* of Chriſt, is the Chriſtian's Glory; it is the Confirmation of our Faith, the Foundation of our Hope, and the Security of all the Promiſes made by Chriſt to his Church; for if Jeſus Chriſt be riſen, then the whole Goſpel is to be believed, then the Church is to be believed, which is promiſed in the Goſpel; the old Teſtament is to be believed, becauſe it is authorized by it; infine, the whole Chriſtian Religion is to be believed, becauſe it is all linked to the truth of the *Reſurrection.* Whence St. Paul declares, that if Chriſt did not riſe from the Dead, his preaching, and that of the reſt of the Apoſtles was to no purpoſe, and our Faith no better, than a Romance; that the Apoſtles would have been Impoſtors, for having taught that Chriſt roſe from the Dead. (ſ)(ſ) 1 Cor. But the truth of our Saviour's Reſurrection, is c. xv. v. beyond all doubt, as I ſhall prove to you more 14. &c. at large in the next Diſcourſe.

And ſo I conclude with the words of St. Peter, *Bleſſed be the God and Father of our Lord Jeſus Chriſt, who according to his great Mercy hath regenerated us unto a lively hope, by the Reſurrection of Jeſus Chriſt from the dead, unto an inheritance incorruptable, and undefiled, and that cannot fade; reſerved in Heaven for you.* (t) Hence we are encourag-(t) Pet. c. ed to bear with Patience, all kind of Afflicti- i. v. 3. 4 ons, Sufferings, and Perſecutions in this World, in Hopes of riſing glorious with Chriſt our Redeemer

deemer, who is our Head, and we the Members of his Body; and as he has made way through Persecution for us, so ought we couragiously to follow him.

ARTICLE

ARTICLE, V.
DISCOURSE. II.
The third Day he rose again from the Dead.

And he rose again the third Day. 1. Cor. c. xv. v. 4.

IN my last Discourse I explained to you, the meaning of these Words in this Article of the Creed, *he descended into Hell:* I also shewed you in part, that our Blessed Redeemer rose again from the Dead on the third Day; But this, is what I shall now prove to you more at large. A lively Faith therefore of this great Mystery; and a Christian Life conformable to it, are the two Points of this Discourse. TheDivis

Never was any Truth opposed with greater Industry on the one hand, nor entertained with greater Reluctance on the other: And consequently, never was any Point of Faith more firmly settled and established, than this Capital Article of the Christian Religion. First of all, P. I.

let

let us consider the Testimony for it, and then the Validity of that Testimony.

The first Witnesses of it, were the Persons who composed the Guards, that attended the Sepulchre; for when the third Day came, viz. Sunday, which they so watchfully awaited, *there was a great Earth quake*, says St. Matthew, (*u*) *and an Angel of the Lord descended from Heaven, and rolled back the Stone, and sat upon it, and his Countenance was as Lightning, and his Garment as white as Snow, and the Guards trembled for fear, &c.* But Behold *some of the Guards came into the City, and told the Chief Priests all that had been done: And they being assembled together with the Elders, resolved to give great Sums of Money to the Soldiers, to say that the Disciples stole away* their Master *while they slept*, which, *if it came to the Governours Ears, they would perfuade him*, and *secure them* from being punished for it. Thus they omitted nothing, which their Malice could invent to hinder the Discovery of the Truth, and to disguise it with a most notorious and injurious Cheat ; injurious, in accusing falsly the Disciples ; and *notorious*, in proving it by Witnesses who said they slept, and therefore by their own Confession, could not know it.

Thus we see, that it was acknowledged by the very Enemies of *Christ*, that his Body was missing from the Sepulchre about the Time, that was prefixed for his *Resurrection;* now could they have produced his Body, but for only one Day after the critical Point, it would have knocked the whole Scheme on the Head, and it is certain, they took Care enough whilst they had it in their power to keep it so ; But unfortunately, all

(u) Mat. c.xxviii. v. 2.3. 4.

ibid. v. 11 12. et 13. 14.

all their Care was fruſtrated, in Spite of all their
Caution; *His Diſciples* ſay they, *came by night and
ſtole him away, when the Guards were aſleep.* (w) (w)Mat.c.
What, is it poſſible, that they ſhould be all a xxviii. v.
ſleep? This is very inconſiſtent with the *Roman* 13.
Diſcipline, as well as very improbable in itſelf.
Beſides, the Buſineſs, which muſt neceſſarily be
done on ſuch an Occaſion, moſt have awak-
ed ſome of them at leaſt, who might have alarm-
ed the reſt, tho' they had ſlept as ſound, as Imagination can conceive. In ſhort, he muſt do
more than ſleep, who cannot ſee the extreme
Weakneſs of this Evaſion.

As for pretending, that the Diſciples ſtole
away the Body of our Lord in order to make
the World believe, that he was riſen, nothing
can be more abſurd than this, as appears
plainly from their being backward in believing
themſelves that he was riſen: even the Women,
who are commonly more credulous, did not believe, or ſo much as think of his Reſurrection,
for *they bought ſweet Spices,* ſays St. Mark (x) in (x)c. xvi.
order to anoint his ſacred Body, and did not v. 1.
doubt, but that they ſhould find it in the Sepulchre; their only concern was, how they ſhould
*roll away the Stone from the Door of the Sepulchre for
it was very great,* (y) but when they came to the (y)Mark
Sepulcre, *they ſaw the Stone was rolled away,* c. xvi. v.
and were ſurpriſed, when they beheld the 3. 4.
Place empty, where he had been laid, and heard
the Angel ſay, *he is riſen he is not here;* (z) they (z)Mat.c.
ſaw he was not there, and tho' the Angel, told xxviii. v.
them he was riſen, yet they would not believe, 6.
Death had made ſo deep an Impreſſion in their
minds, that nothing could ſuddenly efface it.

Mary

Mary Magdalen runs to the Disciples *Peter* and *John*, and instead of telling them, *the Lord is risen,* she complains, *They have taken away the Lord out of the Sepulchre; and we know not where they have laid him,* (a) she still believed he was dead. And while *she stood without the Sepulchre weeping, she turned back and saw Jesus standing, but not knowing him, and supposing him to be Gardener, said unto him, Sir if thou hast taken him away, tell me where thou hast laid him, Jesus said unto her Mary.* And by this time her Eyes and Ears were open; she knew his Voice, and saw it was her Master. *And Jesus met* the other Women, *and said, all Hail, and they came up to him and took hold of his Feet, and adored him.* (b) They saw, they heard, and felt him, and by that means, they made a Shift with much ado, to yield to the concurrent Testimonies of their Senses, and so at length believed him.

(a) John c. xx. v. 2. idem. v. 11. 12. 13. 14. 15. 16.

(b) Mat. xxviii. v. 9.

The Men were yet more incredulous then the Women; although our Saviour had foretold them his Resurrection, their Minds and Hearts were so possessed and troubled with his being dead and buried, that there was no room left for the least Thought, that ever he would rise again; tho' Mary Magdalen had told them, a second time, *that she had seen the Lord, and that he was alive,* but *they would not believe her,* says St. Mark. The other Women, *told* the same *to the Eleven, and to all the Rest,* but their W*o*rds *seemed to them no better than idle Tales,* and therefore they *did not beleive them.* (c) 'Tis true we read, that upon the Women's Message there were two of the Disciples, viz. Peter and John, who had the Curiosity to *run to the Sepchre* (d) They both

John c. xx. v. 18. Mark c. xvi. v. 11.

(c) Luck c. xxiv. v. 9. et 11. (d) John c. xx. v. 4.

both *went in* and *saw*, and they *believed*, he was
not there, but yet they did *not believe*, that he was
rifen again from the dead, as St. John affures us,
(e) they only wondered what was become of (e) c. xx.
him, for we read particularly of St. *Peter*, that v. 6. 8. 9.
he, *went away* wondering in himfelf at that, which
was come to pafs. *(f)* (f) Luc:
 The very fame Day, Jefus appeared to two c. xxiv.
of his Difciples, as they were walking to a Country Village, a few Miles diftant from Jerufalem,
called *Emmaus;* he difcourfed with them, and
yet *they* knew him not.*(g) we hoped*, faid they, that (g) Luc.
Jefus of Nazareth who was a Prophet *and mighty* c. xxiv.
in Works and Words, whom *the Chief Priefts* con- v. 13. et
demned *to Death, and crucified, was He that fhould* 16
have redeemed Ifrael. Here take notice, they *hop-* ibid. v.19
ed it once ; but now, they quite defpair : Then 20. 21. 25
he reproached them for their Incredulity, and 26. 30. 31
faid to them, O foolifh and flow of Heart to believe. 33. 34. 35
He expounded to them the Scriptures, and
fhewed them that *Chrift ought to have fuffered, and
fo enter into Glory;* but all this did not open their
Eyes : At length when *he was at Table with them,
he took Bread, and Bleffed and broke, and gave it to
them*, then they knew him, and *rifing up the
fame Hour, they went back to Jerufalem, and they
found the Difciples gathered together*, to whom
they declared *that the Lord is rifen indeed. And
they told them what things paffed in the way, and how* v. 34. 35.
they knew him in the breaking of Bread. But St.
Mark affures us, that *neither* then *did they believe
them*. (h) They would not believe the Women, (h) Mar;
neither would they believe their own Brethren ; c. xvi. v.
fo far they were from any Thoughts of making 13.
the Jews believe the *Refurrection*, that they
           knew

knew not how to believe it themselves. And thus, instead of laying their Heads together, and consulting how to propagate this Faith among their Neighbours, we find them so divided among themselves, that although some of them were Witnesses of the Fact, yet they could not believe one another.

If we ourselves had then been living, I cannot imagine, how it is possible for any of us to have been more cautious in giving Credit to it, than the Apostles were. And on the other Hand, if God himself had studied, as I may say, and made it his chief Business to convince them of this great and fundamental Truth; I know not how to guess at any Thing, that could have been more powerful, and more effectual, than what he has already done. He knew their Temper; He saw how hard it was to make them thoroughly believe this Mystery; and therefore omitted nothing, that could any way dispose them, by degrees, to an entire and absolute Assurance of it.

He appeared to the Apostles as they were at Table, and he upbraided them with their incredulity and hardness of Heart, because they did not believe them who had seen him after he was risen, says St. Mark, (i) *He shewed them his Hands and Feet, and while they wondered for Joy, yet they did not firmly believe;* he called for something *to eat,* and although it was otherwise needless and unfit for his immortal State, yet nevertheless to satisfy all doubts, that he was no Spirit or Phantom, he was pleased *to eat before them.* (k) *Now Thomas one of the Twelve was not with them,* as St. John assures us, but when he came, the Disciples told him, *we have seen*

(i) Mark. c. xvi. v. 14

(k) Luck. c. xxiv. v. 40. 41. 43. John c. xx. v. 24.

seen the Lord, but he said to them; except I shall see in his Hands the print of the Nails, and put my Finger into the place of the Nails, and put my Hand into his side, I will not believe. Eight days after this, Jesus came again to his Disciples *and Thomas was with them, then he said to Thomas: Put in thy Finger hither, and see my Hands, and bring hither thy Hand, and put it into my Side, and be not faithless but believe.* Besides all this, he appeared to them *on the shore* as they were fishing. (*l*) These Conversations, he frequently renewed for *the space of forty Days,*(*m*) and *was seen before his Ascension by upwards of five hundred Persons at one Time,* (*n*)

(*l*) John c. xxi. v. 4.
(*m* Act. c. i. v. 3.
(*n*) 1 Cor. c. xv. v. 6.

These things are transmitted to us by four Evangelists, two of whom, were Apostles and Eye-witnesses of the whole Transaction: But during their Lives, the whole Apostolick Council, and the numerous Assembly of the Brethren, who had *seen* Jesus, ceased not to assert it. Now the Question is, whether we are to allow these Testimonies to be good or no.

In answer to this I reply, had the Apostles been artful, designing Men, versed in Knavery and Sophistry; had they been Men of infamous Characters, seditious, turbulent, drunken, and lying Men; or could they have proposed to raise their Fortunes (which is a Scheme inseparably anexed to imposture, and which most of our modern Enthusiasts seem principally to have in View) by the Invention, and Propagation of such a Story, had either of these been the Case, then indeed we might with good Reason call in Question their Testimony: But when on the contrary we find that, they were in general artless and illiterate Men; Men as ill qualified ed by their Intellects to form, as by their Stations to execute great Projects: When I observe, that they were, by the Confession of their Enemies (see Euseb. Hist. Eccles.) singular Examples of Piety and good Life; irreproachable in all other Parts of their Conduct; Lastly, when I consider, that they never once attempted to turn the Scheme of Christianity to their secular advantage; that instead of their striking at Riches and Honours, they were only running on to Infamy and Death; that they struggled with Misery in all it's Shapes, rather than recede from their Assertion of this great Truth of *Christ's Resurrection*; and at last sealed their Testimony with their Blood. Now if we duly weigh all these Considerations, we must certainly do Violence to our own Reason, as well as Injustice to their Characters, not to believe them.

L. ii, c. 23.

Tis most certain then, that the first Asserters of *Christ's Resurrection* did themselves believe it to be true: But perhaps some may say, might not they be deceived and imposed upon? Surely no; had they even been Idiots, which we know was as far from their Characters, as *Knavery* and *Sophistry*; their own Doubts and Incredulity armed them against that: For as I said before, they disputed the Report of the Women, tho' offered in the most serious and solemn Manner. Upon this, they have ocular Demonstration, and because that is scarce satisfactory, *Christ* submits himself to their Touch, He eats and drinks with them, converses with them, and gives such Proof of his perfect Resurrection, as extorts a Confession, even from the incredulous Thomas. There appears then not the least Room for Hesitation or Doubt, that *Christ rose again*

Art. V. *Disc.* II.

again from the Dead, and that really and truly, by a proper Resurrection, as it stands defined in this Article of our Creed. Hence we ought to give infinite Thanks to our Blessed Redeemer, for setting this fundamental Article of our Christian Religion in so clear a Light, that nothing less, than a *Jewish* Obstinacy, or the Principles of modern Saduces, can question the Truth of it.

Now, from what I have proved to you Dear Christians, concerning this Point; 'tis no wonder, the Apostles had a lively Faith of this great Mystery; 'tis no wonder, this lively Faith had such an Influence upon them, as to make them preach boldly, and die chearfully in the Defence of it; tis' no wonder I say, that it made them, and the primitive Christians, live like Men of another World, and esteem this Earth and all things in it, no better than Drofs, or Dung under their Feet; when they considered the *Power of Christ's Resurrection, the fellowship of his Sufferings, and* the great Happiness *of being made conformable to his Death,* (o) that so they might rise with him from the Dead, to a Life of Eternal Glory: For Christ by his Resurrection has confirmed our *Faith* and *Hope,* that we also one Day shall rise with, and that (through his Merits) to an immortal Life. This, is what holy Job formerly believed and prophesied of our Saviour Christ, long before he came into the World, *I know,* says he, *that my Redeemer lives, and at the last Day I shall rise out of the Earth and be compassed again with my skin, and in my Flesh I shall see God,* my Saviour. (p)

Now, Christ was our Redeemer, not only by his Birth and Death, but also by his Resurrection,

P. II.

(o) Phil c. iii. v. 10

(p) Job. c. xix. v. 25. 26.

for

for he came to repair not only the Damage, which Sin had done to our Souls, but also to our Bodies; that is, to raise them at the Time of a general Reward to an immortal Life, to a State of incorruption. We may therefore conclude with St. Augustin, that if Christ has shewn us in his Passion, what we ought to suffer for his Sake, and by his Example; he has also taught us by his Resurrection, what we have to hope for. O Christians! what greater Comfort than to be assured, that after the short Labours of this mortal Life, both Soul and Body (if we lead good and virtuous Lives) shall rise again and be rewarded with a happy Life, which will never have an End. But in order to this, we must endeavour to imitate the Resurrection of our Blessed Redeemer, otherwise, we have just Reason to fear, that what ought to contribute to our Justification and happiness, will by our own Neglect, turn to our greater Condemnation and Punishment.

The Apostle St. Paul frequently puts us in Mind, that we ought to imitate the Resurrection of our Saviour; *Christ*, says he, to the Romans, *was delivered up*, to Death, *for our Sins,* (q) Rom. *and rose again for our Justification.* (q) But how c.iv.v.25. must we imitate our Saviour's Resurrection? This is what the same Apostle teaches us in these Words; *Christ*, says he, *rising from the Dead, dies no more; Death shall no more have Dominion over him, so do you also look upon yourselves as Dead to Sin, and living to God in Christ Jesus our* (r) Rom. *Lord.* (r) As Christ rose to a quite different, to c. vi. v.9. a glorious and immortal Life, so must we rise §1, from

from the Death of Sin, and die no more, that is, we muſt return no more to the ſame ſinful Habits, but lead a new, and more perfect Life. *The old* and ſinful Man, ſays St. Paul, muſt be *crucified with* Chriſt, *that the Body of Sin may be* deſtroyed, to the end that we may be no longer Slaves to Sin *(ſ)* And *as Chriſt is riſen from the Dead, by the Glory of his Father, ſo we muſt alſo walk in the newneſs of Life.* Yes Chriſtians, it is in leading a new, a different, and more perfect Life, that we muſt imitate the Reſurrection of Jeſus Chriſt; for it is in vain to pretend to riſe with Chriſt, unleſs we alſo die with him, that is, unleſs we be dead to Sin, and the Affections of Sin. St. Paul aſſures us, that *Chriſt died for all* Men, *that they who live, may not live to themſelves, but unto him who died for them and roſe again.*(t) If therefore we pretend to live to Chriſt, we muſt die to ourſelves, that is, to our ſinful Habits, our Reſurrection muſt of Neceſſity be accompanied with a change of Life, for if our Lives are as full of Pride, of Vanity, of Intemperance, of Immodeſty, as before, if we continue in the ſame Habits of ſwearing, and curſing, of Drunkenneſs, of Detraction, Anger, Hatred, and Revenge, Injuſtice and the like, how can we pretend to have imitated the Reſurrection of Chriſt? On the contrary, his Reſurrection will be our Condemnation.

(ſ) Rom. c. vi. v. 6

(t) 2 Cor. c. v. v. 15

We muſt obſerve, that the Scripture makes mention of three different Sorts of *Reſurrection*, or riſing from the dead. The *firſt*, is that of *Samuel*, whom the Witch of *Endor*, is ſaid to have raiſed by a certain kind of Cunjuration, and who appeared to *Saul*, as we read in the

firſt

first Book of Kings, or *Samuel*: this was not a real Resurrection, but only in Apparition, or by way of Vision, for St. Augustin assures us, that *Samuel* did not rise again in his own, but only in a fictitious and imaginary, or at most, in an aerial Body. The *second*, is presented to us, by those, whom the Prophets raised to Life, as we read in the third and fourth, or the first and second Book of Kings; or by those, whom our Saviour raised to Life; as the Daughter of *Jairus*, and the Widow's Son of *Naim* mentioned by St. Luke, or *Lazarus* mentioned by St. John. These Persons, tho' they were truly raised from Death to Life, yet it was but an imperfect Resurrection, since they rose to die again. The *third*, is the Resurrection, of Jesus Christ, this was a perfect Resurrection, for he rose to die no more.

There are some, who pretend to rise from the Death of Sin to the Life of Grace, but it is only in appearance like that of *Samuel*, they are not truly risen, they still remain dead and buried in Sin; this is the case of all those, who notwithstanding their Promises, and Protestations, *that Sin shall never reign any more in them*, yet still retain an Affection to their Sins, and remain in the Occasion of them; and so deceive themselves, for such are not risen with Christ; nor do they live to Christ, as long as Sin lives in them.

There are others, who like *Lazarus*, truly rise by the Grace of God, but then it is only for a short time, they soon relapse into their former Sins and Disorders, and so die again. But to have our Resurrection perfect, it must be be like that of our Saviour Christ, we must rise like him, so as to die no more by mortal or grievous Sin, we must continue and persevere in his Divine Grace, we must be constant in our good Purposes, and in the Practice of a new Life; in a Word, in order that our Resurrection may be perfect, we must, says St. Paul, *seek the things that are above---and not the Things that are upon the Earth*, (*n*) that is, we must raise up our Minds to Heaven, and place our Hearts and Affections upon God, so as to make him the sole Treasure of our Hearts and Desires, and not to set our Thoughts and Affections, as alas! too many do, upon the vain and transitory Things of this World! not but that it is lawful, and our Duty to take care of our temporal Concerns, as far as is consistent with our chief Care, viz. the Care of our Salvation; but when the Business of this World, so far prevails, as to hinder the Business of Eternity, and prejudice what we owe to Almighty God, then we become culpable: For when the Love of temporal Things, makes us neglect the Service of God, we plainly shew, that we are buried in the Earth, and that we prefer this World before the next; and it was by seeking the Things, that are upon the Earth, that we incurred the fatal Sentence of *returning into Earth.* (*w*) And it is by seeking the Things that are in Heaven, that we revive into a Spiritual Life, so *that the Life of Jesus may be made manifest in our mortal Flesh*, (*x*) as St. Paul says, that our Conversation, even in this World, may be so pure, our Actions so spiritual, and our Affections so fixed upon the Things above, as to

(*u*) Colof. c. iii. v. 1. 2.

(*w*) Gen. c. iii. v. 19

(*x*) 2 Cor. c. iv. v. 11

express

exprefs a lively Similitude of our Lord's Refurrection. This is the way to have a Share of thofe Bleffings, which our Bleffed Redeemer by his Death and Refurrection, has obtained for his faithful Servants.

ARTICLE

ARTICLE, VI.

DISCOURSE, I.

He ascended into Heaven and sits at the right Hand of God, the Father Almighty.

Jesus --- was taken up into Heaven and sits at the right Hand of God. Mark. c. xvi. v. 19.

OUR Blessed Redeemer *Jesus Christ*, after his glorious Resurrection from the Dead, remained upon Earth for the space of forty Days, *appearing to his Disciples, and conversing with them of the Kingdom of God,* (a) that is to say, instructing them concerning the Establishment and Government of his Church, which is the Kingdom of God upon Earth; and confirming them in the Doctrine he had taught, and the Truth of his Resurrection.

Jesus having now compleated the great Work of Man's Redemption; he was pleased to resume

(a) Acts. c. i. v. 3.

sume his former Glory, and thereupon, *he ascended into Heaven* to take Possession of the highest Honour's, and the Seat of Bliss at the right Hand of his eternal Father: This is, what is exhibited to us in this Article of our Creed; which I shall endeavour to explain to you in this Discourse; wherein I shall shew you, that the Ascension of Christ was predicted by the Prophets, and expresly foretold by himself; and that he did really and truly ascend into Heaven both Body and Soul.

The Divis

P. I. The Time being come for our Saviour's quitting this World, and ascending into Heaven, he was willing that his Disciples should be Witnesses thereof: St. Luke tells us, that *he led forth his Disciples to Bethania, (b)* (a Place near Jerusalem) and from thence to *mount Olivet*, as appears from the Acts, *(c)* imparting to them his last Benediction, and giving them new Assurances of sending down the Holy Ghost to instruct and enable them in the Performance of their *Ministry*. *When he had said these things, even while they looked on him, he was raised up, and a Cloud received him out of their sight. And while they were thus beholding him going up to Heaven, two Men* (that is Angels) *stood by them in white Garments, who said, ye Men of Galilee, why stand you looking up to Heaven? This Jesus who is taken up from you into Heaven, shall so come as you have seen him going into Heaven. (d)*

(b) c. xxiv v. 50.
(c) Acts. c. i. v. 10
(d) Acts. c. i. v. 9. 10. et 11.

Now, Dear Christians, to doubt or call into Question this great Truth of the *Ascension of Jesus Christ*, is in reality denying or questioning the Authority, both of the old and new Testament. Since it is from the Authority of the holy

holy Scriptures expounded by the Church, that we are led to the Belief of this, as well as all other Articles of the Creed.

I shall here pass over in Silence, for Brevity fake, the greater Part of those obscure Paſſages, which neverthelefs were even applied by the Jews. to the *Aſcenſion* of the Meſſiah ; and ſo only mention two, viz. that Paſſage, where the holy Prophet King David, invites all the World to the Joy, of this Event, ſaying, *all the Nations clap hands : make jubilation to God in the Voice of exultation ; becauſe God is aſcended in triumph*. (e) The Prophet Micheas ſays, *He ſhall aſcend opening the way before them*. (f) Let us turn to another ſtill clearer, that clear and pregnant Prediction of the Aſcenſion of Chriſt, which holy David gives us in that Song of Triumph contained in the 67 Pſalm, the greateſt Part of which, is prophetically addreſſed to the Meſſiah, for the Paſſage I refer to, is not applicable to any other Creature ; it is this : *Thou haſt aſcended on high ; thou haſt led Captivity Captive, and beſtowed Gifts on Men.* (g) That is to ſay, Chriſt aſcended with innumerable Angels attending him, and carried with him the ancient Patriarchs and Prophets of the old Law, who had been captive ; and as Man, he received Gifts of God, in and for Man, his faithful Servants. Now the Perſon , to whom theſe Words of the Pſalmiſt are addreſſed, is evidently the Meſſiah ; ſo that they pay but an ill compliment to *David*, who would introduce him (as *Aben Azra*, a Jewiſh Commentator, as ſome others do) as though he was making ſuch a ſolemn Addreſs to himſelf, which in ſuch a Caſe, would become not only fulſome Vanity, but alſo glaring Blaſphemy. And the Author's

(e) Pſ. xlvi. or xlvii. v. 1. et 5.
(f) c. ii. v. 13.
(g) v. 19.

of the Chaldee Paraphrase, do as much exaggerate the Characters of *Moses* and *Joshua*, who would raise them to Honour's, belonging only to the sacred Character of the *Messiah*. For which of those *ascended* thus *on high*? Which of all these, carried his Triumph to the Gates of Heaven, and led in Chains the Powers of Sin and Death, which had reduced all Things else to their Subjection. Or was Advocate powerful enough, to obtain so high and valuable *Gifts for Men*, that even our Lord God should inhabit among them :(ibid) This same Royal Author, having his Heart elated with the clear, though distant Prospect of this great Event, breaks out again, in the close of the 23 Psalm, into these exalted Strains of Triumph: *Lift up your Gates ye Princes, and be ye lifted up O eternal Gates; and the King of Glory shall enter in. Who is the King of Glory the Lord of Power, he is the King of Glory.*(h)

(h)v.8. et 9.

Besides these, there was a constant and standing Prophecy, of the *Ascension* of Christ: For I think a Type may (not improperly) be so called; and it is certain, that the Solemn Entrance of the High Priest into the *Holy of Holies*, was a Figure of this: For so it is Expressly explained by St. Paul; (i) it was indeed the settled Notion of the Jews, that the Body of the Tabernacle, was an Emblem of this lower World, and that the *Holy of Holies*, was an Emblem of the *Heaven of Heavens*. As therefore the Jewish High Priest having offered the propitiatory Sacrifice, did enter into this Emblem of Heaven, so was this our High Priest (after having offered up the great Sacrifice of himself upon the Cross) to enter into the real Residence of the

(i)Heb. c. ix.v.11.12

Art. VI. Disc. I.

the true *Holy of Holies*, or the Heaven of Heavens, to make continual Intercession for his People.

It appears then, both from Types and Prophecies, that this was to be one Characteristick of the true *Messiah*. And as clearly doth it appear, that that same *Jesus*, whom we have already seen in so many other parts of that Character, *who died for our Sins according to the Scriptures, and was buried, and rose again the third Day,* (k) that same *Jesus*, I say, did not leave those Scriptures unfulfilled in this Part, but did also really and truly ascend into Heaven.

(k) 1 Cor. c. xv. v. 3. 4.

But to pass over, what may be farther alledged from the Prophecies and Figures of the old Law: Our Blessed Redeemer Jesus Christ expressly taught his Disciples to expect this great Event, as well before his Crucifixion, as after his Resurrection. When his exhibiting himself to them as *Bread which came down from Heaven,* (l) caused among them a murmuring: What says he, *does this offend you?* What then will you say, when *you shall see the Son of Man ascending where he was before. ibid.* Towards the Close of his Mission, he was in this, as in all other things, more full and particular; and not only declared the Ascent, but explained also the Reasons, for which it was necessary; and in order to console them for the Loss of him, which they always heard mentioned with the greatest Regret, he acquainted them with the Benefits, which would accrue to them from that Circumstance. (m)

(l) John c: vi. v. 59. ibid. v. 62 et 63.

From St. Mark we learn, that *after the Lord Jesus had spoken unto them, he was received up into Heaven,*

(m) John c. xvi. v. 5. 6. 7.

(n)Mar.c. *Heaven, and sits on the right Hand of God.* (n) *And*
xvi.v.18. *whilst he blessed them,* says St. Luke, *he departed*
Luc. c.
xxiv. v. *from them, and was carried up to Heaven,* (o) in the
51. Sight of all who were present. Now how many
of the Disciples were actually present, is not
certain, we may however depend upon the whole
Company of the Apostles; but it is not improbable, but there were others present, of the Number of those, *to whom Jesus had shewn himself after*
(o)Acts.c. *his Passion,* (o) whom St. Luke seems to reckon
i. v. 3. et about a hundred and twenty : But be this as it
15. will, certain it is, that these, as well as the Apostles, ceased not to assert it with equal Confidence,
as they had done the *Resurrection*; and their
Testimony in this Respect has, as just a Title to
our Regard, as in the Case of the *Resurrection*,
where I think I have shewn, that it cannot with
the least Reason be rejected. With regard to
to their own Knowledge of the Fact, they were
undoubtedly very clear in it ; nor could they
be otherwise, having had the strongest Evidence in Proof of it, which could possibly be
given or expected, even ocular Demonstration : It was performed in the Presence of
them all, even while their Eyes were wholly
intent upon him.

Some may perhaps here object, that they
were deceived, that *Jesus* only rendered himself invisible, as he had formerly done on the
(p)Luc.c. Hill of *Nazareth* (p) to avoid the Perfidy of his
iv.v.29.30 Country Men : And again in the Temple,
when the Jews were on the Point of stoning
(q)c. viii. him, as we read in St. John. (q) To this I answer,
v. 29. that they could not here be thus deceived,
as not missing him on a sudden, and so take it
into

into their Heads, that he was Afcended up into Heaven; for they faw him, their Eyes were intent upon him, and their Sight traced him through the Regions of the Air, ſtill gazing after him, even after the Clouds had cut off their Profpect. And that nothing might be wanting to their Satisfaction and Confirmation of this Truth, St. Luke aſſures us, that they received Information of his being Afcended *into Heaven*, from the Inhabitants of thoſe Regions, wherein Chriſt was then received. (See the Acts) c. i. v. 10

From hence it is certain, that thoſe who were 11. then preſent, had fatisfactory Proof of Chriſt's P. II. Afcenfion; and St. Luke, from whom we have this Account, might very probably be of that Number, as being one of thoſe ſeventy two Difciples, whom *Jeſus* himſelf had commiſſioned; (*r*) and moſt likely one of thoſe five hundred (*r*) Luc. Brethren, to whom *Jeſus* is ſaid to have appear- c. x. v. 1. ed at one Time, (*ſ*) after his Refurrection. (*ſ*) 1 Cor. Add to this, that he wrote under the Eye of c. xv. v. 6 St. Paul, and that his Writings were allowed, if not inſpected, by all the ſurviving Apoſtles. With regard to St. Mark, befides the Probability of his having been himſelf an Eye-Witneſs of Chriſt's Afcenfion, for the ſame Reaſons as already urged in Favour of St. Luke, he wrote profeſſedly under the Direction of St. Peter, who at leaſt was beyond all Difpute an Eye-Witneſs of Chriſt's Afcenfion, and who has confirmed that Evangeliſts Account, by his own ſolemn Teſtimony. (*t*) But we have an Evi- (*t*) 1 Pet. dence for the Truth of this Article, who well c. iii. v. 22 deſerves our Attention, viz. *St. Stephen;* his Eyes penetrated farther, than thoſe of the Apoſtles,

Apostles had done at the Time of the Ascension, and saw it in it's full Effect: The Doors of Heaven were opened to him, and he *saw the Glory of God, and Jesus actually standing on the right Hand of God.* (*u*) Now certain it is, had not St. Stephen been thus really honoured, he never would have pulled immediate Martyrdom upon his Head, by such an useless Assertion; the Laws against Blasphemy (in which Light that Assertion was considered) were too rigid in themselves, and too severely executed, for a Man to think of trifling in that Way; nor on the other Hand, could the Vision be merely imaginary, and the Effect of *Delirium* or Madness; for so sudden a Change from a Course of sedate, strong, and well digested Arguments, to Infatuation and Madness, cannot well be supposed; so that *St. Stephen*, must undoubtedly be allowed to be both a competent Judge, and a credible Witness. Besides, if we farther add to this, the exact Accomplishment of those Events, which were professedly to be the Consequence of Christ's Ascension, (particularly the Descent or Effusion of the Holy Ghost) which took Place about ten Days after it, we can no longer hesitate to believe the Truth of this great Article, that Jesus Christ did actually ascend into Heaven.

We must here observe, that Christ Ascended up to Heaven, by a true and local Motion, and not by Means of any foreign or outward Help, as *Elias* did, or by the Ministry of Angels, but by his own proper Virtue, that is, by the sole Act, or Command of his Will: Nor was it his *Divinity*, which took it's flight to Heaven, for that being

(*u*) Acts c. vii. v. 55.

being omnipresent, or filling all Places, could not be subject to the Imperfection of local Motion, that needed not to Ascend into Heaven, where it was always resident, nor could it quit the Earth, as being still present in every Corner of it. But it was his *Humanity*, that Part of him, which was made up of a Body and a Soul; that very Body, with which the Disciples had seen him cloathed after his Resurrection, with which they had eaten, drank, and conversed. For though the Earth be the proper Centre of the Body, and that which is palpable, naturally presses downwards and descends; yet if we consider, that the Body of Christ, after his Resurrection was endowed with all the Qualities of a glorified Body, that is, with *Agility*, *Subtility*, *Clarity*, and *Impassibility*, we may easily believe, that he raised up his Blessed Body from the Ground, with the greatest Facility.

Far be it from us then to suppose, that when Christ Ascended into Heaven, his Body was dissolved and dispersed among the Elements, as some ancient Hereticks, viz. *Apelles*, and his Followers affirmed; who taught, that the Body of *Jesus* was composed only of condensated Air, which reverted upon his Ascension to its primitive State and Form; or that he left it in the Sun, as *Hermias*, *Manes*, and other wild Hereticks of old asserted: For if these Systems had been true, then we should have wanted that Proof of the Capacity of our Nature, for being received into Heaven, which we are now all taught to hope for, and glory in; then it would not have been the Man *Christ Jesus*, but the *Divinity* alone which Ascended; nor would it have been the *Son of Man*, but the invisible God, who appeared to *St. Stephen;* both of which imply the most glaring Absurdities, for so had Invisibility become visible, and that been moved, which was incapable of Motion.*

Now, as the Term *Heaven* is capable of different Acceptations, for according to the Scripture there are three Heavens, viz. *Airy, Starry,* and *Empyreal;* so it is here necessary to add, that it was undoubtedly the highest Heaven, or what the Jews called the *Heaven of Heavens,* into which Jesus Ascended; nay St. Paul assures us, that he Ascended above all the Heavens, (*w*) so that he Ascended to the most high and sublime Place of the Heavens, above the Courts of *Angels, Powers, Cherubims,* and *Seraphims,* as being now to be far exalted above them all, and *to Ascend up where he was before,*(*x*) to enjoy the same Place in his *Humanity*, which

(*w*) Ephes. c.iv.v.10.

(*x*) John. c.vi.v.36.

---

* Besides these horrid Hereticks; *Tertullian* tells us, that there was another Set, who acknowledged the Ascension of our Saviour's Body into Heaven, but affirmed that it remained there in a stupid and unconcerned manner, void of Sense, and without Christ, as a Scabbard is, when it is without a Sword; *Adfirmant carnem in cœlis vacuam Sensus, ut vaginam exempto Christo sedere. De carne Christ.* P. 24. This Doctrine is directly contrary to the present Article of our Creed, which assures us, that our Saviour does not live in a regardless and unactive manner in Heaven, but that since his Ascension, he is *sat down at the right Hand of his Father;* from whom he has received all Power and Authority, which he constantly exercises for his own and Father's Glory, and the good of his Church, and the Government of the whole World; and will still continue so to do, till the general Day of Judgment, when *he shall come from Heaven to judge both the Quick and the Dead.*

he

he had ever done in his *Divinity;* and to be invested as God Man, with that Glory, which as God he shared with the Father, before the World was. *(y)* In a Word, whatsoever Heaven is higher than all the rest, which are called *Heavens;* whatsoever Sanctuary, is holier than all, which are called *Holies;* whatsoever place is of greatest Dignity, in those Courts above, and will admit of being called the most immediate Residence of the Almighty Father, thither did *Jesus* Ascend.

(y) John c. xvii. v. 5.

Thus I have endeavoured to explain to you in part, this great Mystery of Christ's *Ascension.* If what I have already said concerning this great Truth, should seem to some not to deserve Belief, then there is nothing, that can possible be deserving of Belief in the Nature of Things; for whatever Motives are required for believing, are either these, or something, that falls short of them; we Christians, have the Happiness to believe this great Mystery, and what is more, we are taught, that this glorious End is design'd for us, this is our Faith, this our Hope: But then in order to obtain this happy End, we must tread the Steps of *Jesus Christ,* that is, we must follow, and imitate his Example. Now it was by Sufferings, that our Saviour Christ entered into Glory, *(z)* what other Way can we pretend to go? *The Disciple* says our Saviour, *is not above his Master.(a)* On the contrary, it ought to be the Height of his Ambition to follow his Master's Steps. *Christ suffered for us,* says St. Peter, *leaving you an Example that you should follow his steps.(b)* He who pretends to *remain in Christ,*

(z) Luc. 24. v. 26.

(a) Mat. c. x. v. 24.

(b) 1 Pet. c. ii. v. 21.

says

says St. John in his Epistle, *must walk as he walked.* (c)

(c) 1 Epist. John c. ii. v. 6.

How dishonourable then is it, how mean, how pitiful and unreasonable, for any one to pretend to be exempt from labouring and suffering, while we see *Jesus Christ* our Redeemer and King, suffering and even bleeding before our Eyes? I cannot do Penance says one; I cannot fast, I cannot bear such Affronts, as People put upon me says another; I cannot endure the least Sickness and Infirmity, I cannot undergo any Mortification, I cannot suffer any kind of Contradiction says a third. Alas! Christians, who are we, that for us poor miserable Sinners, a new Way to Heaven must be found out? Who are we, that must needs walk upon Roses and Flowers, while Almighty God decreed no other Way, but the Way of Thorns, for his own immaculate and only beloved Son? God grant us a better Spirit, and teach us to conform ourselves to the Example of *Jesus Christ*: Let our Concern be to lead our Lives conformable to the Life of *Christ*. It is Sanctity of Life, that must bring us to the same glorious End we have seen in Him. Dye then to Sin, and endeavour to live to God; aspire to Heaven and let your Conversation be there, and you will partake of this great Mystery of our Saviour's *Ascension*, that is, Adoption among the Sons of God, Society with Angels, and Inheritance with *Jesus Christ* in the Kingdom of Heaven.

ARTICLE

ARTICLE, VI.
DISCOURSE. II.

He afcended into Heaven, and fits at the right Hand of God, the Father Almighty.

Jefus—was taken up into Heaven, and fitteth on the right hand of God. Mark. c. xvi. v. 19.

HAVING proved in the laſt Diſcourſe, that Chriſt did really and truly aſcend into Heaven by Virtue of his own proper Power, and not by any other Help, and that not only in regard to his *Divinity*, for in as much, as he was God, he was never abſent from Heaven, but with regard to his *Humanity*, that is, as Man. I ſhall therefore purſue the Subject of this Article before us, and ſo lay down the Reaſons why *Chriſt* as Man, aſcended into Heaven, in the Form and Manner as I have deſcribed in the foregoing Diſcourſe. And ſecondly, I will explain to you the Meaning of theſe Words, *He ſitteth at the right Hand*

of

of God. Which two points shall make up the Subject of this Discourse.

P. I. To enter upon the Enquiry of the Ends, Motives, and Reasons why Christ ascended both Body and Soul into Heaven, we shall find several. The first was in order to take Possession of the Seat of Bliss for himself and us. The Glory of Heaven was due to him from the very first Moment of his Incarnation; but he deferred the Possession of it for the general Benefit of Mankind, in order to compleat the great work of Man's Redemption: Having paid the Price of our Ransom with the Expence of his most precious Blood, and so happily compleated his Ministry on Earth; he then ascended both Body and Soul, to take Possession of his Kingdom of Glory. It was necessary, that he should still retain his *Humanity* (and not then to lay it aside, as some Hereticks of old pretended he did, as having now no more use for it) and so in quality of God made Man to ascend into Heaven, there to reap the promised Rewards of his Humiliation: For as in the Form of Man, he had gone through all the various Scenes of his Humiliation, so that Form, was to reap the Reward of it. *Being made* says St. Paul, *in the likeness* or form *of man, he humbled himself, becoming obedient unto Death; even the Death of the Cross.* Wherefore (in form or likeness of Man) he was now to be highly *exalted,*(d) and to be set (d) Phil. at Gods *right Hand in the heavenly places, far above* c. ii. v. 7. *all Principality, and Power, and Virtue, and Domi-* &c. *nion, and every Name that is named, not only in this* (e) Eph. *World, but in that which is to come,*---to have *all* c. i. v. 20. *things under his Feet,*(e) and to expect that *his Ene-* &c. *mies*

mies be made his *Footstool*, (*f*) and as holy David says, (*f*) Heb. to be *filled with joy in beholding the Countenance* or c.x.v. 13. presence *of God*, and those *endless Delights*, which are on his *right Hand*. (*g*)   (*g*)Pf. xv.

These Honours and Rewards were not in re- v. 11. serve for the *eternal Word*, who had ever enjoyed them from all Eternity, without a moment's Interruption; but they were in reserve and due to a *suffering and afflicted* Character, which cannot be understood of the eternal and impassible *Divinity*, but of him, who was *Man as well as God*.

Again, *Christ* was anointed to the *regal* Office, as well as to the *sacerdotal* and *prophetical*, so that these Honours were due to him as a *King*: He had hitherto appeared but little in that Character, and enjoyed but few of the Privileges of Royalty: But as his *Kingdom was not of this World*, as he himself assures us, (*h*) so neither (*h*) John was his *Throne* in it. He must therefore ascend c.xviii.v. up into those Regions, which are the Seat of his 36. Imperial Throne.

Now as for us, we could have no other Claim to this celestial Inheritance, than what the pure Bounty of God, was pleased to entitle us to; and even this, we forfeited, by the *Disobedience* of our first Parents. But *Christ* who was by Nature, the only Son of God the Father, recovered our Claim, by substituting another Title, so that what we could not demand in Consequence of our *Creation*, or in Virtue of the divine *Promises*, we may now confidently ask, in the Title of our *Redemption*, and through the Merits of our Blessed *Saviour*. For *we are* (*i*)1 Cor. *bought*, says St. Paul, *with a great Price*, (*i*) or c. vi. v. rather, 20.

rather, the Kingdom of Heaven is purchased for us, with an excessive Price, no less than the Blood of *Jesus Christ*. And now he takes Possession of the Purchase, for Himself and us; and by placing our human Nature, at the right-Hand of his Father, *he has prepared for us,* says St. Paul, *a Seat in his heavenly Kingdom.* (*k*) For where the Glory of the *Head* is gone before, there is Hope, for the rest of the *Members* to follow after; whence the same Apostle teaches, that *we are saved by Faith, through the Grace of God, and not of ourselves, for it is the Gift of God.* (*l*) It is he who made us what we are, and whereas, we were fallen from our primitive Innocence; and from the Dignity, in which we were first created; He moulded us as it were a new, in *Jesus Christ*, restoring us through his Merits, to our ancient Dignity, and original Justice; so that *now we are no longer strangers, and foreigners,* says St. Paul, *but fellow-citizens, with the Saints, and the Domesticks of God.* (*m*) Being made, says the same Apostle, *Co-heirs, and Co-partners, of his Promise in Christ Jesus.* (*n*) In whom, we have already taken Possession of that celestial Inheritance.

Secondly, he ascended into Heaven, that he might appear in our Cause before God, that is, to promote our Interest in what regards our Salvation. Whence St. John exhorting the Faithful, to be careful to avoid Sin, bids them not to despair tho' they have offended so good a God; because says he, *we have Jesus Christ our Advocate with the Father; and he is a Propitiation for our Sins.* (*o*) St. Paul likewise testifies that *Jesus Christ is now at the right Hand of God, making Intercession*

(*k*) Eph. c. ii. v. 6.

(*l*) ibid. v. 8.

(*m*) Gal. c. ii. v. 19.

(*n*) Ephes. c. iii. v. 6.

(*o*) 1 John c. ii. v. 1.

tercession for us. (*p*) as being *a high Priest for ever.* (*q*) And as the Jewish High Priest did once a year enter into the inner Tabernacle, to do that Office for the People in the more immediate Presence of God; so was it necessary, that *Jesus Christ* our High Priest, who had already Sacrificed himself once upon the Cross for us, should enter into Heaven, (of which that Tabernacle was the great type) there to intercede in our behalf. *Let us then approach with Confidence to the Throne of Grace, that we may obtain Mercy and find Grace in Time of need.* (*r*) Not doubting, but that *Christ* who as Man, is *always living to make Intercession for us,* (*s*) by representing his Death and Passion to his eternal Father. How powerful therefore must his Mediation be, when he pleads in our behalf.

(*p*) Rom. c. viii. v. 34.
(*q*) Heb. c. vi. v.
(*r*) Heb: c. iv. v. 16.
(*s*) Heb. c. vii. v. 25.

Thirdly, *Christ* ascended into Heaven, to draw our Hearts thither after him, and to shew us, that his Kingdom, is not of this World. If therefore we desire to reign with him, we must contemn the Riches, Pleasures, and Enjoyments of this Life. For *whosoever,* says St. James, *will be a Friend of this World, becomes an Enemy of God.* (*t*) And by seeking to reign in the Enjoyment of temporal Wealth, forfeits that Kingdom, which is the Inheritance of the just. Whence St. Peter exhorts us to look upon our selves here, *as Passengers or Pilgrims,* (*u*) who have no settled Habitation, and consequently, no Inducements to attach their Affections to the Earth: But are tending daily towards their desired Country, and can expect no continued Rest, till they happily arrive at their Journey's End, that is, to the Place of Bliss, Christ has prepared for them, in his everlasting Kingdom;

(*t*) Jam. c. iv. v. 12.
(*u*) Pet. c: vii. 10.

but we can never hope to come to the Poffeffion, of this Seat of Blifs any other way, than by raifing our Hearts above the Earth, and defiring to be united to God. How miferable then are all thofe, who have their Hearts linked to the Earth, with fo many Chains, that they can no fooner lift them up towards Heaven, but they are prefently drawn back, as if they were going out of their way? How can they expect a Place above, when all that is within them preffes them down to the Earth, and they cannot truly fay with St. Paul, that they *defire to be diffolved and* (*w*) Phil. *to be with Chrift.* (*w*) Wholoever therefore feri- c. i. v. 23. oufly thinks of afcending with *Chrift* to Heaven, muft every day learn to afcend. If the Love of Riches faftens their Hearts to the Earth, they muft work them by degrees, into that indifferency, as to difengage them from that Clog. If Pride or Ambition keeps down their Souls, they muft look into the Emptinefs of all they admire, and learn with Contempt, to fet their Feet upon all that, to which now they are Slaves. If the Follies of Idlenefs, Company, and Diverfions, confine their Happinefs to the Earth, they muft fet the Concern of their eternal State againft them, and thus get above the Power of thefe Charms. If Sloth ties their Feet, or Coldnefs puts a damp on their Spirits, they muft give a feafonable look into Hell, and let the Thoughts of that Fire loofe their Bonds. If worldly Solicitude, or Trouble oppreffes their Minds, they muft ftudy the Gofpel, and by learning to under value what now feems fo weighty, gain new Liberty to their Souls. If all would in this manner look into themfelves,

and

and obſerve what Part of the Earth it is that lies upon them, what Paſſion it is that makes their Hearts captive to this World; and then uſe ſincere Endeavours for recovering their Freedom, there would be thus laid a Foundation of a well grounded Hope, that one Day they ſhall be raiſed above the Earth, and admitted to the Participation of that Eternal Glory which *Chriſt* now enjoys: A Happineſs by which they ſhall be made part of that Kingdom, where God only reigns, and which is not to be obtained, but by thoſe, who here labour to bring themſelves into Subjection to God, and begin that Kingdom here, which they deſire to be conſummated in Heaven.

All ſuch Chriſtians, who follow not this Method, can have no Concern in Chriſt's Aſcenſion, nor can they have any Reaſon, to hope for the Fruits and Benefits thereof: For ſince a State of Sin, without juſt Deſires and Endeavours for amendment, is a State reſembling that of Devils, it cannot be a Preparation for Heaven, but for Hell; what then have ſuch Sinners to do with the Aſcenſion of our Lord? And as for thoſe, who tho' not in the depth of Sin, yet live careleſs of Eternity, having their Hearts crampt with Sloth, or bent on every Thing but God, how little a part have they in the Aſcenſion of Chriſt? If ſelf Love and Eaſe have the Promiſes of Bliſs, then indeed theſe may join in their Hopes; but ſuch Promiſes, are not recorded in the Goſpel. Therefore only thoſe can have any juſt Hopes, who accompany Chriſt in his Aſcenſion, by raiſing their Hearts and deſires after him, and think themſelves unhappy in their Pilgrimage, upon account of the many Hazards and Hindrances in their way to him, and so by earnest, and untired Endeavours strive to remove them; such Persons as these give evident Proof, that their Distance from Christ, is no ways voluntary: In whomsoever then we find these Desires and Endeavours, we may truly say, that such Christians are ascending daily towards Heaven.

Lastly, we might add some other Reasons, why Christ ascended up to Heaven; as first, in order to send down the *Holy Ghost*; 'Tis what he himself declared to his Disciples when he said to them, (*x*)*it is expedient for you that I go: for if I go not, the Paraclete will not come to you: But if I go, I will send him to you.* Secondly, to introduce the Souls of the just, whom he had freed from their Confinement, in *Limbo*, into the Kingdom of his Father. Hence St. Paul says, that Christ *ascending on high he led Captivity captive;* (*y*) that is to say, he took along with him those captive Souls, which had been so long detained in the dark Recesses of the Earth. Thirdly, to rejoice the Angels, and blessed Spirits, with the delightful Prospect of his glorified Humanity.

(*x*) John c. xvi. v. 7.

(*y*) Eph. c. iv. v. 8.

P. II. To proceed now to the second Part of this Article, viz. Christ's being seated *at the right Hand of God the Father*, that is to say, in the highest Place of Heaven, above all created Beings, which is the true meaning of this figurative Expression, *He sits at the right Hand of God the Father Almighty;* we must not imagine or conceive, that God has any human Shape, or that he is circumscribed by any certain, or determinate

terminate Form of an organized Body, consisting of Arms, Hands, Feet, and the rest, as was ridiculously asserted by a Sect of Hereticks in the fourth Century called *Anthropomorphites*, or *Audiani*, from *Audæus* their Founder; who by an absurd Conception of those words, in the first Chapter of Genesis. v: 26. *Let us make Man to our Image and Likeness*, imagined, that God had a human Form, and was composed of Limbs and Members, as Theodoret relates in his Ecclesiastical History. *(z)* There is scarce any thing, against which we are more solemnly cautioned, than such an absurd Opinion, both in the Old and New Testament. Moses bids us take heed and *be careful (for you saw not any Similitude in the Day that the Lord spoke to you in Horeb from the midst of the Fire) lest perhaps being deceived, you might make you a graven Similitude, or Image of Male or Female, the likeness of any Beasts, that are on the Earth, or of any Birds, or Fowls, that flieth in the Air, and the likeness of any thing that moveth on the Earth, or of any Fish that abide in the Waters.* (a) To whom then will you liken God? Or what likeness will you compare unto him? Be sure take care you don't fall under the same Reproach with those, of whom St. Paul says, that *they changed the Glory of the incorruptible God, into a likeness of the Image of a corruptible Man.* (b) For he being a pure Spirit, without any Body at all, it would be absurd in the highest Degree to imagine him to be like a human Body, nothing ought to be farther from our Thoughts: His likeness then consists in the Soul of Man, which is like unto God. We are indeed frequently, even in the

(z) L. iv. c. 10.

(a) Deut. c. iv. v. 15. &c.

(b) Rom. c. i. v. 23.

Holy

Holy Scriptures, told of Gods *Hand, Arm, Eye, Mouth,* &c. as when it tells us, that God wrought the Deliverance of *Israel* with his *Arm: He hath seen it with his Eye: With his Mouth hath he spoken it;* with various Expressions of the like Nature. See Exodus. But these Passages, are not to be understood in the naked and literal Sense: For there are many Things figuratively expressed in the Scriptures, in Compliance with the Customs, Capacities, and Conceptions of those, for whose use they were intended.

c. xv. v. 16, &c.

As to the Expression of *Sitting at God's Right Hand,* we must not Imagine from hence, that Christ is always in a sitting posture; but that by this Metaphor, is signified that Ease, Honour, and Stability of the State of supreme Glory, and sovereign Power, Christ is placed in; and as it is a usual Custom among us; to give the right Hand to a Person, who is equal to us, so *Jesus Christ,* being equally *God* with the *Father,* is said to *sit at the right Hand of God the Father*: And that as Man, he excells all created Beings, and enjoys the highest Honours next to the God-head; I say, next to the God-head, for notwithstanding the Unity and Equality of the Divine Nature, Christ as *Man,* inferior to the *Father;* 'tis what he himself acknowledged. (c) But as I said before, in Respect to his *Divinity,* he is one and the very self same equal God with the Father, and the Holy Ghost, so that we must here consider *Jesus Christ,* as both God and Man.

(c) John c. xiv. v. 28.

It is now Time, that I should come to inquire wherein those Honours are to consist, and what are

are the particular Privileges of *Jesus Christ* thus considered.

By this Exaltation then, *Christ* is in the first Place, even in his Humanity, elevated to a Superiority over the whole Circle of created Beings: He has the Superintendency, and Administration of Heaven and Earth, of Men and Angels, of Spirituals, and Temporals. In a Word, he is put in full Possession, of the last and highest Office, to which he was originally anointed, namely the *Regal*, and from thenceforth became a *King for ever, of whose Kingdom*, either with Respect to Extension, or Duration, *there shall be no End*. (d) O Christians what Honour, what Happiness for us, to know and to be assured, that one of the same Nature with us, has the Keys of Life and Death, of Heaven and Hell, that He governs all, and does whatsoever he pleases. (d) Luc. c. i. v. 33.

The first Privilege of this *Royalty*, was to avenge himself of his more immediate Enemies. This Christ executed in the most remarkable Manner, by desolating the whole Land, which had been the Scene of his Sufferings, and by destroying almost the entire People of the Jews.

Another Branch of his Regality, which Christ was then in Possession of, was the Sole Government of his Church, in which he protects, rewards, and punishes, with an absolute and unlimited Power; He directs it through its several Stations and Degrees, and ordains the several Means, which are to perfect it.

Yet these are but faint Glimmerings of Majesty, if compared with those brighter and more glorious Displays, which he will at the last and
Terrible

Terrible Day of Judgement, exert in the Face of Men and Angels, and which the whole Circuit of Creation shall be Witness to. As yet there subsist many great Enemies, which eclispe the Lustre of this Kingdom; for now *Sin* and *Death,* stand up to make his triumph incompleat, but these at last must fall before him, and *Death* it-self *shall be swallowed up in Victory.* (*e*) Then shall it appear in all it's Dignity; then shall there be no Distinctions of Nations and People; but all the Earth shall be united under him it's natural Lord; then shall Strife and Enmity be forgotten; *Nation shall not rise against Nation, neither shall they be excercised any more to battle.* (*f*) But now alas! his faithful Servants and Subjects, are exposed to various Dangers, to innumerable Oppressions, and Persecutions, and it is often Crime sufficient, to appear to be his Servants: But hereafter there shall be no such thing; not an Enemy, either external, or internal, shall dare to disturb the serene Transports of that happy Reign; for *he shall wipe away all Tears from their Eyes; and Death shall be no more, nor Mourning, nor Crying, nor shall there be any more Pain or Sorrow.* (*g*) Such are the Priveleges annex'd to that Throne, which is situated at the right Hand of God.

(*e*) 1 Cor. c. xv. v. 54.

(*f*) Isa. c. ii. v. 4.

(*g*) Apoc. c. xxi. v. 1.

I shall now close this Article, with a short Review, of what Considerations I have offered upon it: From whence it appears, that He who truly assents to this Article, must believe that *Jesus Christ* did after his Resurrection from the Dead, (with the same Body in which he appeared to his Disciples,) convey himself, by his own effective Power, and by a true local Motion

Motion from the Earth, up into the higheſt Heavens; and did there take Poſſeſſion, of all the Grandeurs of God, that are agreeable to his Merits, and the quality of the Son of God, made Man, and enter upon that Kingdom, whoſe comprehenſive and laſting Authority, ſhall endure throughout all Ages, and at the laſt Day, take in the whole Circuit of Creation.

To conclude, from hence you cannot but ſee, that the Aſcenſion of *Jeſus Chriſt* ought to be a ſubject of great Joy and Conſolation to us; becauſe it is a moſt certain Pledge, and an aſſured Hope, that we ſhall follow him; for he ſaid to his Diſciples, *I go to prepare a place for you.* (h) But then to follow Chriſt, and reign with him in his Kingdom of Glory, we muſt neceſſarily imitate him; this is what both St. Peter, and St. John declare to us. And Chriſt himſelf ſays, *if any one abide not in me he ſhall be caſt forth as a branch, and ſhall wither, and they ſhall gather him up, and caſt him into the Fire.* (i) Therefore to be ſaved and not to be caſt into the Fire, it is neceſſary to abide in *Chriſt*, that is, we muſt walk as he walked, live as he lived, imitate the Virtues which he practiſed, each one according to his Condition and Capacity.

Let us then reſolve from this Moment, to follow *Chriſt*; the Labour in the practice of Virtue, is but little, and the Joy of it will be infinitely great; the Pleaſure of this World which draws us from it, is but ſhort, and the Pains that attend that Pleaſure, will be everlaſting; this preſent Life is ſhort, and the future is eternal; and of this ſhort Life depends an Eternity of Happineſs.

(h) John c. xiv. v. 2.
See the 1 Ep. St. Pet. c. ii. v. 21 & the 1 Ep. St. John. c. ii. v. 6
(i) John. c. xv. v. 6.

B b   ARTICLE,

ARTICLE, VII.

DISCOURSE, I.

From thence He shall come to Judge the Quick, and the Dead.

He commanded us to preach to the People, and to testify that it is he who was appointed by God to be Judge of the living and Dead. Act. c. x. v. 42.

OUR Blessed Redeemer, Dear Christians, has many great and honourable Titles. He is our *Saviour*, he is our *Advocate*, and our *Judge*. In the former Articles, the Apostles have delivered his two first Titles; and in this they propose him as our Judge: We are therefore from this Article of our Creed, to believe that *Jesus Christ* will come again from Heaven, to Judge the Quick and the Dead, that is to say, all Mankind, that ever inhabited the Earth from the beginning of the World, to the End thereof

But

Art. VII. *Difc.* I.

But before we proceed any farther, you muſt obſerve, that there are two Judgments, viz. a private or *particular* Judgment, and a *General* Judgment. Let us now firſt examine and ſee what Grounds we have to believe, that there will be two Judgments, for by proving theſe great Truths, we may the better proceed to their attendant Circumſtances.

That there is a private or *particular* Judgment, exerciſed upon every Soul immediately after her departure out of the Body, is what St. Paul ſeems to ſpeak of where he ſays, that. *it is appointed for every Man once to die, and after this follows Judgment.* (*k*) and this again is proved from the Example of *Lazarus*, and the Rich *Glutton*, mentioned in St. Luke, (*l*) where we read, that one was Sentenced to everlaſting Repoſe, and the other to Eternal Torments, immediately upon their Separation from this World; From hence we gather, that no ſooner is the Soul departed out of the Body, but a dreadful Judgment or Trial will follow, where all the Good and Evil the Sinner has ever done in this Life, muſt be weighed in the Balance of the Sanctuary of the divine Juſtice: And an irrevocable Sentence will paſs upon him, according to his Works, for an Eternity of incomprehenſible Happineſs, or of incomprehenſible Miſery.

P. I.

(*k*) Heb. c. ix. v. 27.
(*l*) Luck. c. xvi. v. 22.

But notwithſtanding this, there is a Day appointed by the Almighty for a *General* Judgment, which ſhall be publick, manifeſt, and univerſal, wherein the Dead ſhall all riſe from their Graves, and ſhall be ſummoned to appear before the Tribunal of Chriſt. *For we muſt all be manifeſted,* ſays St. Paul, *before the Judgment*

Judgment seat of Christ, that every one may receive the proper things of the Body, according as he hath done, whether it be good or Evil. (m) Besides, Almighty God, would for many Reasons, ordain one solemn Day for the *general* Judgment of all : *First*, for the greater Honour of *Christ* our Judge, that as he was publickly in the sight of the World, condemned by the Wicked ; so he might publickly, and in the sight of the whole World, shew his Power and Innocence, and condemn them. *Secondly*, for the greater Honour of the Just. *Thirdly*, for the greater Confusion of the Devils, and damned Souls. And lastly, that the Body and Soul, which have accompanied together in this Life, and both of them concurred jointly in their Works, may meet and be united again, and remain together in Pleasure, or Pain, for all Eternity.

Now Jesus Christ will perform this Office of *Judge*, as he is Man : For as Kings delegate their Authority, to those whom they make Judges to judge, and give Sentence in the Name and Person of the King ; so would God honour the Humanity of Christ, giving him Authority as Judge in his Place according to St. John, *He hath given him Power to do Judgment, because he is the Son of Man.* (*n*) Christ himself often, and expresly declared, that *the Father*, would not execute that Office himself, but had committed all Judgment to the Son, (o) and that hereafter *they should see him come in Glory, and all the Angels with him*, when all Mankind shall be summoned before him, *and then he shall render to every Man according to his Works.* (*p*)

(m) 2Cor. c. v. v. 10.

(n) John. c. v. v. 27.

(o) John. c. v. v. 22.

(p) Mat. c. xvi. v. 27.

Art. VII. *Difc.* I.

The laſt thing this Article points at, is, who ſhall be the Objects of this Judgment? The Perſons who are to be Judged, we are told, ſhall be *the Quick and the Dead;* this Phraſe comprehends the whole Race of Adam; the *Quick*, thoſe who ſhall happen to be alive, when it ſhall pleaſe God to put an End to the World; and *the Dead*, all thoſe who ſhall have died from the Foundation of it, to that Time. This Interpretation is followed by St. Auguſtin and others. Tom. 3. Enchir. ad Laurent. c. liii. p. 225. It may be alſo underſtood of the State of the *Good* and the *Wicked;* the Good or Juſt, who live ſpiritually, by the Life of Grace; and the Wicked, who are Dead in Sin.

What therefore I farther intend in this Diſcourſe, is, to explain to you the *particular* Judgment, we muſt all undergo after Death; and the *Nature* of that Judgment.

P. II.

The Soul is no ſooner ſet at Liberty from her Priſon of the Body, but ſhe is immediately preſented before Almighty God, and a preciſe Inquiry is made, into her whole Life, from the firſt uſe of Reaſon to the laſt Gaſp. No Friend to aſſiſt her with Advice, no Advocate to plead her Cauſe; but left to herſelf, ſhe is to abide a rigorous Trial; wherein, as nothing can hurt her but the Evils ſhe has committed, ſo ſhe muſt expect no Comfort, but what the Teſtimony of a good Conſcience affords.

Inquiry will then be made, how we have employed the ſeveral Talents intruſted to our Care; and it will be expected, that the Advantage gained, be equal to the Number and Quality

lity of what has been put into our Hands. If ten Talents were intrusted to our Care, we must make it appear, that we have gained other ten; if five, other five, and so in proportion. If it should be proved against us, that instead of making a right use of what was received, we have been idle, and contented ourselves with hiding our Talents; much more if it be made appear, that we have prodigally squandered them away, in compliance with our evil Inclinations; we shall certainly fall under the Sentence of the wicked Servant mentioned in the Gospel, *cast out the unprofitable Servant, into exterior darkness, where there shall be weeping and gnashing of teeth* (*q*) (*q*) Mat. c. xxv. v. 30.

But let us consider what these Talents are. In the first place, we were created and sent into this World for no other End, but to serve God, and Work out our Salvation; and for this Reason, the several Faculties and Qualifications of Soul and Body, were bestowed upon us, only as conducive and applicable to that purpose. Hence we may be assured, that a strict Account will be exacted, concerning the manner in which they have been employed. Inquiry will be made, whether our *Will, Memory,* and *Understanding,* have been so directed, as to be subservient to the great End, for which they were designed. Has that noble Prerogative, the *Understanding,* by which we are raised to an infinite Distance above our fellow Animals, has the Understanding I say, reserved it's Sovereignty free from the Delusions of the *Flesh,* the *World,* and the *Devil?* Has our *Memory,* faithfully recorded the immense Obliligations

gations due to Almighty God, and been ever-mindful of his all-feeing Prefence, even in the moſt hidden Corners of the Earth? Has our *Will*, always executed the Dictates of Reafon inlightened by Religion, and not obſtinately turned, to what our cool, and deliberate Thoughts, have fo juſtly condemned? It will likewife be demanded, what ufe we have made of our *Time, Health*, and *Subſtance*, and whatever Talents or Means, the Divine Goodnefs, has favoured us with in our feveral Stations, throughout the Courfe of our mortal Life. Our *Time*, that precious, but much neglected Treafure, whofe fmalleſt Portion, rightly employed, is capable of purchafing eternal Happinefs, how have we employed it? Shall we be able to make it appear on our Examination, that in proportion, to the duration of our Lives, we have fet a part a due fhare for our Advancement in the Way of Virtue, and not fuffered worldly Affairs, or criminal Exceffes, to ingrofs that, which the Almighty Giver, defigned as a means of gaining Heaven? As to our *Health*, can we truly fay, that we have never wafted it by a Conduct, which not only as Chriſtians, but even as Rational creatures, we ought to have abhorred? Our *Subſtance*, only lent us by Providence, have we foolifhly fquandered it away, or wickedly hoarded it up, without reflecting, that even a Cup of cold Water, given with a right Intention, fhall not lofe it's Reward? Without confidering, that at the laſt Day, the Reprobates will be reproached, with having refufed Meat to the Hungry, and Clothes to the Naked.

We

We shall be likewise examined, concerning our Compliance, with the mutual Duties we severally owe, to each other. *Married Persons* will be examined, whether they have observed their Matrimonial Vows, how far they have made good their Promises, of loving, and cherishing each other in all the Difficulties usually attending that State of Life. *Parents* must give an Account, what care they have taken in the Education of their Children; in procuring them such Instructions, as were absolutely necessary for training their minds to Piety, and Devotion in their tender Years; How diligently they have watched over their Behaviour, and prevented the growth of Vice in their Souls; and above all, whether they have edified them by good Example, or brought them acquainted with Sin by a contrary Conduct. *Masters and Mistresses* will be examined, in what manner they have behaved towards their Servants, whether they have used them with Tenderness and Compassion, being made according to the same Image and Likeness of God, and designed by him, for the same Eternal Happiness with themselves; whether they have set an edifying Example before their Eyes, and allowed them sufficient Time and proper Opportunities, to look after the Concerns of their Souls, which cost the Redeemer of the World, the same immense Price, as those of their Masters and Mistresses. *Servants* will be called to a strict Account, concerning their Obedience and Fidelity to their Masters or Mistresses; whether they have been equally careful of every thing, committed to their Charge, as they would have

been

been in their own Concerns, neither wafting them themfelves, nor fuffering them to be fquandered by others. *Tradefmen*, or Perfons, engaged *in Bufinefs*, will be examined whether they have ufed any unlawful means, to encreafe their Gain ; whether they have been contented with a fair and honeft Profit, dealing with others as they are willing to be dealt with themfelves, without having Recourfe to any Contrivances for impofing on the Judgment of thofe, with whom they are concerned. The *Minifters* of Chrift's Church will be ftrictly examined, whether they have given good and edifying Example to the Laity, and according to the very belt of their Abilities informed their *Flock*, of their feveral Duties to God, and their Neighbour ; whether they have endeavoured to print in their Minds the great, and terrible Truths of the Gofpel, without foftening in the leaft, the Severity of God's juft Judgment on thofe, who rebel againft him. And *the Flock* on the other Hand, muft give an Account what Profit, and Advantage they have made of the feveral Inftructions, they have from time to time received. Thefe are, among many others, part of the Inquires, to which we muft anfwer at our *particular* Judgment.

On the Tribunal will be feated an Almighty Judge, whofe Knowledge nothing can efcape, whofe Eye pierces the darkeft Recefles of the Soul, and views in a clear Light the moft filent Motions of the Heart. There he will clearly read all that ever paft in Man, even the moft fecret Thoughts, tho' now buried in deep Oblivion. Not a word, which has fallen from our Lips,

Lips, since we arrived at the use of Reason; not an individual Action of our Lives, nor the least Omission of the Duties we are obliged to perform, but must be weighed in the Scales of the divine Justice: Those Scales which will be held in the unerring Hand of God, will admit of no false Weights to favour the poor Delinquent; no plausible Excuses to palliate what is bad in itself; but will assign to every thing it's proper Quality, and the due Reward it justly deserves. Even our best Actions, all the Good we have ever done, must be tried in the Balance of the Sanctuary; if they are found too light, if a right Intention was wanting, if any worldly Views influenced the performance of Actions, otherwise just and holy in themselves, they will be adjudged deficient, and consequently being short of the divine Standard, must be set aside as nothing worth. Good God, how different are thy Judgments from those of Men! What shall I say of the dismal Apprehension and Terror, which will certainly seize the wretched Criminal, when he considers that all lies at Stake, that upon the Event of this one Trial, all depends? When an Estate is to be recovered or lost, what Solicitude, what Anxiety doth not each Person concerned usually undergo? When Life or Death is depending, the Agony often suffered, whilst the Trial remains in Suspence, is little inferior to that, which is the forerunner of Death itself. But in the Case before us, not an Estate, not a wretched Life, which Nature itself would demand in a few Years; But an Eternity of Happiness, greater then the Heart of Man can possibly conceive, or never ending Misery, exceeding

ceeding all Imagination, is then going to be finally determined. O Christians! what will then be your Thoughts? what will you then be willing to give for a few of those precious Moments, which you now so lavishly throw away? How will you at that instant wish you had taken the Warning, which has been so often given to you to prepare for so rigorous a Trial; to lay up a Treasure of good Works, which alone can enable you to stand before an inexorable Judge, without withering away with Dread and Expectation of your eternal Doom!

Walk, says our Saviour Christ, *whilst you have the light that the darkness overtake you not.* (r) *For the night cometh when no Man can work.* (s) While you remain Dear Christians, on this side the Grave, you have the Light of Religion, by which you are enabled to advance in the way of Virtue, and consequently to approach nearer to the Kingdom of Heaven. But when the Night of Death is once come, there is no farther Opportunity of working out our Salvation; you must then stand or fall, by the Condition in which your Soul is found, when separated from the Body.

(r) John c. xii. v. 35.
(s) John c. ix. v. 4.

If we desire to provide against that important Scrutiny, which we know we cannot possibly avoid, now is the time; from this Instant let us set about the great Work. But if we are so senseless, as to delude ourselves with the notion of doing it hereafter, whom can we blame but ourselves, if we are surprised when we least expect it, and find ourselves before the all-seeing and just Judge, without the Testimony of a well spent Life to offer in our Behalf? To-morrow,

morrow, that stupid, that fatal Refuge of poor indolent Wretches, what Mischiefs, what irreparable and endless Woes has it not occasioned! Build not therefore on *To-morrow*, which is not yours to dispose of, which if trusted to, will insensibly draw you on till Life can yield no more, and leave you in the immense Ocean of Eternity, amazed and confounded at so unexpected an Alteration. No, let each of us, with Heart as well as Lips, cry out with holy David, *now I have begun, this Change is the work of the most High.* (t)

(t) Pf. lxxvi. v. 11.

ARTICLE

ARTICLE, VII.
DISCOURSE. II.

From thence he shall come to judge the Quick and the Dead.

We must all stand before the Judgment Seat of Christ. Rom. c. xiv. v. 10.

THE highest Grandeur, Dear Christians, or the lowest State of Life, shall not exempt any Man from this *General* judgment; for the Prince and the Beggar shall be upon a level, and there shall be no distinction of Rich or Poor; but only of *Sheep* and *Goats*, of *Just* and *Wicked*, for as the Apostle says, *with God there is no respect of Persons.* (u) We are all equally his Creatures; the highest Honours, are but his Donations; strip the King of his Robes, and the Beggar of his Rags, and you will not know which is which; an Empire cannot enoble a Man's Soul, nor can a Dungeon vilify it. And this being truly the Case, we are all upon a level,

(u) Acts. c x. v. 34

level, unless one gain the the Pre-eminence by Superiority of *Virtue* and good Works. Earthly Grandeur is so far from being a Plea of Exemption from Judgment, that it is a strong Argument in proof of it, for it sets those who enjoy it beyond the reach of human justice, and the use they make of that Privilege is too often such, as cannot be attended with impunity always, without manifest violence done to the Divine Attributes. How vain are the great Men's Hopes of Partiality in that impartial Court, where *Virtue* shall be the only true Stamp of *Nobility*, and *Deeds*, not *Titles* shall determine his Reception.

I have

---

* Now contrary to this Article of our Belief, there were formerly certain detestable and wicked Hereticks, viz. the *Marcionites*, and *Gnosticks*, who held, that there were two Gods. The one a just and severe God, who was the Creator of the World. *See Tertull. de Præscript. adverf. Hæret. p.* 82. *et* 95. *See also Origen in his* 1st. *and* 2d. *Book of Dialog.* The other a good and merciful God, who was the Father of our Lord Jesus Christ, and that he and his Son were all Pity, Grace, and Love; and that the Son's design in coming into the World, was only to save those, from the Severity of the Creator of the World, who should fly unto him; and though they should be the most abominable Sinners, yet he would never condemn, or punish them: Which monstrous and horrid Tenet, opens a Floodgate to all Licentiousness and Impiety, for if God be only *good* and not *just*, who will ever obey his Commandments, and especially such of them, as are contrary to Men's sensual Inclinations, and carnal Passions? For if there be no fear of a future Punishment, the Sensualists and Voluptuous, are certainly the wisest and most prudent Men; and it would be a most unaccountable Folly, to mortify the Flesh, or renounce the World, in order to obey that God, who is not at all displeased with any of our disobedient

I have already spoke in the foregoing Discourse concerning the *particular* Judgment, what therefore I here design, is to lay before you the [The Divine]

disobedient Actions, and being not displeased, will never punish us, tho' we freely plunge ourselves into all sorts of Debaucheries and Impurities. But in contradiction to this destructive Tenet of all Religion and Piety, our Rule of Faith declares, that there is but one God, as I have before proved; and that he is not only *Good*, but that he is also *Just*; that he is a *Judge*, as well as a *Saviour*; and that Jesus Christ did not only die and rise again for the good of all Mankind, but that *he will also come to Judge the Quick and the Dead*; to examine into the Behaviour of all Men, and to reward them suitable to to their Deeds, as *Tertullian* observes, *advers.* Marcion. L. iv. p. 221 : And St. Irenæus says the same thing in these Words ; *Venturus Salvator, eorum qui salvantur, et Judex eorum qui judicantur, et mittens in ignem æternum transfiguratores veritatis, et contemptores Patris sui et adventus ejus.* L. iii. c. 4. p. 172.

From hence we believe, that all Men are free and voluntary Creatures, not forced by any superior Agent, but freely determining themselves to all their Actions; for Judgment implies a Freedom and Liberty in the Person judged, as St. Justin Martyr writes; *for if*, says he, *it be determined by Fate, that this Man shall be good, and the other wicked, then neither is the one to be commended, nor the other to be blamed ; so neither would the just Man deserve a Reward, if he was made good, and did not of himself choose the good ; neither if he was wicked, could he be justly punished, except he voluntarily made himself so.* Apolog. ii. p. 80. For a righteous and just Judgment as our Saviour's will be, doth necessarily imply a liberty and freedom of every Action that shall be judged. So that by this Article of our Creed, we believe that Man is a free and voluntary Agent, acting without constraint or force, and therefore he shall at the Day of Judgment receive a Sentence from Jesus Christ either of Bliss or Wo, suitable to the Works which he did here on Earth, whether of Piety or Wickedness, Obedience or Disobedience. But we may here observe, that the *Liberty* of Man, and his

the several Circumstances of the last and *General* Judgment, which this Article of our Creed seems chiefly to point at; which will be at the End of the World, when Heaven and Earth shall pass away, and all things be dissolved. The *Harvest* is expresly said to be the *End* (*w*) *of the World.* (*w*) And the Day of Judgment is every where in Scripture said to be the *last Day,* that is, the last time there shall be any such Distinction as Day or Night, when Time itself shall be no more, but all be swallowed up in the boundless Ocean of Eternity.

(*w*) Mat. c. xiii. v. 39.

P. I. But although that Day be actually fixed, and appointed by Almighty God, for *he hath appointed a Day,* (says the Apostle) *wherein he will* (*x*) Acts: *Judge the World.* (*x*) Yet when this will be, is beyond the reach of human or even angelick Wisdom to know; for *of that Day and Hour no one knoweth, no not even the Angels of Heaven.* (*y*) The Jews have indeed a Tradition derived (as they say) from *Elias,* that the Duration of this World is to be just six Thousand Years; but as this does not come under my present purpose, so I shall say no more of it, only so far, it seems to contradict the above assertion of a general Ignorance of that Point; besides, there is such a Disagreement among Chronologers concerning the Age of the World, that we are entirely at a loss with regard to the true and exact Date of its Creation: The Defenders of

(*x*) Acts: c. xvii. v. 31.

(*y*) Mat. c. xxiv. v. 36.

his being judged according to his Works, were formerly denied by other Hereticks, viz. the *Valentinians* and *Basilidians.* See their detestable System mentioned by *St. Irenæus.* L. i. c. 1, as also by *Tertullian* in his Book *adverf. Valentin.*

each

each Opinion, proceed upon nothing but Conjecture, and are far from being satisfied in themselves of their being in the right. And when we have pushed our Discoveries to the farthest, *when shall these things be?* (z) Is a Query which shall not be revealed, but by the thing itself. In the mean time, he who lives always prepared for it, knows enough; for he knows, let it come when it will, it cannot take him at a Disadvantage. (z) Mat. c. xxiv. v. 3.

Now as to the Place where the last and *general* Judgment will be held, the Scripture seems to insinuate, that it will be the Valley of *Josaphat*, where it says, *I will gather together all Nations, and will bring them into the Valley of Josaphat, and I will plead against them there.* (a) The Valley of *Josaphat* is near *Jerusalem* and Mount *Calvary*, so that it is probable, Christ will exercise the Severity of his *Justice*, where he shewed such Tokens of his *Mercy*; a sad Remembrance to the Jews, who put him to Death, and to Wicked Christians, who have crucified him by their scandalous Lives. (a) Joel. c. iii. v. 2.

The Prophet *Sophonias* speaking of this last and Terrible Day, delivers himself in the following Manner: *That Day is the Day of Wrath, the Day of Calamity and Misery; the Day of Darkness, Clouds, and Whirlwinds.--- In the fire of his Zeal the whole Earth shall be destroyed.* (b) (b) Sop. c. i. v. 15.

We read in St. Luke, the following remarkable words of our Blessed Redeemer, concerning the great Miseries, which will be the Forerunner's of the last accompting Day: *There shall be Signs*, says our Saviour Christ, *in the Sun and the Moon, and in the Stars, and upon the Earth, dis-*

trefs of Nations, through the Confusion occasioned by the roaring of the Sea and it's Waves; Men withering away through fear and Expectation of what shall come upon the whole World. For even the Powers of Heaven shall be shaken. And then they shall see the Son of Man coming in the Clouds with great Might and Majesty. (c) Thus we see when the *general* Judgment draws near, the very Signs of it's Approach will be so very dreadful, as to raise such a Consternation and Horror in the Minds of Men, that the bare Apprehension of what is to follow, shall Cause them to wither away for Fear! And as these Miseries arise from the approaching total Dissolution of Nature, so they themselves will be introduced by an universal Confusion of all Order and Regularity throughout the whole Earth, and the utter Abolition of all the Comforts and Conveniences of Life. All created Beings shall conspire, and exert their utmost Force against that wretched Creature Man; and even Men with implacable Fury and Madness shall oppress each other, till the whole Earth becomes one Scene of Horror and Confusion. It is true, the Design of Providence in the Creation of Mankind, was, that they should be a mutual aid and assistance to one another, for their advancement towards the Kingdom of Heaven: The several Elements, and all other Creatures were produced, that Men, by making a right use of them, might be the better enabled to work out the Salvation of their Souls: But as this Order of Providence, has been so many Ages in a great measure perverted, by the depraved Appetites of human Nature, making a wrong use of every thing, in

(c) Luck c. xxi. v. 25.

direct

direct Oppofition to the Intention of their univerfal Lord and Maker, it is therefore highly confonant to divine Juftice, that Men fhould mutually revenge on each other the Caufe of God.

When the day of Judgment draws near, Seditions, Tumults, and Civil Wars will break out on all fides; nothing to be feen or heard of but Murders, burning of Cities, plundering of Provinces, utter Ruin and Deftruction, with all the dreadful Confequences of a fharp and bloody War. Thefe of courfe will be fucceeded by Famine and the Want of all thofe Neceffaries, without which, Life itfelf becomes a Burthen. Parents will no longer have any Tendernefs for their Children; Children will forget all Duty and Regard for thofe, to whom they owe their Birth; the beft Friends will be eftranged from each other, an univerfal Depravity will banifh all the focial Ties of civil Life; fo that Kindred, Friendfhip, the mutual Love of married Perfons, and all the Allegiance due to the common Weal, will all vanifh from the human Mind. What wonder then, if many are fwept of by raging Peftilences, in fuch prodigious Numbers, that the living will fcarce fuffice to bury the Dead, from whofe corrupted Carcaffes, new Plagues will arife, fpreading Horror and Defolation throughout the Earth.

But all this, is only the beginning of their Sorrows. For now the Elements united in the common Caufe of their Creator, pour out their baneful Influences, continual Lightening fwift as Thought, fhall dart it's fubtle Fire, reducing to Afhes what ever it touches; and Claps of Thunder will follow, ſhaking the whole Earth to it's very center, accompanied with dreadful Storms, Whirlwinds, laying whole Countries entirely waſte. The Sea no longer keeping it's ancient Bounds, ſhall break out like a Deluge upon the Land, with ſuch a prodigious Impetuoſity, that the very Roaring of it's Waves ſhall ſtun, and confound thoſe who live at the greateſt Diſtance. The Sun's bright Orb ſhall loſe it's Splendor, affording only ſome glimmering Light, ſufficient to diſcover the woful Deſolation, in which the World is involved: And the Moon and Stars quite obſcured, ſhall fall, that is, confound the beauteous Order, in which they have hitherto moved for ſo many Thouſand Years. In this horrible Confuſion, Man withering away through Fear and Apprehenſion, a furious Torrent of liquid Fire, ſhall pour along the Surface of the whole Earth, devouring every thing it meets, and reducing the whole to one undiſtinguiſhed Heap of Aſhes. O ye great and powerful ones of this World, where are now your gaudy Trappings and pompous Equipages? Ye Kings and Princes, where are now your gilded Palaces, your ſtately Gardens and extenſive Plantations? Where are now your golden Thrones and glittering Diadems, your warlike Stores, and fortified Cities, your numerous Armies, and powerful Fleets? All, all vaniſh in Smoke, not ſo much as their very Ruins to be diſcovered!

Every thing on the Face of the Earth being thus deſtroyed, and Nature cloathed a new, the Day of Judgment ſucceeds. That Day of Comfort to the Juſt, and Terror to the Wicked;
that

that Day, wherein our Saviour bids his Faithful Servants *lift up their Heads, for that their Redemption is near at Hand*. (d) Then they shall see, says the Scripture, *the Son of Man coming in the Clouds with great Power and Majesty*. v. 27. Before Him will be carried his heavenly Standard, the Holy Cross, shining brighter than the Sun, Millions and Millions of Angels encompasing the Judge on all sides, and all Mankind assembled before him in two distinct Companies, wherein the Sons of Adam are once more brought upon a Level, and all former Distinctions of Birth or Fortune, are entirely reduced to this only Difference, of the *just* being placed on his Right Hand, and the *wicked* on his Left. But alas, how little do they resemble each other! the one with chearful and joyful Countenances, looking up to their Redeemer, whose Life was their Pattern, whose Cross their only Comfort in this World; the other, calling out to the Mountains to fall and cover them, that they may be screened at any rate from that terrible Tribunal, which is upon the Point of adjudging Soul and Body, a wretched Victim to the Flames of Hell. The one appearing in glorious Array, accompanied with their Angel Guardians, and cheared from time to time, with the amiable Looks of their Blessed Redeemer; the other in hideous Confusion, foul and loathsome to behold, terrified with the Stern and tremendous Regards of an offended Majesty; mocked, scorned and derided by the Devils, to whose infernal Malice and implacable Revenge they are just going to fall a Prey for all Eternity. Poor Wretches! what will they

(d) Luck c. xxi.
28. ibid. v. 27

they think of themselves, when they compare the happy Condition of the Juſt with their own woful Situation? Will they not through the Anguiſh and Bitterneſs of their Souls, cry out as we read in the Book of Wiſdom. *Theſe are the Perſons, at whom we formerly ſcoffed. Fools that we were! we looked upon their Lives a folly, and their End ignominious; but ſee, they are now numbered among the Children of God, and their Portion is with the Happy. We have wandered therefore from the Path of Virtue, and wearied ourſelves in the Ways of Sin and Iniquity, and have walked in crooked Paths, without knowing the way of the Lord. What has our Pride availed us, and what has our boaſted Riches afforded? They are all vaniſhed like a Shadow, like a Ship at Sea, or an Arrow flying through the Air, of which not the leaſt Track appears?* (e)

(e) Wiſd. c. v. v. 3. &c.

After theſe two Companies have conſidered their ſeveral Circumſtances, the Almighty Judge will proceed to the Trial: the Subject of our Indictment will relate to our perſonal Behaviour in the reſpective States, in which God has placed us in this World; we muſt then give an Account of all our Thoughts, Deſires, Wiſhes, Affections, Words, and Works, though never ſo ſecret; the Intention, Motive, and Circumſtances of them; the uſe of our Will, Memory, and Underſtanding; all the Faculties of both Body and Soul; the uſe of God's holy Graces; the Neglect of doing Good, and miſpent Time; and not only our own Sins, but thoſe of others, which we have any ways occaſioned; for our Saviour aſſures us, *that nothing is hid that ſhall not be revealed, nor ſecret*

secret that shall not be known. (f) When the Examination or Trial is over, the Judge will proceed to the definitive Sentence, which will separate them for ever, never to behold each other more. To those on the right Hand, *Christ* will say with an amiable and inviting Countenance, *Come ye blessed of my Father, possess the Kingdom prepared for you from the beginning of the World.* (g) O Christians! what Joy and Delight must arise in their Breasts, when they find the Promises of their Blessed Redeemer fulfilled; that they who give a cup of cold Water out of a charitable Motive, shall not lose their Reward; that the Measure they gave to others, is now to be heaped up a hundredfold to them again; their Mortifications and Self-denials are rewarded with Crowns of eternal Glory; their Patience and Humility entitled to a share with the Son of God himself, in his heavenly Kingdom; their virtuous Lives, their Triumphs over Sin and the Devil, to be the Subject of celestial Hymns sung before the Throne of the Almighty. With these glorious Sentiments, they mount aloft conducted in Triumph to the Possession of Heaven, there to reign Body and Soul in everlasting Bliss, as long as God shall be God.

Nothing now remains, but the dismal Sentence to be pronounced against the Wicked; they already read it in the terrible Countenance of their offended Judge: *Go ye cursed into everlasting Fire,* he will say, *prepared for the Devil and his Angels.* (h) O dreadful Sentence! to depart from God, by losing him and all that is Good; never to see God's Face, nor ever to enjoy

(f) Mat. c. x. v. 26.

(g) Mat. c. xxv. v. 34.

(h) Mat. c. xxv. v. 41.

enjoy his Favours, this is that Hell of Hells, which the Divines call *Pain of Loss*. But then not only to lose all Good, but also to be sunk for ever into the Abyss of everlasting Evils, without any hope of Comfort, is that *Pain of Sense*, which even the worst of Sinners, cannot firmly believe without trembling. O miserable wretched Creatures! How much better would it have been for you, never to have been born! Or rather, how much better would it have been, to have spent your whole Lives in Tears and Groans, in Pain and Affliction, than thus to fall a Victim to the just Anger of Almighty God! But, it is too late to think; you gave the Preference to the Devil before your Creator, and now you must receive your Wages from him, whom you chose for a Master: You neglected to lay up a Treasure of good Works, by relieving according to your Abilities, those who stood in need of your Assistance; by not curbing your own vicious Inclinations, and not complying with the Duties of a Christian: Go therefore, reap the bitter Fruits you have sown.

You have heard, Dear Christians, the Sentence which Truth itself declares will be pronounced at the last Day on the two great Divisions of Mankind; the one placed on his right Hand, and the other at his left; and no doubt, you sincerely intend to be in the Number of the former. But let me conjure you, as you value your precious Souls, not to content yourselves with empty Wishes. Alas! how many have formed the same Intention in their Minds, and notwithstanding will find themselves

at

at the laft day, on the wrong fide of the Judgment feat! for, *not every one who fays to me Lord, Lord, fhall enter into the Kingdom of Heaven; but he who does the Will of my Father who is in Heaven.* (*i*) If therefore you would effectually provide for your Safety in that great Day, *do the Will of your heavenly Father*, make his holy Commandments the Rule of your Lives; ftudy to know your Duty in the feveral Stations, in which God has placed you, and be earneft in the Performance of it. Affift your poor and diftreffed Neighbour, chearfully according to your Abilities, without Oftentation or feeking Applaufe of Men. Thefe are the Means, the only Means, to fecure a Place at the Right Hand of the heavenly Judge.

(*i*) Mat. c. vii. v. 21.

E e ARTICLE,

ARTICLE, VIII.

DISCOURSE, I.

I believe in the Holy Ghoſt.

The Holy Ghoſt, whom the Father will ſend in my Name, He will teach you all things. John. c. xiv. v. 26.

IN the foregoing Articles of the Creed, the Apoſtles inſtruct us in what we are to believe, relating to the *Firſt*, and *Second* Perſon of the Bleſſed Trinity: In this Article they exhibit or preſent to us the *Holy Ghoſt*, who is the *third* Perſon in that ſacred Union, and together with the *Father* and the *Son*, makes up the adorable undivided Trinity; this therefore teaches us, what we are to believe of the *Holy Ghoſt*, the third Perſon.

To this Article, is again prefixed the initial *Credo I believe*, which is virtually underſtood in every Article, and every portion of each Article, as well as in theſe two. But as I formerly
said,

said, so I here observe again, that *to believe*, is an Act indispensably necessary to Salvation, for *without Faith it is impossible to please God*. (k) Therefore we cannot be saved with out it.

(k) Heb. c. xi. v. 6.

Before I enter upon the explanation of this Article, it will be necessary to put you in mind once more of the Definition of *Faith*; St. Paul calls it *the Substance of Things hoping for, the conviction of Things that appear not*. (l) What then must we say of all those, who pretend to try revealed Truths by the Standard of their own Conceptions, and will believe nothing that is superior to their own reasonings; now it is certain that this excludes all *Faith*, for when a Belief arises from the Evidence of things seen and known, it is not a Belief of *Faith*, but of Knowledge and Conviction. The Christians Faith must be grounded upon the Words and Revelation of God, without presuming to scan them by our weak Capacity. For the *Blessing* is due only to *those who have not seen and yet have believed*. (m) Nay a seeming impossibility is so far from being an Obstacle, that the Merit of Faith rises in Proportion to the apparent Difficulty in the Object; when therefore the *Mysteries* of Religion, which we cannot comprehend are proposed to our Belief, we readily assent to them upon the Word and Veracity of God, to whom nothing is impossible, as we know he is Omnipotent, and can do more than what we can conceive; so that to disbelieve what God has revealed, and his Church declared, because we cannot comprehend it, is to deny the *Omnipotency* and Power of God. But some will say, they cannot comprehend how such things can be

(l) Heb. c xi. v. 1.

(m) John. c. xx. v. 29.

be which seem to them impossible. What then? Are they ever the farther from being true? 'Tis certain that we cannot conceive or trace *Eternity*, is God therefore not Eternal? Nor can we conceive the *Unity* and *Trinity* of God; nor is it necessary we should; for were there not some things in Religion, which carried with them some *Mystery*, there would be no room for *Faith*, and the whole of Righteousness would be resolved into that of the *moral Law*.

But notwithstanding the Difficulties some make in believing or asserting to revealed Truths; yet even these very Mysteries came attended with such Evidence in the Proofs of the Revelation, as we cannot reasonably or safely reject. We give our Assent to many things, (which we declare appear very strange and surprising to us,) upon the sole Word to Testimony of a Man, of whose Veracity we have a good Opinion. *If then we received the Witnesses of Men, the Witness of God is certainly greater*; (*n*) our Motives to believe in Man, are his Knowledge and Truth, and that he is not deceived, and that he will not impose a Lie upon us, and deceive us. Now both these Motives do most strongly persuade us to an implicit Faith in the word of God, in whom these respective Qualities do reside in the highest and most extensive Perfection, for he can neither deceive nor be deceived. As to what some may object. How shall we know these things to be the word of God? I answer, that the Authority of the sacred Scriptures, and the general Concurrence of the greatest and wisest Men of the Church of God, in all Ages down to us,

(*) John. c. v. v. 9.

with

Art. VIII. Disc. I.

with the Authority of the Church in their Interpretation, is a sufficient motive of our Belief; besides an almost infinite Number of other Arguments, that may be urged in Proof of the Truth of the Christian Revelation from Prophecies, Miracles, the Excellency of the moral Precepts of the Gospel, and from all the Circumstances attending the Establishment of the Christian Religion.

There are some People who pretend to say, that they cannot believe or assent to the Testimony of the Scripture, when they think it derogates from God's Honour, as in the Belief of the Blessed *Trinity*: Now I think they may as well call in question the *Incarnation* and *Death* of our *Saviour*, since nothing can seemingly derogate more from God's Honour, than such a debasement; and yet whosoever calls in question these great *Mysteries*, is no Christian, but a down right Infidel; for it is the Christian's Duty to believe and assent to whatever God has revealed, and his Church declares, because it is not for us to dispute the *Word* of our *Creator*, any more than his *Will*.

The *Holy Ghost* is the third Person of the Blessed Trinity, who *proceeding from the Father and Son*, together with the Father and the Son is *one God*; and therefore, *together with the Father and the Son is worshipped and glorified* (o)   (o) Symb. Atha.

Now what we mean by the Term *Ghost*, is the same as *Spirit*, or Spiritual Essence, distinct from Corporeity; and the Epithet *Holy*, is added as well in respect to his Office, which is that of *Sanctification*, as to distinguish him from all other Beings, that are called Spirits.

There

There are two great Promises which God made to those, who live under the *new* Law, that is as Christians. The one was to send his *only Son*, that we might place all our hopes in him; and the other to send the *Holy Ghost*, that Men might live by the Spirit of God. We have already seen how God has accomplished the first Promise, in sending his only begotten Son to save the World; now we are to see the Accomplishment of the second, in sending the Holy Ghost.

The Holy Ghost in Scripture is called the *Gift* of God, as it were by excellency his Gift, which comprises all other Gifts, and without which, all other Gifts profit nothing. The Holy Ghost, and the Promise of the Holy Ghost, is appropriated to the new Law, and belongs only to Christians, to them the Holy Ghost is sent, and thus all Christians ought to live by the Spirit of God.

What therefore I intend in this Discourse is, *first*, to explain to you what we ought to believe of the Holy Ghost. And *secondly*, what it is to live by this Holy Spirit. We believe that the Holy Ghost is true God, equal to the Father and the Son. We also believe there are three Distinct Persons in the most Adorable and Blessed Trinity, and that the three are only *one God*, though each of the three be truly God. But in the first place, it will be necessary to consider what the Catholick Faith teaches; and opposes against the Rashness of those, who call in question this great Mystery of our Faith, as delivered to us in St. Athanasius's Creed; for there we are taught,

The Divis
P. I.

that

that the Catholick Faith is this, that we worship one God in Trinity, and Trinity in Unity: neither confounding the Persons, nor dividing the Substance. For there is one Person of the Father, another of the Son, and another of the Holy Ghost: But the Divinity of the Father, and of the Son, and of the Holy Ghost is one and the same, such as the Father is, such is the Son, and such is the Holy Ghost. The Father Uncreated, the Son Uncreated, and the Holy Ghost Uncreated. The Father Eternal, the Son Eternal, and the Holy Ghost Eternal, and yet there are not three Eternals, but one Eternal: So likewise the Father is Almighty, the Son Almighty, and the Holy Ghost Almighty. So the Father is God, the Son is God, the Holy Ghost is God, and yet there are not three Gods, but one God. For as we are obliged by the Christian Faith, to acknowledge every Person by himself to be God, so we are forbidden by the Catholick Religion, to say there are three Gods. The Father is made of no one, neither created nor begotten; the Son is of the Father alone, not made nor created, but begotten; the Holy Ghost is of the Father, and of the Son, not made, nor created, nor begotten, but proceeding. There is therefore one Father, not three Fathers, one Son, not three Sons, one Holy Ghost, not three Holy Ghosts. And in this Trinity, nothing is before or after another; nor one greater or less than another; but all three Persons are Co-eternal, and Co-equal, so that in all things, as has been said above, both Unity in Trinity, and Trinity in Unity is to be worshipped.

By

By this Profession is to be regulated the Faith of this Myſtery; it was compoſed in the firſt Ages of the Chriſtian Church when *Arius*, with his numerous and powerful Followers, had with equal heat and impiety oppoſed this Article of the Catholick Faith, as it had been taught by the Apoſtles and delivered down by the Paſtors of the Church, who to ſatisfy the Charge given them by Chriſt, *of taking care of his Flock*, aſſembled in the firſt General Council of Nice in the Year 325, and there publiſhed the Faith of this great Myſtery of the Bleſſed Trinity, as it had been received, and ſetting a Mark upon *Arius*, as a Wolf that deſigned to devour the Flock, prevented the growth of his Impiety at that time, and by pronouncing *Anathema* againſt him, left a Rule, by which all ſucceeding Ages might be ſecured againſt his deteſtable Errors. And has ever ſince been uſed by the Catholick Church as a Standard, by which the orthodox Chriſtians, as to this Point have been diſtinguiſhed, from the Abetters of Hereſy. And as the Faith of this Myſtery has been thus delivered, ſo it ought to be received by all Chriſtians, as the Church of England profeſſes in their 39 Articles.

Again it may be here neceſſary to prove that the Holy Ghoſt is a true and real *Perſon*, and not a bare *Quality*, as the *Socinians* and ſome other Hereticks have held.

For that muſt be a *Perſon*, to whom *perſonal* Actions are expreſsly and ſtrongly attributed; now *perſonal* Actions are expreſsly attributed to the *Holy Ghoſt*; therefore the Holy Ghoſt muſt be a Perſon, and not a *Quality*; for what we mean

mean by a *Person*, is that which conftitutes an individual Rational Being. The *Holy Ghoft* both *receives* and *executes* a Commiffion, in confequence of which, he perfoms the following feveral *perfonal* Actions. " The Comforter the Holy
" Ghoft, whom the Father will fend in my
" Name, he fhall *teach* you all Things; he
" will *teftify* of me : --- And when he is come
" he will *reprove* the World; he will *guide* you
" into all Truth; for he fhall not fpeak of
" himfelf, but whatfoever he fhall *Hear*, that he
" fhall fpeak: And he fhall *fhew* all things to
" come, he fhall glorify me, for he fhall re-
" ceive of mine, and fhall fhew it unto you."
(*p*) All which Words are nothing Elfe, but fo many Defcriptions of a Perfon. A Perfon *hearing*; A Perfon *receiving*; a Perfon *teftifying*; a Perfon *fpeaking*; a Perfon *reproving*; a Perfon *inftructing*. &c.

(*p*) John c. xiv. v. 26. et 16. v. 8. 13. 14.

Again to *fpeak* and *hear* are perfonal Actions; but what is ftill more, this Confeffion of our Faith is founded on the facred Form, which was by Chrift himfelf enjoined to be ufed at our Baptifm; we are Baptifed, *in the Name of the Father, and of the Son, and of the Holy Ghoft.* (*q*) Now the Father and the Son, are both acknowledged Perfons; therefore the very Conjunction of him with two allowed Perfons, does prove the Holy Ghoft to be more than a *Quality*: In a Word, a true, real, aud diftinct *Perfon*.

(*q*) Mat. c. xxviii. v. 19.

Laftly, upon our Saviour's afcending up out of the River *Jordan* after his Baptifm, there was fuch a Manifeftation of the *Holy Spirit*, as puts the Thing paft difpute; for his Defcent and Appearance was vifible; it was the *Token* given to

the

the *Baptist*, whereby he should know the Messiah : (r) *I saw the Spirit*, says St. John, *coming down from Heaven as a dove, and he remained upon him* (ibid. 32.) Now a visible *Quality* is a much greater Mystery, than what our modern Scepticks cavil at. What I have now to prove, is, that the Holy Ghost is not only a *Person*, but a divine Person.

(r) John. c. i. v. 33.

We believe the Holy Ghost to be consubstantial to the Father, and the Son, and that he proceeds from them both, and is equal in all things to them, and therefore he is truly God: This is *first* proved from the Creed itself, where the Form of our Belief is expressed in the same way, in regard to all the three divine Persons : *I believe in the Holy Ghost*, as well as *in the Father* and *in the Son.* * Secondly, from St. Peter's Words

---

* Several of the Primitive Fathers make a great Distinction between *believing* and *believing in ;* for to believe God, is to believe all to be true, that he has revealed ; but to *believe in God*, is to love him, and put our whole trust in him as our last End ; and from thence they prove the Divinity of the Holy Ghost, and intimate to us, that the Apostles did on this account, omit to prefix the Preposition *in* before the other Articles, which immediately follow this, as it is observed by *Ruffinus* (who lived in the fourth Century) in his Exposition of the Apostles Creed. 35. p. 575. where he observes, that " it is not said, we believe in the Holy Church,
" or in the Remission of Sins, or in the Resurrection of
" the Body; for if, says he, the Preposition of *in* had
" been added, it would have had the same force with
" what went before. But now in these words, where
" our Faith in the Divinity is declared, it is said to be
" *in God the Father*, and, and *in his Son Jesus Christ*, and
" *in the Holy Ghost ;* but where the Creed speaks of
" Creatures, and Mysteries, the Preposition *in*, is not
" added

Words to Ananias, *why hath Satan tempted thy Heart to lie to the Holy Ghost? Thou hast not lied unto Man but to God.* (*f*) Here you see the Holy Ghost is called God. Thirdly, from St. John in his first Epistle, where he says, *there are three that give Testimony in Heaven, the Father, the Word, and the Ghost, and these three are one.* Fourthly, from the Form of Baptism, where the Holy Ghost is equally numbred with the *Father* and the *Son*, which ought not to be, if he was not God. Lastly, from St. Paul's second Epistle to the Corinthians, where he thus concludes his Epistle, *The Grace of our Lord Jesus Christ, and the Love of God, and the Communication of the Holy Ghost be with you all.* (*t*) From hence we prove the Holy

(*f*) Acts. c. v. v. 3. 4. John c. v v. 7.

(*t*) c. xiii v. 13.

" added; as we do not say, we believe in the Holy
" Church, but that we believe the Holy Church, not
" as *in* God, but as a Church congregated by God,
" and we do not say *in* the Forgiveness of Sins, nor *in*
" the Resurrection of the Body, but the Forgivness of
" Sins, and the Resurrection of the Body: Therefore
" by this Preposition the *Creator* is distinguished from
" the *Creatures*, and *divine* things seperated from *human.*"
So that the not fixing the Preposition *in* before *the Holy Catholick Church*, and the other Articles which follow, directs us to believe them after another manner than the precedent Articles, before which, the Preposition is prefixed; for on the former we are to believe in as God, whilst we are only simply to believe the latter, as Mysteries revealed by God; or as St. Augustin says, that the Creed obliges to believe the Church, but not *in* the Church; for the Church, says he, is not God, but the House of God; *Ecclesiam credere, non tamen in Ecclesiam credere debemus, quia Ecclesia non Deus est, Sed Domus Dei est.* Tom. 10. Serm. de Temp. 181. p. 535. By all which it appears, that the Ancients observed a great difference in the Manner of their believing the several Articles of the Creed, laying a great Stress upon the Preposition *in.*

F f 2 Ghost

Ghoſt to have the ſame divine Nature with the Father and the Son, as alſo to be a different Perſon from them both: So that we ought to glorify and worſhip him equally with the Father and the Son, as the laſt End and Object of our Affections; and therefore the *Macedonian* Hereſy, was condemned by the Church in the Year 381, which denied the Divinity of the Holy Ghoſt.

But we are not only to believe that the Holy Ghoſt is truly God, but we muſt alſo believe that the *Holy Ghoſt* is given to Men, and that he dwells in Chriſtians, to make them live by the Spirit of God; I ſay the Holy Ghoſt inhabits among Chriſtians, not only by his *Grace* or *Gifts*, but by his perſonal Preſence. This God has promiſed by the Prophets *Iſaias* and *Joel*, whoſe Words St. Peter has quoted in the Acts of the Apoſtles,(*u*) to make this Effuſion of his *Holy Spirit* among Men. This Promiſe our Bleſſed Saviour confirmed, and even verified, when he ſent the *Holy Ghoſt* upon the Apoſtles and Diſciples on *Whitſunday*, being then aſſembled together at Jeruſalem. Here Almighty God in a miraculous and ſenſible Manner, manifeſted the coming of the Holy Ghoſt, for thoſe who had received him, ſpoke in different Languages, and all Jeruſalem were Witneſſes of the Miracle; and there was at that Time a great Concourſe of different Nations at Jeruſalem, each Nation heard theſe Men ſpeaking in their own Language *the Wonders of God*; which ſtruck the Jews with Fright, Shame, Confuſion, and Aſtoniſhment, ſeeing on a ſudden Men who were before weak, ignorant, timorous, become

(*u*) c. ii. v 17.

Acts: Apoſt. c. ii. v. 11.

Art. VIII. Disc. I.

come zealous, fervent, and active to all Good; they heard, I say, a Company of illiterate Men, speaking the Languages of all Nations, and disputing with the learned, and making themselves admired by all for Wisdom. Men chosen from amongst the meanest of the People, all on a sudden are capable by the inflamed Eloquence of their Discourse, to touch Men's Heart's with Compunction, and raise their Minds to Heaven, who before were full of Vice. Those who a little before were hated and persecuted, are now on a sudden admired. And long after this, the Holy Ghost continued to give in the same miraculous Manner the Gift of Languages and Prophecy, and has continued often to do the same for the Conversion of Infidels.

But the Holy Ghost is now still as ready to descend upon us, as he was upon the primitive Christians; when the Samaritans received the *Holy Ghost* by the *Imposition* of the Hands of St. Peter and John, as we read in the Acts of the Apostles: (w) So the *Imposition* of the Hands *(w)*c.viii. of our Bishops in *Confirmation*, are as powerful to give the *Holy Ghost*, as were the Hands of the Apostles; provided we approach with the same Dispositions as the Samaritans did; this has ever been the constant Belief of the Catholick Church in all Ages down to us.*

To

---

* It may perhaps seem strange to some, that as there is so much declared in the Creed relating to the *Father* and the *Son*, so little should be said concerning the *Holy Ghost;* but it must be observed, that there is a sufficient

and

P. II. To come now to my second Point, wherein I shall endeavour to shew you, what it is to live by the Spirit of the *Holy Ghost*.

It is easy for Men of all Religions to pretend they have the Holy Ghost within them: Every Fanatick, and Enthusiast, pretends to the Spirit of God; but it is only an interior Light, always within, but never appears without by good Actions; these Men have received the Holy Ghost in their own Dreams and Fancy, but those who have truly and really received the Holy Ghost, by the Imposition of the Bishop's Hands, don't boast of interior Lights which are never seen, but they shew it outwardly by their good Lives. If we have the Spirit of God, says St. Paul, let us live by the Spirit of God; those who have this Holy Spirit within them, shew it by the Fruits. For as Mankind before the coming of the Holy Ghost, were tepid and unactive to all Good, so now they are zealous, fervent, and active to all Virtue. The *Holy Ghost* gives us new Life by infusing Charity into Man's Heart, which is the Life of the Soul, and moving Christians to every good Work that Merits eternal Life.

The

and manifest Reason, which is, because there was not then so great a Controversy in the Primitive Church, concerning the Divinity and Person of the Holy Ghost; for though the *Gnosticks*, and *Macedonians*, or *Pneumatomachists* blasphemed Him, yet their Assaults were more furious and violent against the *Father* and the *Son*, which obliged the Church to use her greatest care for the preservation of that part, which was most attacked, as *St. Epiphanius* observes in his Book, *adverf. in Har.* 74, *adverf. Pneumatoach. p.* 384.

Art. VIII. *Disc.* I.

The presence of this Divine Spirit, in the first Place, banishes all Vices from the Soul, and then endows her with his *Gifts* and *Fruits.* Here let us consider what these Gifts and Fruits of the Holy Ghost are, that we may know what it is to live by the Spirit of the Holy Ghost. The Gifts of the Holy Ghost are these seven, enumerated in the eleventh Chapter of the Prophet Isaiah, and second Verse. *First, Wisdom,* which teaches us, to direct our Lives and Actions to God's Honour and Glory, and the Salvation of our Souls, and opens our Eyes to see the Vanity of this World. *Secondly, Understanding,* which makes our Faith lively, and enables us to penetrate into the Mysteries and Truths of our Christian Religion. *Thirdly, Council,* which discovers to us the Snares of the Devil, and teaches the most ignorant Persons in dark and dubious Cases to chuse that, which is best both for themselves, and the Honour of God. *Fourthly, Fortitude,* which enables us to overcome or surmount courageously all the Difficulties of Temptations, and to undergo all Dangers for God's sake. *Fifthly, Knowledge,* which teaches us to know, and to understand the Will of God, and to comply with it. *Sixthly, Piety,* which makes us zealous, and fervent in the Service of God. *Seventhly, the Fear of God,* which curbs us from Sin, and makes us obedient to his Law, and fearful of loosing his Favour.

The Fruits of the Holy Ghost are reckoned up by St. Paul, in his Epistle to the Galatians (*x*) these twelve. *First Charity,* which fills us with the Love of God, and our Neighbour.

(*x*) c. v. 22

Secondly,

Secondly, Joy, which enables us to serve God with Chearfulness. *Thirdly, Peace,* which keeps us unmoved in our Minds, amidst the Storms and Tempests of the World. *Fourthly, Patience,* which enables us to suffer all Adversities for the Love of God. *Fifthly, Longanimity,* which is an untired Confidence of Mind in expecting the good Things of the Life to come. *Sixthly, Goodness,* which makes us hurt no Man, but do good to all even to our Enemies, and there is no clearer Proof of the Holy Ghost abiding in our Souls, than this Spirit of *Goodness.* *Seventhly, Benignity,* which causes a certain Sweetness in our Conversation and Manners, so as to profit, and advance others in Virtue thereby. *Eighthly, Mildness,* which allays in us all the Motions in Passion and Anger. *Ninthly, Fidelity,* which makes us punctual Observers of our Covenants and Promises, and even strengthens our Faith, so as not to be shaken by Persecution, or staggered with Doubts. *Tenthly, Modesty,* which observes a fitting Mean in all our outward Actions, even as to our Words, Dress, and Conversation. *Eleventhly, Continency,* which makes us not only temperate in Meat and Drink, but in all other sensible Delights. *Twelfthly, Chastity,* which keeps a pure Soul in a pure Body.

Now as these are the Divine Fruits and Virtues of the Holy Ghost; you have in them the Picture of a Christian Life. When I see in Christians, this Mildness of Spirit, this Sweetness of Nature, this Goodness of Manners, this Heavenly Life: These Fruits of the Holy Ghost, it is a true Mark that he abides in that Soul;

Soul; becaufe the Tree is known by it's Fruits, and there is nothing fo happy as fuch a Soul; where Peace, where Joy, where Charity, where Goodnefs, where the Holy Ghoft has made his abode, he banifhes from thence all Vice, and finful Pleafures, and continually moves the Soul to all Good, and fortifies her againft all Temptations, both interior and exterior: Nothing fo happy, as fuch a Soul, where the Holy Ghoft refides, and fupports Man's Infirmities by fo many Divine Virtues, and ftrengthens him with celeftial Comfort; fuch a Soul no doubt, becomes great and happy by the Prefence of the Holy Ghoft, and that in no fmall Degree, but in a Manner fuitable to the Spirit of God.

O! I wifh I could fee the Fruits of the Holy Ghoft among all Chriftians, always zealous, fervent, and active in all Good; doing good to all, mild to all, patient with all, keeping Peace and Concord with all, fervent in Piety, active in all good Works, difcreet in all their Words, and prudent in all their Ways; nothing can be more happy under Heaven, than fuch a Society of Chriftians. And what hinders us from being fo? Thefe Virtues do not feem to be fuch infuperable Mountains, but that all may practife them if they pleafe; Why cannot you love Peace, and confequently keep it with all Men? Is any thing more defirable to a Man than his own Peace? What great Mortification would it be to you, to have the Joy of a quiet and ferene Confcience, the eafe of Patience, the quiet of Contentednefs? What great harm would it be, what great Task, to be somewhat more discreet and cautious in your Words, to shew more Goodness of Nature, and Sweetness of the Holy Ghost? Are all these likely to gain us the ill Will of Men? No Christians, these Virtues of the Divine Spirit are conformable to our very Nature, and nothing but a perverse Temper will refuse to put them in Practice.

The works of the Flesh are opposite to these Fruits of the Holy Ghost: These are all unclean viz. Luxury, Enmities, Contentions, Envy, Drunkenness, Gluttony, Immodesty, and the like; now where this Spirit is, I may safely pronounce, the presence of the Holy Ghost is banished from that Soul; for St. Paul declared, that those Christians who do these Things, shall not inherit the Kingdom of God. *(y)* What can be more afflicting than to see among Christians, who profess to live by the Spirit of God, nothing but the Works of the Flesh, instead of the Fruits of the Holy Ghost?

(y) Ephe. c. v.

It is not surprizing that Christians, by their Sins and Vices should banish the Holy Ghost from their Souls, by whom they were sanctifyed? and if we banish this Holy Spirit thence, tell me what Spirit think you will succeed in his Abode? Since St. Paul assures us, *if any Man has not the Spirit of Christ, he is none of his*, *(z)* and if he be none of his, whose then must he be? O! Dear Christians, enter now into yourselves, forsake and abandon those Vices, and evil Ways, which make the Holy Ghost abandon you, which banish from your Souls this God of all Comfort, this Author of all Grace and

(z) Rom. c. viii. v. 9.

and Sanctity, this Cause of all Virtue and Happiness; and thus you will have the Comfort to hear at the last Day from the Mouth of your Blessed Redeemer, *Come you blessed of my Father, &c.*

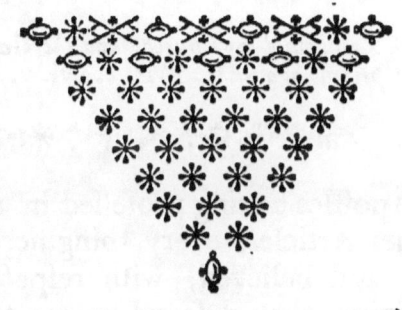

ARTICLE, IX.

DISCOURSE. I.

The Holy Catholick Church, the Communion of Saints.

Upon this Rock I will build my Church, and the Gates of Hell shall not prevail against it. Mat. c. xvi. v. 18.

THE Apostles having professed in the eight former Articles, every thing necessary to be known and believed, with respect to the Blessed Trinity, they descend now to the Article of *believing* the Holy Catholick Church. Which Article, is no less necessary than any of the former: For by believing the *Catholick Church*, we come to the Knowledge of the Truth of the foregoing Articles, and to understand rightly all the Articles of our Christian Belief. And therefore as St. Augustin has observed, (Pf. 30) the Prophets have spoken in more plain and clear Terms of the Church of Christ,

than

than they have done of Chrift Himfelf, and the Reafon is, becaufe the Authority of the Church, is the Guide by which we are to be directed in all Things, which we believe of Chrift; and all true Believers are kept in the Unity of the true Faith, which was founded by Chrift; which true Faith continues always inviolable by a continual Obedience to the Church of Chrift. This then being the End and Intention of this Article; let us now come to the Declaration of it.

We profefs in this Article of our Creed, to *believe one Holy Catholick Church, and Communion of Saints*, which feemingly contains two Points, which I fhall treat of feparately.

There is nothing of greater Importance, than the Belief of this Article, if Chriftians would but fincerely underftand what is meant by *believing the Catholick Church;* this Belief would fave many Nations from the horrid Ship wreck of Herefy; it would appeafe the whole War of Religion, and give Peace to Chriftianity; it would confute old Herefies, and prevent new ones, if they would but believe the Creed; that there is but one true Church founded by Jefus Chrift, and planted by the Apoftles, and which all are bound to be *Members* of, and which all are bound to *hear*, as well as *believe*, and that this Church is in all Ages *holy*, as the Creed which confeffes it to be holy, is in all Ages true. This proves that the Church never ceafed to be *the Communion of Saints;* and never was corrupt in her Faith.

What I defign in this Difcourfe, is *Firft*, The Divifion, to explain to you what is meant by the *Term Church;*

Church; and *Secondly*, to shew you that the true Church of Christ, is the *one Holy Catholick Church*.

P. I. Now as for the *Term Church* according to it's Etymology in the *Greek*, 'tis a Congregation, or Assembly of People called together, and is sometimes taken for the Place where they meet; but in the Scripture Language it constantly relates to the Worshipers of God, sometimes in a more narrow and contracted, sometimes in a larger and more extensive Sense; viz. The Congregation of *Christians* in any particular City, is called the Church of that City; thus the Church of *Jerusalem*, *Smyrna*, *Athens*, *Ephesus*, *Corinth*, *Rome*, &c. Nay even Assemblies in private Houses, are sometimes thus dignified; as *the Churches in the Houses of* Aquila and Priscilla, (*a*) *the Church in the House of* Nymphas, (*b*) *In the House of* Philemon. (*c*)

(*a*) Rom. c. xvi. v. 3. 5.
(*b*) Col. c. iv. v. 15.
(*c*) Phile. c. i. v. 2.

These different Appellations, are not designed to signify different Societies either as to *Faith* or *Government*, but only the different Districts, where the Faithful assembled, under the same universal Church, and were so distinguished, in the Apostolical Letters, accordingly as there was Occasion of being instructed in their respective Duties; a different Address being requisite, to make a proper Application of what they were to be informed of: So that all these different Churches, were in effect one and the same; the Church of *Corinth*, was the Church of *Christ*; so were those at *Antioch*, *Thessalonica*, and wherever the Christian Doctrine had taken Root. For whatever Hereticks started up, they were said to make a *Division*

Division, not in the Church of *Alexandria*, *Rome*, &c. But in the Church in general : For they were so much they same, as St. Paul tells us, that *if one Member suffered, all the Members suffered with it; or if one Member was honoured, all the Members rejoyced with it.* (*d*) This is the Church which falls under our present Consideration, and not any particular Branch or Member, but the universal Church in what parts of the World soever dispersed, who hold the same Faith of *Christ*, in the Unity of the same Spirit. So that the Church which Christ established on Earth, was a Congregation of People baptized, and united together, by believing and professing the same Faith, which he had taught; and governed by lawful Pastors and Bishops, subordinate to the Vicar of Christ upon Earth, as he had appointed. It being suitable to the Divine Wisdom, that in establishing such a Community, a Regulation should be observed, to prevent the Inconveniences of Errors in Belief, and Disobedience in practical Duties.

(*d*) 1 Cor. c. xii. v. 26.

But some may object and say, how can the Church of Christ be known by *Faith*? Since Objects of Faith are obscure and lie not within the Cognizance of our Senses. To this I answer, that the Church, as it is a visible Being, is not an Object of *Faith*, but only known by the Senses and Reason, and by the undeniable Marks it carries both in the Scripture and the Creeds, of it's being *One, Holy, Catholick,* and *Apostolical,* which are answerable to all the Requisites, that Prudence can suggest, to submit to it's Authority. Now what we mean by the Object

Object of Faith in the Church, is the Divine Authority conferred upon it, in being directed by the Holy Ghost, having a Power of binding and loosing, and producing Grace, by means of the Sacraments. These are invisible, and the Object of Faith only; and of this we have a parallel case in our Blessed Saviour, whilst he was upon Earth, his *Humanity* was the Object of Sense and Reason, but his *Divinity* was the Object of Faith.

From hence we may see, that three Things are requisite to become a Member of the true Church of Christ, viz. *First*, that the Person be baptized either *actually*, or in *desire*: *Secondly*, that he believes the Doctrines which *Christ* delivered; and *Thirdly*, that he be obedient to the *Authority*, which Christ placed him under. But alas! there are many, who pretend to be Members of Christ's Church, who are divided in their Faith, teaching Doctrines directly contrary to one another, and by separating themselves into different Congregations, and not paying Subjection to the same Authority, but either to none, or to that of their own choosing; all this does not seem consistent with the Wisdom of so wise a Legislator; for if every civil Community is provided with Rules against Divisions, certainly the God of *Peace* and *Unity*, would not establish a Church to be exposed to all the Inconveniences of Errors and Disobedience; and therefore whoever do not believe all that *Christ* taught; and will not obey the *Authority* which he appointed, they are not true Members of his Church; and of Course they are not in the Way to Heaven, for our

Saviour

Art. IX. *Disc.* I.

Saviour has declared, that *he who believes not shall be condemned.* (*e*) And again, that *he who will not hear the Church, let him be unto thee as a Heathen and a Publican.* (*f*) Perhaps some will say, that this Doctrine is very severe, and uncharitable, as it seems to insinuate that none can be saved out-of the Catholick Church, notwithstanding nothing can be abated of it, since it is the Doctrine of the Gospel of *Jesus Christ,* and it is what the Catholick Church has constantly taught, that no one can be saved unless he be a Member in the Catholick Communion, either *actually* or *virtually,* that is, either in *fact* or in *desire,* for there is no sure way to Heaven out of the Catholick Church. This *general* Rule of the Catholick Faith, that none are saved out of the Communion of the orthodox and universal Church, (except where is *invincible ignorance*) follows by a plain and necessary Consequence from the Scripture, as well as from the Apostolical and Nicene Creed. For that there is but *one* true Church and Religion, is very plain and evident from the Scripture: St. Paul in his Epistle to the Ephesians says, there is but *one God, one Faith, and one Baptism.* (*g*) And for this Reason has Almighty God, sent *some Apostles, some Evangelists, and some Pastors and Doctors,* that the mystical Body of Christ, that is, the Church may be built and perfected, so as to be *one Body,* that we may all meet and agree in the same Doctrine and Sentiments, in *one* and the same *Faith,* and may not be like little Children, wavering and changeable as the Winds, tossed to and fro, with various and different Notions and Opinions, and not know-

(*e*) Mar. c. xvi. v. 16.
(*f*) Mat. c. xviii. v. 17.

(*g*) c. iv. v. 5.

H h ing

ing where to fix and settle; on which Account, be sure says the same Apostle, that you be careful and solicitous, how to preserve *Unity*, Peace, and Concord. *(h)* In like manner, in his first Epistle to the Corinthians, *I beseech you Brethren*, says he, *in the Name of our Lord Jesus Christ, that you all speak the same thing, and that there be no Divisions among you.* *(i)* And in the 14th Chapter of the same Epistle, he says, that *God is a God of Peace*, of Unity, *and not of Dissension*, and Discord. *(k)* And in reality, if different Principles, if contrary Religions, if any but *one Faith*, was to be allowed of, the Church of God, the Kingdom of Christ, would be soon overthrown, dissolved, and reduced to nothing. According to what our Saviour himself says, that every Kingdom that is divided against itself must fall to Desolation and Ruin. *(l)* But it is to be observed, that it is not only the Faith and Doctrine of the Church, that is to be ever *one* and the same, but the Church herself is likewise to be *one* Body, *one* Society of Men, *one* Communion, *one* House, *one* Fold, *one* Flock, under *one* Pastor; and as in a natural Body the Members must be united together to make up one Body, so must the Faithful be all united together in one Communion to make up Christ's *one* Mystical Body, of which he himself is the invisible Head, and they the Members.

Again, if Christ has only *one Holy, Catholick, and Apostolick Church,* which *is the Communion of Saints;* if he has only *one* Church which *is built upon a Rock, and against which the Gates of Hell shall not prevail;* *(m)* If he has only *one* Church, which

(h) ibid. v. 11. 12. 13.

(i) c. i. v. 10

(k) v. 33.

(l) Mat. c. xii. v. 25.

(m) Mat. c. xvi. v. 18.

Art. IX. Disc. I.

which is the *Pillar and Support of Truth*. (*n*) And with which he promised to continue *always to the End of the World*. (*o*) And which is therefore the Church of all Ages, as well as the Church of all Nations; if he has only *one* Church to which *the Lord added*, and adds daily, *such as shall be saved*: (*p*) Then it is at least a *general* Rule of divine Faith, that none are saved out of the Communion, of this Church; nay setting aside *invincible Ignorance*, the Rule is *universal*, and without Exception.

This Doctrine of the Catholick Church is so unquestionable, that the greater part of Christians, and reformed Churches, of what denomination so ever have taught the same. Calvin says, that *out of the* " *Bosom* of the visible Church
" no Remission of Sins, no Salvation is *to be*
" *hoped for*. (*q*) Beza, the great Disciple of Cal-
" vin says, *there is only one true Church: And*
" *there always was and always will be a Church, out*
" *of which there is no Salvation*. (*r*) Trelactus
" says, it's a thing absolutely Necessary, if we
" will be saved, to embrace the Communion of
" the Catholick Church, out of which there
" is no Salvation. (*f*) The learned Bishop Per-
" son, Bishop of Chester, in his Exposition of
" the Apostles Creed, says that the Necessity
" of believing the holy Catholick Church ap-
" pears first in this, that *Chrift* has appointed
" it as the only way to eternal Life. We read
" at first, says he, that *the Lord added to the*
" *Church daily such as should be saved*; (*t*) and
" what was then daily done, has been done since
" continually: *Chrift*, never appointed two
" ways to Heaven, nor did he build a Church
             " to

(*u*)1 Tim. c. iii. v. 15.
(*o*)Mat.c. xxviii. v. 20.
(*p*) Acts. c. ii. v. 47.
(*q*) L. iv. Inst.Cap. 1. §. 4.
(*r*) In Confess. Fidei. c. v. §. 2.
(*f*) L. ii: Instit. de Eccles. part. ii. §. 10.
(*t*) Acts. c. ii. v. 47.

"to save some, and make another Institution for other Men's Salvation. *There is no other Name under Heaven given among Men whereby we must be saved, but the Name of Jesus.* (u) And that Name, is no otherwise given under Heaven then in the Church. As none were saved from the Deluge, but such as were in the Ark of Noah, framed for their Reception by the command of God; as none of the first born of *Egypt* lived, for such as were within those Habitations, whose Doorposts were sprinkled with Blood, by the Appointment of God for their Preservation; as none of the Inhabitants of Jericho could escape the Fire and Sword, but such as were in the House of Rahab, so none shall ever escape the eternal Wrath of God, which belong not to the Church of God." (w)

The Protestants of *Switzerland* say, in their Profession of Faith : " We have so great a value for being in Communion with the Church of *Christ,* that we say, those cannot have Life in the sight of God, who are not in Communion with the true Church of God, but separate themselves from it." (y)

The Protestants of *Scotland,* in the Year 1568 in their Profession of Faith say : " We believe in one God, the Father, the Son, and the Holy Spirit; so we firmly believe that there was from the beginning, that there now is, and that to the end of the World there will always be, one Church, which is the Catholick, that is, the Universal Church, out of which Church there is neither Life, nor everlasting Happiness."

(u) Acts. c. iv. v. 12.

(w) P. cccxlix.

(y) Confess. Helvetia. c. 17. An. 1556. et in Synt. Confess. F. di. Genevæ An. 1654. P. 34

The *French Huguenots*, in their Catechism on the tenth Article of the Creed say, " Why is this Article of forgiveness of Sins put after that of the Church? Answer. Because no one obtains Pardon for his Sins, unless he be first incorporated with the People of God, and continue in Unity and Communion with the Body of Christ: For none of those who withdraw themselves from the Communion of the Faithful, to make a Sect a part, ought to hope for Salvation, as long as they continue separated from them."

The Church of England, in the 18 of the 39 Articles says, *they are to be had accursed who presume to say, that every Man shall be saved by the Law or sect which he professeth, tho' he be diligent to frame his Life according to that Law, and the Light of Nature.* Art. 18. Thus you see, that it is not only the Catholick Doctrine, that *none are saved out of the Catholick Communion,* but it is also the Doctrine of all reformed Churches.

As to what is objected, that *this Doctrine is uncharitable,* I answer it is not, nay I affirm it to be the reverse: For is it not Charity to publish, what the Word of God, the Creed, and Tradition of all Ages, obliges us to think, concerning Salvation out of one Catholick and undivided Communion? Is it not Charity to put them in mind, that no Religion is safe to any one, because he and his Fiiends were bred up in it, because it suits best his Interest, and is the prevailing Religion of the place? Was it not Charity in St. Luke to tell us that *the Lord added daily to the Church,* In one undivided Communion, *such as should be saved?* (z) In like Manner (z) Acts. c.ii.v. 47

Manner, is it not Charity in us to declare openly, that People cannot be saved without Baptism, nor without keeping the Commandments of God, for in all this, we declare nothing from ourselves, but from the word of God. True Charity always was, and always will be, unknown practically to those who want it. Wicked Men think it highly uncharitable to have their Pleasures disturbed, by the unwelcome news of Death and Hell. Can any thing appear more uncharitable to Infidels or Unbelievers, than these words of Christ himself, *he who believes not shall be condemned.* (*a*) And will not Hereticks always think those words of our Saviour Christ Uncharitable, *he that will not hear the Church, let him be unto thee as a Heathen or Publican.* (*b*) But must not saving Truth be told, because we are pretty sure before hand, that it will not be believed? Must Charity neglect it's Duty, because Heresy is deaf, true Charity flatters not, nor does it invent new ways to Heaven, but does all it can to help all thither according to the old way, the only Way? On which account it admonishes, proves, and endeavours to convince all People of the Mistakes, and Errors in which they are engaged. And it is plain to the World, that this is what the Ministers, and Preachers of the Catholick Church have continually done, even to the Loss of Thousands and Thousands of their Lives: So that this very charge of Uncharitableness against us, is not only groundless and weak, but is in itself Uncharitable in the highest Degree.

As to what some do alledge, that the Scripture assures us, *that a Remnant of all Religions shall be saved*

(*a*) Mark c. xvi. v. 16

(*b*) Mat. c. xviii. v. 17.

Art. IX. *Difc.* I. 239

faved; to this I anfwer, that the Scriptures no where fay fo. But Men who are refolved to live and die in Error, will never want a Text for it. The Prophet *Ifaiah* 'tis true fays, that a Remnant only of the *Jews* was to return from *Babylon.* (c) And St. Paul quoting thefe Words of *Ifaiah*, tells us, *tho' the Number of the Children be as the fands of the Sea, a Remnant,* (that is a fmall part of them) *fhall be faved.* (d) Which Remnant the Apoftle himfelf explains of fuch of the *Jewifh* Nation, as at that time by entering into the Church were faved, by God's Grace. (e) But what relation has this, to the faving of a Remnant, of all Religions, of Chriftians, Jews, Turks, and Pagans. *(c)* Ifa. c. x. v.20. 21. 22.

(d) Rom. c.ix.v.27.

(e) Rom. c. xi. v. 5

We muft here take notice, that the Catholick Church which was eftablifhed by Chrift, will continue to the End of the World; notwithftanding the little regard that is paid now a Days to Religion; the prodigious Increafe of Atheifts and Infidels; the Multitude of lukewarm, and tepid Chriftians; tho' all thefe bid fair for the fulfilling of our Saviour's Prediction, that, *when he comes, he fhall hardly find Faith upon the Earth.*(f) Yet we muft reft in full Affurance, that no Storms or Perfecutions whatfoever, fhall prevail fo far as totally to overthrow, or deftroy it; for we have the Affurance and Promife of our Saviour Chrift, that he will be with his Church to the End of the World; *behold I am with you to the End of the World,* fays our Bleffed Redeemer. (g) And the Prophet Daniel tells us, that the Kingdom of *Chrift fhall never be deftroyed, but that it fhall ftand for ever.*(h) Again, as we believe in the Creed; fo every Article thereof muft

(f) Luck. c. xviii. v. 8.

(g) Mat. c. xxviii. v. 20.
(h) Dan. c.ii.v.44.

must always be true, therefore there must always be a Holy Catholick Church, the Perpetuity of which will remain to the End of the World.

But what is still farther to be observed is, that the Church of Christ is always *visible* and known, for our Blessed Saviour compares it, to a *City placed upon a Hill, which cannot be hid* (*i*) Now it is certain nothing can be more conspicuous or visible than a City placed upon a Mountain. The Prophet *Daniel* calls it *a great Mountain which fills the whole Earth.* (*k*) and the Prophet *Isaiah* calls it a Mountain upon the *Top of Mountains*, and says, *that* all Nations shall flow unto it. (*l*) The learned Doctor *White*, calls the Church of Christ *a visible* Church. (*m*) Besides, how can the universal Church of Christ be invisible or unknown, since she always professes her Faith; and Terms of her Communion and has Ministers preaching, baptizing, and administering the Sacraments: These are all outward and sensible Actions, which are inconsistent with an invisible Society of Men. Therefore the Church of *Christ* must of Necessity be always *visible*, and not *invisible*, as some would have it, upon account of their being convinced, there were none of their Religion or way of thinking, to be seen or heard of in the World three hundred Years ago.

P. II. I now come to the outward or visible *Marks*, by which the Church of Christ may be known, the chief are expressed in the present Article of the Creed under our consideration, viz. the *Unity, Sanctity, Catholicism* or *Universality* of the Church. But perhaps some will say, if these are

(*i*) Mat. c. v. v. 14.

(*k*) Dan. c. ii. v. 35. 44.

(*l*) Isa. c. ii. v. 2.
(*m*) See his defence of the Way. c. xxxvii.

are the *Marks* of the true Church of Chrift, how fhall we account for the Behaviour of thofe, who ftand off, and are not convinced by fuch plain Proofs, and cannot fee the City, that is placed upon a high Hill, nor find out the Way *wherein Fools cannot Err*, for fuch the Church of God is defcribed to be in the holy Scriptures, (*n*) and it is inconceivable, that fuch Multitudes of Men of the greateft of Penetration, Learning and Zeal, fhould not difcover, and own the Church recommended by fuch advantageous Circumftances. To this I anfwer, that it is a melancholy Reflection to confider the Blindnefs and Stupidity of Judgment, which is occafioned in Mankind, through Pride, Intereft and the Love of Pleafures. We can but admire the Stupidity of *Praroah* and the learned *Egyptians*, who could not, or would not difcover the Finger of God in fo many Miracles, that were wrought among them by Mofes and Aaron? What a thick Veil of Darknefs was thrown over the Jews, when they would not acknowledge the Meffiah; and the undeniable Proof of his Miracles made no impreffion upon them? Could there be a greater Stupidity, than that of the whole World, when they adored Stocks and Stones and acknowledged the vileft Creatures to be their Gods? And what wonder is it, if Hereticks fhould lie under the fame Infatuation, and not fee the Church, tho' reprefented to them with fo many outward Marks?

We now proceed to confider the Marks, that are attributed to the true Church of Chrift, viz. It's *Unity, Holinefs*, and *Catholicifm* or *Univerfality;* As to it's Unity I have already fpoken

(*n*) Ifa. c. xxxv.

en of it; it remains then that we should see, what right the Church of Christ has to the Epithet of *Holy*.

In the *first* place it is certain, that the Church of Christ has a right to the Epithet of *Holy* from its Founder, who was most truly and eminently so. *Secondly,* it has an undisputed right to the Denomination of *Holy* from the Institution, which how much soever it be abused, can never cease to be both holy and perfect: God *called us*, says St. Paul, *with a Holy calling*. (*o*) And it was the Intention of our Institution that *every one*, should *depart from Iniquity who nameth the name of our Lord*. (*p*) It calls upon us and exhorts us to be *Holy;* it points out the Way to *Holiness*, and if we are not Holy, it is our own fault, by a violation of it's Ordinances; we may abuse this Institution, but we cannot destroy the Institution itself: *Christians* may be uncharitable; but the Church of Christ is nevertheless a charitable Church: The Doctrine it delivers, tends to Holiness. The Lessons are such as are agreeable to Reason, and serviceable towards making Men good, both good Neighbours, good Subjects, and good Christians. *Thirdly,* it has appointed and provided us with Instruments, and means of becoming Holy, viz. The use of the Sacraments, which are the Channels of Grace. *Fourthly,* It abounds with the Fruits of *Holiness*, even visible to the Eye, in Numbers of her Members: But we are not obliged from the Words of this Article, to believe that all or every one, who constitutes the visible Church of Christ is realy Holy: The Church may be properly called

(*o*) Tim. c. i. v. 9.
(*p*) ibid. c. ii. v. 19.

called Holy, notwithstanding the Wickedness and Corruption of some of it's Members.

Let us now examine and see how the Church of Christ is *Catholick*, which Word signifies *Universal*. The Church of Christ is called the Catholick or Universal Church, upon account of the ancient Prophets foretelling it's Universality; as also because in the Apostles Days the Christian Belief was preached over several Parts of the World; and in all the first Ages, the true Church was always known by the Name *Catholick*, to distinguish it from all false Churches, as it appears by the Writings of the ancient Fathers; hence the *Donatists* and some other ancient Hereticks coveted to be esteemed and called *Catholicks*, but St. Augustin and the orthodox Party, shewed the absurdity of their Claim: *First*, because the Donatists, made a particular Society, were confined only to *Africa*, and by consequence could not be the Catholick or Universal Church. *Secondly*, because their distinguishing Name, was taken from those Persons who were Authors of the Defection, as *Montanists, Manichees, Palagians, Arians, Novatians*, &c. *Thirdly*, because those who were indifferent Persons, called none Catholicks, but such as were in Communion with the Universal Church. *Fourthly*, those very Hereticks themselves were so convinced, that they had no right to that Appellation, that they seldom called themselves by that Name, and if they were asked, to shew a Person the Church or Chapel where Catholicks assembled, they durst not point at their Schismatical Meetings, but sent them to those who communicated with the

Churches abroad. These are St. Augustin's Reasons. (*q*) And may be applied to all the modern reformed Societies, as *Lutherans, Calvinists, Hugonots, Anabaptists, Methodists,* &c. But it must be observed, that the Word *Universal* is here to be taken comparitively to all other Societies or Sects, and chiefly as to *Time, Place,* and *Doctrine,* in these three respects, the Church is Universal, and no other. Heathens are not under our Consideration, but only those Bodies who believe in the true God, and were separated from the Church Universal. *First,* it is Universal as to *Time,* because the true Church of Christ must be as ancient as the Apostles, that is to say, prior in time to any Body or Society of Men divided from it. *Secondly,* it is Universal as to *Place,* having flourished in many parts of the Earth in every Age, since it was established. *Thirdly,* it is Universal in *Doctrine,* always teaching the same Faith in all parts of the World, and the same Creed being always it's Rule; and all it's Members yielding Obedience to the same Authority.

(*q*)See.St. Aug.cont. Ep.Fund. c. xli.et l. vera Relig. c. vii.

I shall now close the first part of this Article as usual, with a short Review of what Considerations I have offered upon it; from whence it appears, that he who truly assents to this Article, must believe that Christ has a Church upon Earth, and that we are bound to believe and obey her; and that there is only *one* true Church or Congregation of faithful People; and that this Church is *One, Holy, Catholick,* or *Universal;* and we believe that this holy Catholick Church is, and always was a *visible* Church, and that it will continue to the End of the World;

World; we also believe that out of this one, holy Catholick Church, or Communion, there is no hope of Salvation: Thus far we believe of this Article, which I shall conclude with these Words of St. Augustin; that "there is
" not any thing which a Christian ought to fear
" so much, as to be separated from the Body
" of Christ, which is the one Catholick Church;
" for if he be separated from the Body of Christ, (r) Aug.
" he is not a Member of Christ, and if he be tract. 27.
" not a Member of Christ, he is not nourish-
" ed with his Spirit. (r)

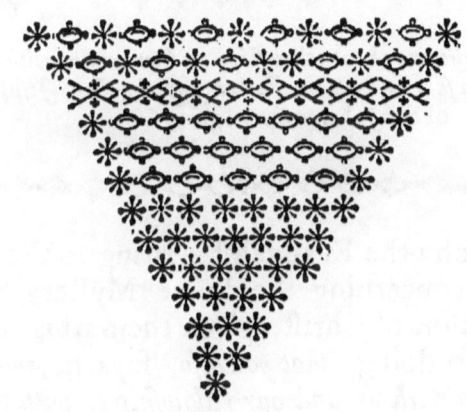

ARTICLE.

ARTICLE, IX.

DISCOURSE, II.

The Holy Catholick Church, the Communion of Saints.

That you also may have fellowship, or Communion with us, and our fellowship is with the Father and the Son Jesus Christ.
1 Epist. of St. John. c. i. v. 3.

ST. John the Evangelist writing to the Faithful concerning the divine Mystery of the Incarnation of Christ, gives them this Reason for his so doing, *that you also,* says he, *may have fellowship with us, and our fellowship is with the Father and the Son.* Now this Fellowship is placed in *the Communion of Saints;* which I shall explain to you in the *First* part of this Discourse; and *Secondly,* I shall shew you that the Authority of the Catholick Church is of divine Institution, and by Consequence, that she is *Infallible* in her Doctrine.

1 Epist. John c. i. v. 3.

In

In this Article of our Creed, the Catholick P. I.
Church is called *the Communion of Saints*, or an
Affociation of thofe, *who are called to be Saints*,
that is, whom the divine Providence, *has thought
fit to make partakers of the Inheritance of the Saints
in Light*, as St. Paul expreffes it. *(f)* For tho' in *(f)*Col.c.
this *Communion* there are feveral bad and wicked i. v. 12.
Men, yet their Vocation is that of Sanctity,
and as St. Ambrofe obferves, *the Root* fays he,
is holy tho' the Branches are fruitlefs. *(t)* All Chrif- (t)Ambro.
tians allow that the Apoftles were a company l.8.inLuc.
of *Saints*, tho' there was a Devil among them,
viz, *Judas*. The Faith which they preached
to the World, is called the *Faith delivered to the
Saints* ; and the Chriftian Churches were called
the Churches of the *Saints*, even at a time when
there were many Impieties practifed among
fome of them: But we muft here obferve, that
as the Church of Chrift is not barely nominally
Holy, but really and truly *Holy*; fo likewife are
it's Saints, not in Name only, but really Saints.
For by the Tenour of the Gofpel it appears,
that they only are to be ranked in that Clafs, who
are *Sanctified by Chrift Jefus* ; and who therefore are holy both with refpect to their *Faith*,
and with refpect to their *Lives and Converfation*,
by endeavouring to imitate him, who called
them to be *Saints*, that as he is *Holy*, fo may they
alfo be *Holy* in all manner of Converfation ;
abounding in every good Gift. Thefe are the
Saints of the Church of Chrift, and thefe are the
Saints on whom we are required by this Article
before us to turn our Attention. The former
part of this Article, obliges us to affent to the
Exiftence of fuch *Saints*; but this requires us to
believe

believe that thefe *Saints* have Communion or Fellowfhip not only with God and his Angels, (as fome would have it) but even with the Saints in Heaven, and with each other whether living or Dead.

To enter now upon the Subject relating to thefe Terms, *of the Communion of Saints*, the meaning is this, that there is a ftrict Union and Communion among the Saints with each others Prayers and good Works; who are all united in one and the fame Faith, one and the fame Spiritual Intereft; in one and the fame Hope; all receiving the fame holy Sacraments and Rites; and worfhip God *with one Mouth, and one Heart*; and the Reafon is this, becaufe the Church of Chrift is as it were one Body, and all the Members of it live by the fame Spirit of the *Holy Ghoft*, who keeps them together in that holy Union and Communion. And as all the Members of the Body concur and help to the Good of each other, fo every Member of Chrift's Church helps to the good of the reft and receives good by the reft, partaking reciprocally of each others Prayers and good Works. *I am partaker with all them that fear thee and keep thy Commandments*, fays the Royal Prophet. (*u*) And in the Lords Prayer our Saviour has taught us to pray, that every one fhould afk in the Name of all, faying, *give us our daily Bread, and forgive us our trefpaffes*.

(*u*) Pf. cxviii. v. 63.

But it muft be obferved that all thofe who are not in the ftate of Grace, that is to fay, who are guilty of any grievous or Mortal Sin (unrepented of) lofe in a great meafure the Benefit, which they would otherwife receive by the good
Works

Art. IX. *Disc.* II.

Works of others, as long as they remain in that state; for tho' they are Members of the Catholick Church, yet as they want the Life of Grace, so they receive no farther assistance from them, than in order to get out of that bad state. The Benefit which is reaped by the good Works of others, is participated or shared by every one in measure and proportion to the Disposition which he has for it, and according to the Intention of him who performs the Work; for as we are more or less in his Intention, so do we partake more, or less Benefit by the Works which he does; from hence we may see, what a Happiness it is to be in the Communion of the Church of Christ, and in the state of Grace, so that we may cry out with the Royal Prophet, *Blessed are they who dwell in thy house O Lord.* (*w*)

This Communion or Participation among the *Saints* with each others Prayers and good Works, is not only with regard to the Living, but also with respect to those, who are departed this Life in Righteousness; and the Reason is, because they are always a Part of Christ's Flock, and Members of his Mystical Body the Church. For as Christ died for all Men, and all are redeemed with the Price of his precious Blood, so all compose the Body of his Church, who are united to him by *Faith* in this World, or by *Charity* in the next. St. Augustin says " that the Church in *general*
" does not only include all the Faithful, who as
" yet are detained in this World; but also the
" Saints in Heaven, who help us by their
" Prayers; and as we are designed to be partakers of the same Glory, so at present we are
" united

(*w*) Ps. lxxxiii. v. 5.

"united by the same Tye of *Charity*, which ter-
"minates in the Worship, and Love of one
"God." (St. Aug. in Enchir. c. lvi.) Again he
says, "that the Souls of the Faithful departed
"are not excluded from the Communion of
"Saints, as they are a Part of the Kingdom of
"Christ ; otherwise it would be in vain, says
"he, to be mindful of them at the Altar." (St.
Aug. l. 20. de Civi. Dei. c. ix.)

The Catholick or Universal Church is divided into three Classes, (but they are all one and the same Church) viz. the *Triumphant*, the *Suffering*, and the *Militant*. The *Triumphant*, are those Blessed Saints who are eternally happy in Heaven ; The *Suffering*, are those Souls who are now Suffering under the *Rod of Justice*, for the expiation of those Sins or Faults, which they had not fully satisfied for in this Life, and thus wait for their Delivery. The *Militant*, are the Faithful here upon Earth, who are engaged in the heat of Battle, and surrounded on all sides with implacable Enemies : So that they must either fight against these Enemies, viz. the *Devil*, the *World*, and the *Flesh*, or be overcome. Now between these different Classes or Tribes, (if I may call them so) there is a certain Communion or Intercourse of Charity conformable to their Station. The Blessed in Heaven pray for the Faithful on Earth, and the Faithful on Earth give Praise and Thanks to God for their Glory, and they honour them, and beg their Prayers or Intercession ; The Faithful on Earth pray for one another ; they are united under the same *invisible* Head *Jesus Christ*, and under the same *visible* Head to avoid Schism, in the

same

Art. IX. *Difc.* II.

same Faith to avoid Herefy; and in the same Sacraments and Sacrifice, and Bonds of Love, whereby they partake of each others Merits and Prayers of the Univerfal Church. The Faithful on Earth also offer up their Prayers and Supplications to Almighty God, in behalf of their deceafed Brethren, who are in the *Suffering* ftate, commonly called *Purgatory*, under the juft Hand of God, to be purified from their Sins, before they can enter Heaven: For Death, which is only a Separation of the Body and Soul, cannot diffolve that Myftical Union between the Members of the Church, and Chrift their Head, fo that being ftill Members of the fame Church with us, they may be affifted by the Suffrages, Almfdeeds, and good Works of the Faithful on Earth; and this Charity for the departed Souls, was very much practifed in the primitive Church, and commended by the ancient Fathers, (*x*) and particularly by St. Auguftin (l. de cura pro Mort.) who fays, it is not to be doubted, but that the Souls of the Faithful departed are helped by the Prayers and good Works of the living, offered up for that End. (*y*) Hence we may conclude, that *it is a holy and wholfome Cogitation to pray for the Dead, that they may be releafed from their Sins.* (*z*) Befides it is clearly proved from the Doctrine and Practice of the Jewifh Synagogue, that they looked upon it as a pious and wholfome Charity and Devotion to pray for the Faithful departed. Whence the learned Proteftant " Doc- " tor Jeremy Taylor writes thus, we find fays " he, that the Jews did pray and make Offer- " ings for the Dead. Now it is very confiderable

(*x*) See Tertul. L. de Cor. c. iii. et L. de monog. c. 10. St. Cypri. Ep. 1. Ed Oxon. fee St. Chryf. de Sacerd. L. 6. p. 424. Ed. Montfau- con.

(*y*) St. Aug. Serm. 32. de verbis Apoft.

(*z*) 2. Mach. c. xii. v. 46.

K k 2 " that

"that since our Blessed Saviour did reprove all
the evil Doctrines and Traditions of the
Scribes and Pharisees, and did argue concerning the Dead and the Resurrection, yet
he spoke not a word against this publick practice, but left it as he found it; which he who
came to declare to us all, the will of his Father would not have done, if it had not
been innocent, pious, and full of Charity.
The practice of it, says he, was from the beginning and was universal. (*a*)

(*a*) Dr. Jer. Taylor. L. of proph. c. i. Sect. 20. n. 11. p. 345.

This is the blessed Effect of *the Communion of Saints*, that as we are all Partakers of the same Hope, we may love, help, and assist one another; and not be unmindful of those who are gone before us; That such as are obnoxious to the divine Justice, may find Relief by our Prayers: And such as have received the Reward of Eternal Glory, may help us by their Prayers or Intercession, not that we ever pray to them as we do to God, (as some pretend we do) but we only beg, that they would pray or intercede to the Throne of divine Mercy for us, since what might otherwise be justly refused us, in Punishment of our Sins, may be granted through *the Merits of Jesus Christ*, and the Intercession of his Saints; for *the Prayer of the Just Man availeth much*, as St. James testifies. (*b*) And the example of St. Paul sufficiently confirms it, for in his Epistle to the Phillippians, he says, that *in all his Prayers he makes Supplication* for *them with joy;* (*c*) and can we imagine, that the Prayers of those blessed Souls, who are perfected in Glory, are less efficacious; or that being inflamed with divine Love, they are less charitable, and solicitous for the Salvation of those, who are daily exposed to threatening

(*b*) Ia. c. v. v. 16.

(*c*) c. i. v. 4.

Dangers

Art. IX. *Disc.* II.

Dangers, and surrounded on all sides with implacable Enemies? Certainly those glorified Saints are still Members of Christ's Mystical Body, and as such cannot be unconcerned for the Welfare of those other Members, which tho' divided by the different Circumstances of Place, and state of Being, are yet united by *Faith* and *Charity* in *Jesus Christ;* so that as there is naturally a Communication between the Parts or Members of the same Body, by which the Body is supported and maintained; so between the Members of Christ's Mystical Body which is the Church, there is a Communion of Prayers and good Works, by the help whereof, each particular Member is aided, according to it's respective Wants; and the whole Body is cemented together by *Charity which is the Bond of Perfection.* (d) Much more might be said on this Subject, but as it is not my design in this work, to enter into any Point of Controversy any farther, than what is absolutely necessary, so I shall decline it, and take leave of this Point of the Article, though very brief, yet sufficient to instruct the Christian in what he ought to know, concerning *the Communion of Saints.* Let us then proceed to the second and last Point, which relates to the *divine Authority* of the Catholick Church, which we prove from this Article of the Creed under our present Consideration.

(d) Col. c. iii.v. 14.

Every Article of our Creed is of *divine Authority*, and we are by this Article, bound to believe the Catholick Church; it therefore follows that the Catholick Church is of divine Authority, and that we are bound to believe and obey her, as she has her Authority from God; and therefore she must be *infallible* in her Doctrine.

P. II.

But

But before I enter upon any Argument to prove the Infallibility of the Catholick Church, it will be proper to let you see what is meant by it; when therefore we say that the Church is *infallible*, we understand that it is so assisted, so guided, and directed by the holy Ghost, that she shall never be deceived or deceive her Children in Matters of *Faith*. Thus all agree that the Church was infallible in the Apostles Time. That is, that the Apostles, tho' they were but Men, and of themselves subject to Error, and Deceit, yet they were so guided by the Spirit of Christ, that they could never be deceived in misapprehending his Doctrine, nor deceive their Followers in delivering it to them; and hence it was, that whatsoever the Apostles proposed as the Doctrine of Christ, the Christians received and submitted to it, how opposite soever it might appear to their Senses. Now whatsoever is confessed or acknowledged of the Church in the Apostles Days, is also to be extended to all succeeding Ages; I mean that the Church of Christ at all Times, and in all Ages, has this Assurance, this Protection, and Direction of the holy Ghost, which renders her *infallible* in her Decisions, and her Children most secure in their Belief, as I shall prove to you from the holy Scripture, and.

Firſt from the Words and Promiſes of our bleſſed Saviour, but you muſt obſerve, that theſe Promiſes are not limited to the Apoſtles only, but extended to the Church of Chriſt to the End of the World. Our Saviour tell us that *he will build his Church upon a Rock, viz. that the* (e) *Gates of Hell ſhall not prevail againſt it,* (e) that is, the

(e) Mat. c. xvi. v. 18.

the Powers of Darkness, and whatever Satan can do, either by himself, or his Agents. For as the Church is here likened to a House or Fortress, built on a Rock; so the adverse Powers are likened to a contrary House or Fortress, the Gates of which, that is, the whole Strength and all the Efforts it can make, can never be able to prevail over the City or Church of Christ. By this Promise we are fully assured, that neither Idolatry, Heresy, or any pernicious Error whatsoever, shall at any time prevail over the Church of Christ. And our blessed Redeemer, when he gave the Apostles a Commission *to go and teach all Nations*, and knowing at the same Time the difficult Task they would have upon their Hands in the Propagation, and planting of his Gospel among so many Enemies, he assured them for their Comfort, that he and his holy Spirit should remain with them, (not for three or four hundred years) but to the End of the World, *Behold*, says he, *I am with you all Days even to the consummation of the World.(f)* From hence it is plain, that these Promises cannot be limited to the Apostles only, because they were not to last to the End of the World. How then could the Catholick Church ever go astray; having always with her Pastors (as is here promised) Christ himself, who *is the way, the truth, and the Life.* (g) Again he promised them the holy Ghost, *the Spirit of truth, who should remain with them for ever*; And our Saviour says, that when *the Spirit of truth shall come he shall teach them all Truth (h)* so effectually, that his Church might always be what is stiled by St. Paul, *the Pillar and ground of Truth.* (i)

(f) Mat. c. xxviii. v. 20.

(g) John c. xiv. v. 6.

(h) John c. xvi. v. 13.

(i) 1 Tim. c. iii. v. 15.

Now

Now if the Church was *Fallible;* if at any Time she could fall into Error; if she could be deceived, and deceive her Children; if she was mistaken concerning revealed Truths; then the Promises of Christ would have failed; then the Gates of Hell would have prevailed against the Church; and then she would be no longer the Pillar and Ground of Truth; then our Saviour might be said to have forsaken the Church; then the holy Ghost would have failed to teach and direct the Church. But it is impossible that the Promises of Christ should fail; it is impossible the Holy Ghost should at any Time, neglect or be wanting in his Office of Teacher and Director, therefore at all Times and in all Ages, the Church of Christ is, and ever has, and ever will be *Infallible.* St. Paul confirms us in this Doctrine, in his Epistle to the Ephesians, (*k*) he foresaw that Heresies would happen, that Men of corrupt Minds should fall from the Faith, he therefore forewarns us of this Danger from wicked Men; he also acquaints us with what Christ has done to secure his Church from their Attempts, and to settle his Faithful in a right Belief; *he gave,* says St. Paul, *some Apostles, some Prophets, some Evangelists, some Pastors, and Teachers for the perfecting of the Saints, for the work of the Ministry, for the Edifying of Christ's Body till we all meet in the Union of Faith, that henceforth we be no more like Children tossed to and fro, and carried away by every wind of Doctrine, by the Craft, and Slight of Men to deceive us.* (*k*) Here you see, that Christ has left in his Church *a perpetual* Succession of orthodox Pastors, and Teachers, to preserve the Faithful in Unity

(*k*) c. iv. v. 11. 12. et 13.

Unity and Truth. If these Pastors and Doctors which Christ has appointed for our Guides, were not assisted by his infallible Spirit, then they could give no Settlement to the Faithful, nor Security to our Faith, we should still be subject to be tossed to and fro by every wind of new Doctrine, whilst even they that teach us may lead us into Errors, and occasion the Mischief, which St. Paul says, they were appointed to preserve us from. What Security then of our Faith from such Pastors, and Teachers, who may, and for any thing we know, have led us into Errors? Who instead of the Doctrine of Christ, may have taught us Doctrine quite opposite to Christ.

We find in the Gospel most terrible Threats pronounced against those, who will not hear the Church. But can we think that our Blessed Saviour, would oblige us under the severest Penalties, to hear Teachers who may deceive us? That he would command us to follow Guides, who may lead us into Precipices? How unreasonable is such a Command? How fatal is such an Obedience? To submit our Judgment to the Decisions of a Church, which we own to be *Infallible*, and which we believe is directed by the Holy Ghost, is thought by some to be blind Obedience; a slavish Subjection, an irrational captivating of our Understanding: But what is it then, to be obliged to hear, and obey a Church, which we ourselves esteem to be *fallible*, that is to say, may Err? This indeed is most dangerous, and most irrational. Since therefore our Blessed Redeemer commands us to hear and obey the Church, we may conclude it is *Infallible* ; that it can neither be deceived, nor deceive us in matters of Faith.

A second Proof of the *Infallibility* of the Church, I take from the constant Judgment and Practice of the Church itself, in the primitive and purest Times. As the Apostles esteemed themselves to be guided by the Holy Ghost, in the Decision they made at their Council in Jerusalem where they declared, that *it seems good to the Holy Ghost, and to us:* So also have their Successors, in their general Councils, assumed to themselves a like *Infallibility*. They believed themselves to be directed by the same Spirit of Truth; and therefore they proposed the Decrees they made in Matters of Faith, as so many Oracles of the Holy Ghost; and the Faithful received them, as so many Articles of their Belief; and whosoever denied what they defined, was looked upon as much an Heretick, as he that should have opposed any Decree of the Apostles; or as he that should have rejected any Article of their Creed, or Proposition of the holy Scripture.

Acts. c. xv. v. 28.

Thus the first general Council of Nice, which was held in the year 325, made a Creed, and obliged all Christians to receive and profess it, and condemned and anathematized as Hereticks, all those who dissented from it's Doctrine. And what more convincing Proof could they give, to shew that they believed themselves *Infallible*, than this proceeding? For had not the Fathers of *Nice* esteemed themselves to be so directed, and guided by the Spirit of Truth, that they could not be deceived in misapprehending the Doctrine of Christ, by what Warrant

rant could they presume to make a Creed? By what Authority could they require all Christians to embrace and profess the Doctrine of the Creed? With what Justice could they condemn as Hereticks, all those who diffented from it?

And as for as those, who receive this Creed of the Fathers of *Nice*, who believe and profess it as the Doctrine of Christ; with what Security can they do this, if they esteem themfelves *fallible*? We may give great Deference to the Opinions of an Affembly of wife Men; but to receive their Decifions, as fo many Articles of our Faith, to make their Determinations a Part of our Creed, unlefs we own them *Infallible*, is to impofe upon ourfelves, and run a great hazard of embracing the Errors of Men, inflead of the Doctrine of Chrift. You fee therefore from the Behaviour both of the Paftors, and People, the Church was efteemed *Infallible*, and the Decrees of our general Councils were received, as fo many Oracles of the Holy Ghoft.

A Third Argument for this *Infallibility* of the Church is, that without it we can have no true Faith; we can have no certainty of our Belief; all will be but Opinion: How firmly foever we may feem to affent to the Doctrine propofed, yet if we confider things well, we shall find ourfelves under fome Fear, fome Apprehenfion, that we may be in the wrong, and that what we believe, may be falfe.

For *firft*, if we hold that the Church is *Fallible*, then fhe may be deceived, and deceive us in the Conveyance of the holy Scriptures, she may receive and propose to us for the Word of God, some Apocryphal Writing, and instead of Divine Truths, impose upon us the Inventions of Men. Whence it follows, that our Assent to those things, cannot have the Firmness and certainty of Divine Faith, that is, it cannot make us *Infallibly* certain, or assured of the Truth of them; because we shall have this check on our Minds, the Church from whence we receive these Scriptures is *Fallible*: She may have been deceived in her Judgment of them, and therefore for any thing we know, all that we now assent to, may be false; and instead of the Doctrine of Christ, we may have entertained Errors opposite to Christ.

Secondly, tho we suppose as most certain, that we have the Word of God, yet unless the Church be assisted by some *Infallible* Directions of the Holy Ghost, how can we be assured, that we have the true Sense of it? How can we be assured that we do not interpret the Words of Christ contrary to his Sense and Meaning? The Scripture you will say, is plain in all Points necessary to Salvation, and every serious, and sincere Reader, may find out Truth sufficient for his Direction and Salvation. And yet you know, that St. Peter tells us, there are in the Writings of St. Paul, *Things hard to be understood, and which the unlearned, and unstable wrest, as they do also the other Scriptures to their own Destruction.* (*l*) And what St. Peter complained of in his Days, has been the Misfortune of all succeeding Ages. For as you know, the *Arians, Nestorians, Eutychians,* and other Hereticks by their Interpretations, made the Scripture the
Ground

(*l*) 2 Epi. Pet. c. iii. v. 16.

Ground of their Herefies; and from the Oracles of Truth drew Arguments for the greatest Errors: And we cannot queftion, but that among them, there were fome fincere and well minded Perfons, who read the Scripture with great Application, and yet inftead of finding all Points neceffary to Salvation, they eftablifhed Tenets inconfiftent with Salvation.

And if we lay by the *Infallibility* of the Church, we muft own they had as good Grounds, as we can pretend to. They had the Letter of the Law; they had the Gofpel, they had Underftanding; they had a difcerning Judgment; they had a right Intention; they ufed Induftry, and what have we more to rely on? Thus, Dear Chriftians, you fee that unlefs the Church be *Infallible*, unlefs the Holy Ghoft provides, that the Paftors and Doctors of the Church fhall not mifinterpret the Scripture, we can have no Certainty of our Belief, and confequently no *Divine* Faith. Without this, the *Arians*, *Neftorians*, and all other Hereticks had as good a Plea, as the Catholick Church.

Hence follows another difmal Confequence, that by denying the *Infallibility* of the Church, we not only deftroy our Faith, by taking away all Certainty from it, but alfo open a Gate to all Schifm, Sects, and Herefies: For if the Church be *fallible* in her Interpretation of the Scripture, any new Sect may eftablifh Doctrines contrary to her Tenets, and fhe has no means left either to vindicate herfelf, or cenfure them; for by owning herfelf *fallible*, by confeffing that fhe may be deceived in her Interpretation of Scripture, fhe is forced to acknowledge, that it

The CREED EXPLAINED.

is poffible fhe may be in the Wrong, and thofe fhe condemns may be in the Right. And with what Juftice then can we cenfure any Diffenters? What Affurance can we have, that the Doctrine we teach is the Faith of Chrift, rather than that of the Sect we condemn? We alledge Scripture, they alledge Scripture; we tell them their Interpretation is falfe, they return us back the fame Compliment; we pretend to have the Confent of the primitive Church, they make the fame Claim. And thus we may difpute and wrangle out our Lives; but what Means for poor Chriftians to come to the Knowledge of Truth? Among fo many, and fo oppofite Interpretations of Scripture, how fhall they be able to judge which is the Right? How fhall they diftinguifh the Doctrine of Chrift from the Errors of Men.

Can we think, that our Bleffed Redeemer would come from Heaven to teach us, and not leave us fome certain Means, whereby we might come to the Knowledge of his Doctrine? Can we think, that he would oblige Men under Pain of eternal Torments to embrace his Faith, and not afford them fome *Infallible* Rule, whereby they may diftinguifh it from the Illufions and Inventions of the Devil? O Dear Chriftians, let us correct fo wild, fo extravagant an Imagination! Let us call to Mind all that he has done to eftablifh his Church; let us remember the Promifes, by which he has engaged to protect his Church; let us remember he has promifed to be with his Church to the End of the World: He has promifed to fend the Holy Ghoft, the Spirit of Truth, which fhall teach her

all

all Truth, and remain with her for ever: He has promised that the Gates of Hell shall never prevail against his Church; if we believe these Promises have not failed, nor can fail, we must then necessarily conclude, that the Catholick Church is so protected by Christ, so directed by the Holy Ghost, that she cannot be deceived in Matters of Faith, that she cannot fall into Error; in a Word, that in this Sense, she is *Infallible*.

You who are so happy as to be Members of the Catholick Church, give Praise and Thanks to Almighty God for having made you Members of his holy Church; but then remember to live in such a manner, as becomes a Member of the Church of God: In the first place, believe with an entire Submission all Decisions and Articles of Faith; renounce and abhor all those Errors that oppose the Belief of the Catholick Church; be true to all her Precepts and Commands, taking them as from God, as if you heard him say, *he that heareth you, heareth me:* Live in perfect Unity and Concord with all your fellow Members, as our primitive Ancestors were *all of one Mind, and one Heart.* Be *you holy as God is holy:* Holiness becomes the House of God, and all that dwell in it: Let the Head Christ Jesus, the Apostles and Martyrs, Confessors and Virgins, who have been so eminent for Sanctity, animate you to every Virtue. O Christians! bring not upon yourselves that terrible Sentence, *He that pollutes the Temple of God,* through sinful living, *him shall God destroy.* As you profess to believe the *Holy Catholick Church,* let no Persecution,

nor

nor even Death itſelf, deter you from it; 'tis the Church which Chriſt eſtabliſhed; remain then firm and conſtant in it to your laſt Breath, that you may come to the Enjoyment of God, with your fellow Members in the Kingdom of Heaven.

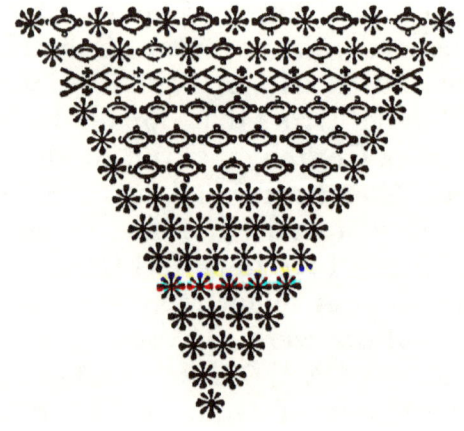

ARTICLE.

ARTICLE, X.

DISCOURSE, I.

The Forgiveness of Sins.

Whose Sins you shall forgive, they are forgiven them. St. John c. xx. v. 23.

BY this Article of our Creed we are *first* to believe, that God is both *able*, and *willing* to forgive us our Sins; *Secondly*, that he has given a Power to the Ministers of his Church to remit, or absolve Sinners (upon certain Conditions) *in his Name*, from their Sins: For tho' it is God alone, that can forgive Sins as the *principal* Agent, yet he may employ others as *Instruments* to confer Grace, and by Consequence to forgive Sins.

It may appear needless for me to explain to you, what is meant or understood by the Term *Sin*, since every Christian who has the least knowledge of his Religion, understands it to be, any voluntary *Thought*, *Word*, or *Deed*, against the Law

Law of God; or any lawful Superior; and therefore it includes all human Laws either Civil or Ecclesiastical, which are God's Laws radically, for as St. Paul says, *he who resisteth Power, resisteth the Ordinance of God.* (m) But by the Term Sin in a stricter sense we generally understand the Violation of the Ordinances or Commandments of God, who is the Supreme Legislator, for *had it not been for the Law,* says St. Paul, *I had not known Sin;* (n) for were there is no *Law,* there is no *Transgression.* Therefore *whosoever committeth a Sin transgresseth the Law,* says St. John, (o) so on the other hand, whosoever transgresseth the Law, committeth Sin.

(m) Rom. xiii. v. 2.

(n) Rom. c. vii. v. 7.

(o) 1 Ep. c. iii. v. 4.

That there has always been a *Law* in force for the Rule of Man's Actions, is no ways necessary to prove to a Christian, since such a Law has been promulgated by Almighty God himself (under the severest Penalties and Vengeance against those who violate it) at sundry times, and in divers Manners. Besides Mankind has always had a *Law written in their Heart, their Conscience bearing Witness,* to the fitness or unfitness of an Action, *and their Thoughts in the mean while accusing or else acquitting them.* (p) Whatsoever then is opposite or contradictory to this Law, whether by *Commission* of any thing which is by that prohibited, or by the *Omission* of any Duty which is by that enjoined, such Action or Omission constitutes the Person offending a Sinner, and is that particular kind of Guilt, which we are here to understand by the Term *Sin.*

(p) Rom. c. ii. v. 15.

Now as no Christian ever yet called in question the Ability or *Power* of God in forgiving

us

us our Sins, fo it will be needlefs to offer any Proof that there is fuch a Power in God. And the fame may be faid to every Chriftian with regard to his divine *Will*, or readinefs to forgive us our Sins; fince all Chriftians believe that God fent his eternal and beloved Son into the World to be our *Redeemer*, to free us from Sin and Hell. Here let us for one Moment call to Mind, the fcene of Mifery and Ignominy which Jefus Chrift fuffered for Love of us,' and for our Redemption; all which we have already explained in the fourth Article of the Creed; fo that this alone, is a fufficient Proof of the *Willingnefs* of God to forgive us our Sins.

There are feveral Chriftians who deny, that the *Power* of abfolving from Sin is granted to Men; for fay they, this is a Prerogative belonging *only* to God. The Jewifh Scribes and Pharifees had formerly the like Notion, but they were feverely reprehended for it, and put to confufion by our Saviour Chrift; for when our Saviour (as we read in St. Matthew and St. Mark) had told a Man who was Sick of the Palfey, that his Sins were forgiven him, fome of the Scribes and Pharifees who were there prefent, concluded immediately, in their Hearts, that this was Blafphemy, *this Man*, fay they, *Blafphemes*, for *who can forgive Sins except God alone?* But our Bleffed Redeemer, who came on purpofe into the World for the Remiffion of our Sins, was prefently touched at this wrong Notion of the Jews, and therefore before they could even fpeak their Thoughts, he faid to them, *why do you think Evil in your Hearts? For to let you fee that the Son of Man has power on Earth.*

P. I.

Earth to forgive Sins, he turns to the sick Man saying, *arise take up thy Bed and go into thy House.* (*q*) The Jews Dear Christians, were here under two Mistakes: In the first place they thought, our Saviour was not *God;* and in the second place, they thought that being *Man*, he could not forgive Sins; therefore our Saviour Christ, for our Instruction concerning the Remission of Sin, was pleased on this Occasion (in some degree) to pass by the first Mistake, and more expresly to confute the second; on which Account we ought to take Notice, that he does not say, to let you see that I am God, or to let you see that in Quality of *God*, I can forgive Sins; But to let you see that in Quality of *Man* upon Earth, I have Power to forgive Sins.

Some perhaps might expect, that our Saviour would have used (against the Scribes and Pharisees to prove himself God from their own Principles) some such Argument as this; you grant that he who forgives Sins is God; now by this Miracle which I have wrought; I shew you that I can forgive Sins, consequently according to your own Principles, it follows that I am God. But our blessed Redeemer did not openly make use of this Argument; For altho' tacitly and in fact, especially in discovering to the Jews their own Thoughts, he made it sufficiently appear that he was God, the Searcher of Hearts: Yet in the curing of the Man Sick of the Palsey, what he more expresly made appear was, that even in Quality of *Man*, he had Power to forgive Sins; this being the Intention of the Miraculous Cure: *To let you know*, says he, that (not only the Son of God but also) *the Son of Man has Power* even *upon Earth to forgive Sins,*
arise

(q) Mat. c. ix. St. Mar. c. ii.

arife Sick Man *take up thy bed and go into thy Houfe.* Upon this as it is related in the Chapters above cited, all the People were aftonifhed and feized with fear, and all *glorified Almighty God,* not becaufe God himfelf had fuch Power which they knew before, but becaufe, *he had given fuch great Power* even to Men.

Now, as from the *Divinity* of our Saviour down to his *Humanity,* is derived and defcends an unlimited Power of remitting Sin, fo from our Saviour, who is our Head, down to the Minifters of his Church who are his Members, is alfo derived and defcends a Power of remitting all Sins, of what kind foever they be, not indeed in their Name, or by their own Authority, but in the *Name,* and by the *Authority* of God. Does not our Bleffed Redeemer himfelf fufficiently imply and infinuate this Comparifon, when he faid to his Difciples mentioned in St. John; *as my Father fent me, fo I fend you?* Yes he certainly does; and to let you fee that this fending was in order to the remiffion of Sin, he *breathed* upon his Difciples, *and faid to them; Receive ye the Holy Ghoft, whofe Sins you fhall forgive, they are forgiven them, and whofe Sins you fhall retain, they are retained* (r)

c. xx. v. 21.

All which is conformable to that Divine Promife, which Chrift made to his Apoftles in general mentioned in St. Matthew, (*f*) *Amen I fay to you whatfoever you fhall bind upon Earth, fhall be bound in Heaven; and whatfoever you fhall loofe upon Earth, fhall be alfo loofed in Heaven.* It is alfo conformable to the Promife, which he made more particularly to St. Peter mentioned in St. Matthew,

(r) John c. xx. v. 22. 23.
(*f*) c. xviii. v. 18.

Matthew. To thee I will give the Keys of the Kingdom of Heaven, and whatsoever thou shalt bind upon Earth, shall be bound in Heaven, and whatsoever thou shalt loose upon Earth, shall be loosed in Heaven. (*t*)

(*t*) Mat. c. xvi. v.19.
John c.xx
Mat.c.xvi

It is to be first observed, that from the Words of Christ, mentioned in St. John and St. Matthew, that the Power which our Saviour gives, reaches and extends to all Sins whatsoever without Exception; and Secondly, that our Saviour does not say whose Sins you shall *declare* to be forgiven are forgiven them, (as some would have it) but he expresly says, whose Sins you shall *forgive*: And consequently hereby, Power is given to the Bishops and Priests of God's Church, not only to *declare* Mens Sins forgiven, but a true and real *Power* in the name of God to *forgive* them.

Hence here appears a great difference between the Priests of the *New* Law, and those of the *Old*; for the Jewish Priests mentioned in Leviticus, had not power to cleanse and cure even the Leprosy of the Body, but only to inspect and declare who were infected with it, and who not, and to distingush between Leprosy and Leprosy: Whereas the Priests of the *New* Law or Testament, have Power over the Leprosy of the Soul, viz. Sin, and this not only to say it is cleansed, but positively to cleanse it, not only so as to *declare*, but also to *effect* and perform it's Remission and Cure.

Levit. c. xiii et 14.

Again we must observe that our Saviour Christ, speaks not only of *forgiving*, but also of *Retaining* Sins, from whence it plainly appears that People must *confess*, and discover to the Priests all the grievous or Mortal Sins of their Life,

Life, howsoever hidden and secret they may have hitherto been, and the Reason of this is, because without this *Confession*, it is impossible for a Priest to be a competent Judge, he cannot see any difference between Men's Consciences, he cannot tell what Penance to impose, he knows not whether to give Absolution, or withhold it; in a word he cannot discern whose Sins are to be *forgiven*, and whose to be *retained*.

Lastly we must take notice of *the Keys of the Kingdom of Heaven*, given to St. Peter (*u*) and his Successors; for what can this mean, but that when the Gate of Heaven is shut against us by Sin, we must go to the Successors of St. Peter, that is to say the Bishops and Priests of of the Church, that by these Keys they may again open to us the same blessed Gate; for who but Christ, or those to whom he has given the Keys, can open that heavenly Gate? The Ministers of the Church of England, in the Communion service, exhort the People to come first to them, for *absolution*: And in the Visitation of the sick, they expresly declare, that *Christ has left a power in his Church to absolve all Sinners*, and accordingly after *a Special Confession*, the Minister is ordered to absolve the sick Person, in the very Words which the Roman Catholick Church makes use of viz. *I absolve thee from all thy Sins, in the Name of the Father, and of the Son, and of the Holy Ghost. Amen.*

(*u*) Mat. c. xvi. v. 19.

Is it not then surprising after all this, that the Ministers of the reformed Churches should reject the Sacrament of *Penance*, (but alas! when People will follow their own whims, and reject the

the Authority of the Church, what can we expect but Contradiction and Inconsistency) since nothing can be more reasonable than to believe, that the Church of Christ has a power from God to forgive Sins, *in the Sacrament of Penance.* For why has his Providence and Goodness given us the *Sacrament of Baptism?* Is it not because we were all born in Sin? And therefore we all stand in need of this Sacrament, to free us from the Slavery of the Devil, and the *Original* Sin we were born in. Now every one knows that after Baptism, People often relapse into Sin again, and often commit even far more abominable Sins, than what they did before Baptism: Therefore there is as much need for a *Sacrament* after Baptism in order to restore us again to the Favour of God, and preserve us from eternal Damnation, as there was before: And what *Sacrament* can this be, but *the Sacrament of Penance?* For as to *the Lord's Supper,* or *the Holy Communion,* it's Property, is not to raise us to Life, when dead by Sin; but divinely to feed us when alive, that is to say, when we are in the state of Grace; for so holy is this *Sacrament,* that our Sins must be first forgiven us, before we ought to approach to it. For let that Man look to himself, who leaves behind him his Nuptial Garment, and brings his Sins along with him to this most adorable Banquet, for thus in eating, he eats his own Damnation, says St. Paul. *(w)*

(w) 1 Cor. c. xi. v. 28

But perhaps some will say, that after Baptism, a Person being grown up may obtain Pardon or Remission of his Sins, without any *Sacrament* at all, viz. by Faith, and inward Sorrow,

of

of Mind *alone*. To this I anfwer, that fuch a Plea will not fuffice; becaufe Jews, and Heathens, when in like manner grown up to Maturity of Age and Judgment, before they are baptized, might at this rate pretend to be faved without having Baptifm either *actually* or in *defire*, by inward *Faith and Contrition alone*. But alas! inward Contrition, and other Difpofitions are feldom fo perfect, as to be able *alone* to juftify Sinners; and therefore for the common Good of Mankind, and to fupply the Defects, Imperfections, Infufficiency, and Inabilities of our ordinary Difpofitions, and to make Salvation as eafy to all Mankind as poffible, it was neceffary our Bleffed Redeemer fhould inftitute two reconciling *Sacraments*, viz. that of *Baptifm* for all Mankind; and that of *Penance* for fuch as fhould relapfe after Baptifm.

Again it may be farther urged, that this Power given to the Church, is an Ufurpation of the divine Authority; and that it is an encouragement to Perfons to commit Sin, feeing that the Bifhops and Priefts have a Power to abfolve whom they pleafe; nay farther, why may they not give them leave to fin?

To all this I anfwer, that it is rather an acknowledgment of the Divine Power, becaufe an Inftrument has no Virtue of itfelf, but derives all it's Efficacy from the principal Agent, whereof there is a plain Inftance in working Miracles, where God is honour'd and his Power illuftrated by thofe, who cure Diftempers, and raife the Dead, by being the Inftruments he employs for thefe Purpofes. As for Popes, Bifhops, and Priefts, having a Power to forgive whom

whom they pleafe, or to give Perfons leave to fin; thofe are ignorant furmifes, and down-right Calumnies: For the Power of abfolving from Sin, is granted with fuch Reftrictions, that no one is capable of receiving any Benefit thereby, but only fuch as bring proper Difpofitions with them.

Let us now examine and fee what thofe Difpofitions are. The *firft* is, that a Sinner muft be inwardly, and fincerely forrowful for having offended fo good a God. *Secondly*, he muft make a firm Refolution not to offend God any more. *Thirdly*, he muft humbly and fincerely declare all his mortal or deadly Sins by Confeffion. *Fourthly*, he muft be refolved to reftore the good Name, or Goods of others, he has unjuftly detained. *Fifthly*, he muft promife to avoid the Occafions of finning, &c. Thefe are the Difpofitions or Conditions, which the Minifters of God's Church require of the Penitent in order to obtain a valid Abfolution; for whofoever approaches to the Sacrament of Penance without thefe or the like Difpofitions, inftead of obtaining Pardon or Forgivenefs of his Sins, he makes himfelf guilty of a great Sacriledge.

I have here laid open the Truth of the Catholick Doctrine on this Point, left any one fhould be loft through Ignorance, I heartily wifh all may find Mercy; But I muft affure all thofe who pretend to approach to the Sacrament of Penance, without true and fincere Repentance, that they never will be juftified from their Sins; for the leaft a Sinner can do to have any Hopes of Pardon, is to enter into thofe Difpofitions

Art. X. *Disc.* I.

Dispositions above mentioned, he must also endeavour to apply or make use of the Remedies, which his Confessor shall prescribe to him; these are the Conditions of Pardon, without which no one can obtain it. I therefore wish that all Sinners may so perform these Conditions, as to partake of that great Mercy offered them by Almighty God in the full Pardon of their Sins; which is the Blessing I pray God of his infinite Mercy to grant to all.

ARTICLE.

ARTICLE X.

DISCOURSE. II.

The Forgiveness of Sins.

Whose Sins you shall forgive they are forgiven. St. John. c. xx. v. 23.

IN the foregoing Discourse I proved to you in part, that God is both *able* and *willing* to forgive us our Sins, and that he has left a *Power* in his Church to absolve all penitent Sinners from their Sins.

The Divis. What therefore I intend in this, is to inforce and illustrate the foregoing Arguments in support of the great Truth of this Article of our Christian Belief; and to lay before you the infinite Goodness and Mercy of Almighty God towards Sinners, on which alone is grounded all our comfortable Hopes of Salvation.

P. I. You here see Dear Christians, that *the Remission of Sin* is made one principal Article of our Christian Belief; so that it is not lawful to
doubt

doubt of this great Truth, upon which the Salvation of all Christians depends. We read in the Gospel, that our blessed Saviour Jesus Christ ordered his Apostles to preach to all Nations *Penance and Remission of Sins, (x)* from whence it is plain, that in the Church of Christ there is *Remission of Sin*, which Power he imparted to his Apostles just after his Resurrection, as we read in St. John. *(y)* And it is to be observed that *the Remission of Sin*, is no where to be found but in the Catholick Church, for St. Augustin says, that the "Remission of Sin " is not given but in the Holy Ghost, and " therefore it can only be given in that Church, " in which the Holy Ghost resides." *(z)* To which the Promises of Christ were made, and which through a lawful Succession of Pastors, continues to enjoy those *Prerogatives*, which were originally granted by *Christ*, to his Apostles, and in them to the Ministers of his Church in all future Ages. For as the Apostles were mortal and not permitted to abide always upon the Earth, so it was necessary that others should succeed in their stead, invested with equal Power, and sent by the same Authority, *for the perfecting of the Saints, for the work of the Ministry, and for the edification of the Body of Christ. (a)*

(*x*) Luc. c.xxiv.v. 47.

(*y*) c.xx. v. 23.

(z)St.Aug Serm. ii. de verbis Dni.c.xx.

(a) Eph. c.iv.v.12.

This Power of forgiving Sins, is one of the greatest Blessings which our blessed Redeemer has left to his Church. For if we consider the Frailty and Corruption of human Nature, and the dismal Consequences of Mortal Sin, we shall be easily convinced not only of the *Convenience*, but of the *Necessity* of this *Power*; for the Support of our Faith, the Recovery of Divine Grace,

Grace, and the everlasting Salvation of Mankind. For by every Mortal or Deadly Sin, we incur the Displeasure of God, we deprive ourselves of his holy Grace; we become obnoxious to the Rigour of his Justice; we forfeit our Title to the Kingdom of Heaven, and make ourselves guilty of eternal Damnation. It was therefore becoming the infinite Goodness and Mercy of God, to leave to his Church such a Power of absolving from Sin; hence the Prophet Isaias pronounces, that the *People who dwell therein*, (that is to say in the Church of Christ) *shall have their Iniquities taken from them*. (*b*)

(*b*)c.xxxiii. v. 24.

But notwithstanding the *Necessity* of this *Power* in the Church of absolving from Sin, and invincible Evidence of it's Institution by Jesus Christ; yet there is nothing more exposed to Ridicule, by modern *Sectaries*, than the practice of *Confession*, for it is traduced by them, as a piece of Priest-craft or mere human invention, in order to gain Money, but notwithstanding all this, they do at the same time profess to believe *a Remission of Sin*, as they read in the Gospel of such a *Power* vested *by Christ* in his Apostles and their Successors; so they cannot but see that *Confession* must naturally follow from it by a necessary Consequence, for how can the *Ministers* of the Church exercise the *Power* of *binding* and *loosing*, and pronounce Sentence? Unless they first know the state of the Sinners Conscience; neither could they prescribe such Remedies, and give such Advice as would be necessary for the Penitents Cure, or Amendment; unless they first knew the particular Qualities and Condition

Condition of the several Sins the Penitent commits, which cannot be without *Confession*; so that we conclude with Saint Augustin " that " to pretend it is enough to confess to God " *alone*, is making void the Power of the *Keys* " given to the Church, and contradicting the " Gospel, and making void the Commission of " Christ" (c)

(c) Hom. xlix. St.

Besides we find the Practice of *Confession* was ordained by God himself, both in the *old* Law, as well as the *new*, for we read in the Book of Numbers that Almighty God expresly commanded, that *when a Man or a Woman shall commit any Sin, that Man committeth, and by negligence shall have transgressed the Commandment of the Lord, and offended, they shall confess their Sin, and restore the Principle itself.* Now this *Confession* and *Satisfaction*, according to the best Interpreters of the Scriptures, was a Figure of the *Sacrament of Penance*. *Secondly*, St. James commands us to *confess our Sins one to another;* (d) from hence we may gather, that it is not enough to confess to God *alone*, but that we must also confess to Men, tho' not to every Man, but to those whom God has appointed, and given power in his Name to remit Sin. *Thirdly*, we find from the practice of the primitive Christians, that *many*, says St. Luke, *who believed came and confessed their Deeds.* (e) To this I know that some will object and say, that this was only a general Declaration or confessing themselves Sinners; but I answer, that we must here observe with *Grotius*, that it is a different thing for Men to *confess their Sins*, and to confess themselves Sinners.

Mat. c. xvi. v. 19

c. v. v. 6 7.

(d) c. v. v. 16.

(e) Acts c. xix. v. 18.

We

P. II. We must acknowledge that the Goodness and Mercy of God has been very great towards Sinners; from the beginning of the World, he knew the Frailty of human Nature; the Phortness of Man's Life; and the dreadful Punishments of the other World; therefore he casts an Eye of Pity and Compassion upon Sinners; he does not cut them off in their Sins, but gives them Time to repent, he forbears patiently with them; he is slow to punish, and inclined to pardon; he admonishes them continually; he invites them sweetly, and pardons them graciously. Let every Man reflect upon his own Life; whether he has not experienced the Sweetness of God's Mercy; whether he has received one Mercy, or a Thousand; whether God has not often spared him when he was in Sin; and where had he been now, if God had cut him off in his Sins?

But the Mercy of God towards Sinners, is yet more clearly revealed to the World by *Jesus Christ;* there was nothing more remarkable than his Mercy to Sinners, both in his Life, and Doctrine: As to his Life and Conduct among Sinners, he was called even the Friend of Sinners, which signifies he was their only Hope. And his Doctrine was as remarkable in this Point, as his Conduct; for what means the *Parable* of the *Publican* preferred before the proud *Pharisee,* a Man loaded with Injustices and other Crimes, to return from one *Knock* of his Breast into his House justified? What means the *Parable* of the Man who fought the lost Sheep, with so many remarkable Circumstances of his leaving Ninety nine to look after *one,* his

bringing

bringing him back upon his shoulders; the Congratulation of his Friends and Neighbours upon it? What means the *Parable* of the prodigal Son? Why is he painted out in such lively Colours, to have wasted his substance, as well as his Virtue among Harlots, and became as I may say a Swine among Swine? Why at his return does his Father go out to meet him and make such rejoicing? All these *Parables* are Inventions to express the Conversion of a Sinner; the Joy shewn in the Gospel at these Conversions, is the Joy of Heaven, and those who in the Gospel repine at them are Figures of the Devils, to whom the Conversion of a Sinner becomes a new Hell. In a Word these remarkable Parables of the Justification of the *Publican*, the lost *Sheep* found, the *Prodigal Son* returned, are written in the Gospel with design to render the Mercy of Jesus Christ to Sinners, the most remarkable Part of his Life and Doctrine. And therefore we ought always to remember, that Jesus Christ came into the World to save Sinners; for them he died and spilt the last drop of his most precious Blood: This is the ground work of our Pardon, and the Doctrine of the Remission of Sins; the Grounds of that pardon, are the *Merits* of *Jesus Christ*, and the *Mercy* of God; and in Consequence of this Faith, there is no Sinner, tho' never so wicked, but by the Mercy of God may be justified, and become a Saint in the Kingdom of Heaven; and there is no Sin, of which a repenting Sinner ought not to have certain Hopes of Pardon in the Church of God.

The CREED EXPLAINED.

Now this Doctrine of the Remission of Sins is a great Motive for Sinners to repent, and is the greatest Hope and Consolation we can have in this World. Though I know there are some so perverse, as to take it in a quite contrary Sense: For the Libertine will say, that if there be Hopes even at the last Day of our Lives, and Repentance never comes too late, we may follow our own Pleasures a little longer, not without pardon at last.

But tell me, Dear Christians, did ever one single Person arrive at Heaven by following this Libertines Doctrine, except the good Thief, and he was converted at the first call, and yet he is the only one the Scriptures make mention of; therefore it is a certain Proof, that the Libertines Doctrine is not good, for are there not thousands fallen into Hell and Damnation by following the same Doctrine? Then it is most certain the Doctrine is bad; for how can this be a Reason to make the *Mercy* of God a Motive to *continue* in Sin, and not to *repent* of Sin, can bitter and sweet come out of the same Fountain? I here propose the Goodness and *Mercy* of God, as a Motive for Sinners to repent, Libertines propose the same *Mercy* for a Reason, why they continue in their Sins; this is the Cunning and Artifice of the old Serpent, who fights as industriously against our *Penance*, as he did against our *Innocence*; but alas! here is our fatal Mistake; Sinners hope in the *Mercy* of God, but they do not reflect that they destroy this *Hope* by a continuance in their Sins; for thus they abuse every day that Mercy, which they acknowledge to be all their Hopes; not reflecting

reflecting that when they turn this *Mercy* into Anger and Justice, they destroy their own Hopes. They cry we may repent on the last Day; this is very true, but I question whether ever any one did so, who wilfully deferred his Repentance till the last Day, in hopes then of Pardon; for suppose such a Sinner should fail to repent on that Day, can he repent on the next? O Christians, take heed left you put off so long your Repentance, till there is neither Time or Pardon left, and thus you be found to have believed in vain, this great Truth of the Remission of Sins.

I have here laid before you the Promises of Pardon, which Almighty God has made to Sinners, when ever they shall return to him; I have also made manifest the Goodness and Mercy of *Jesus Christ* towards Sinners; I have laid open the Doctrine of the Remission or Forgiveness of Sins; and the Joy there is in Heaven at the Conversion of a Sinner; all which, I think is more than a sufficient motive for us to repent, in order that we may partake of the Pardon offered us, and not to expose ourselves to the uncertain Hopes of a death Bed Repentance.

How long Dear Christians, shall we doubt and waver on this clear Case? Shall we all our Lives be fluctuating, and balancing between Heaven and Hell, as if the Choice was dark and difficult? Shall we always live among the Swine with the Prodigal, with the Drunkard, with the Luxurious and Debauched, with the Detractor, the Swearer, &c. and never return to the House of our Father who is in

Heaven? Can Christians live all their Lives long, separated from God their only Hope? Will they never more think to have Part with their Blessed Redeemer? Will they always do the Works of the Devil, and never more seek the Justification of *Jesus Christ?* Will they always continue to heap up Wrath against the Day of Wrath? Will they always remain in Death, on the brink of Hell, and never more think of Heaven, their blessed Country, and of God whom they have lost? O Prodigal Sinner, return without delay to the House of your Father, and do no longer feed with the Swine; sure *Pardon* is promised; *Mercy* is great; your Conversion shall be the Joy of Heaven, and the Mortification of Hell, and will be a new Glory to yourself. You have a thousand Examples to encourage you, thousands of Sinners who have been justified, and led the remainder of their Lives in Innocence, and thus ended their Days in Peace: Heaven is full of justified Sinners, for it is a certain Truth, that many who are now reigning in Heaven with Jesus Christ, were once great Sinners upon Earth; the greatest Sinners therefore by following their Example, may become glorious Saints in the Kingdom of Heaven.

And as this Doctrine of the Forgiveness of Sins, is the Hope of all Sinners, so it is also the great Consolation and Support of our frail Life; for was it not for our *Faith* or Belief in the Forgiveness of Sins, and in the Goodness and Mercy of God, how could such frail Mortals support Life? For when we consider our Sinful and mortal Condition; the Frailty of
human

human Nature, and shortness of Life; the dismal Consequence of Sin; and that by one only grievous Sin committed all is lost; all we have gained by the Death and Redemption of Jesus Christ is lost, both Grace and Glory; all the Merits of our past good Works are all lost by one Mortal Sin; this Consideration of human Misery, and so desperate a Chance of Salvation, must needs hold us in great Anxiety; but when we turn our Thoughts, and consider that there is Pardon and Remission of Sins, by true Repentance, and the Sacrament of Penance; O this raises our Hope, it creates Joy, and gives Peace, and obliges us to render immortal Thanks to Almighty God.

But if this Truth be so comforting, this Faith in the Forgiveness of Sins, so prevailing a Support to our frail Nature, let us not mistake the Conditions, which I have already mentioned, that ought to be performed on our part, lest we believe in vain the Remission of Sin. But perhaps some will say, how shall we know who those are that do repent, and who not. I will tell you Dear Christians, it is not so difficult as some imagine; at least to frame a very probable Guess; for as our Saviour Christ says, *the Tree is known by it's Fruit*, and Man by his Works, and the Penitent by worthy Fruits of Penance; in a Word, the Cause is known by it's Effects. If the Sinner finds, that after the Sacrament of Penance, his Life is even worse than before, that he no sooner repented, but returned again to the Vomit, that he was no sooner risen with Christ, but in the Grave again; no wise Minister or Pastor in
God's

God's Church, ever did or can say, that such a one was a true Penitent. Habitual or scandalous Sinners, who neither mend in the whole nor in part, who neither mend nor endeavour so to do, by applying the Remedies prescribed to them, nor will quit the Occasion of their Sins; those we are certain, have not performed the Conditions of the Promise of Pardon; and therefore have great Reason to fear, that they were not justified in the sight of God; for who can believe that a Man justified in Jesus Christ, can immediately turn to the Works of the Devil? That a Man can immediately shift from Sin to Sanctity, and from Sanctity to Sin, and that in a few Hours time, he should Work all these stupendous Alterations in his Soul; this is making us judge of Man, quite differently from all we know of him, and make him act in this Matter of Repentance, quite against his Nature and Custom in all other parts of his Life.

To conclude this Discourse from what has been said concerning this Article; we firmly *believe*, that God is both *able* and *willing* to Forgive us our Sins; and that he has given a *Power* to the Ministers of his Church to absolve or remit from all Sins, and the Punishment of them *in his Name*, in the Sacrament of Baptism and Penance; and therefore we hope by an humble Compliance with the Divine Institution in these two Sacraments, to be partakers of this great Mercy; which is what I pray God of his infinite Goodness to grant to all.

ARTICLE,

ARTICLE, XI.

DISCOURSE, I.

The Resurrection of the Body.

This corruptible Body must put on incorruption, and this Mortal Body put on Immortality. 1 Cor. c. xv. v. 53.

BY this Article of our Creed, we are in the *first* place indirectly put in mind of our *Mortality*, that *we must all die*, and *secondly*, we are to believe that at the last Day of Judgment, we shall all rise again with the same *individual* Bodies, in which we lived in this World before, though in many respects changed and altered from their former state, (for if we were not to rise with the same *identical* Bodies, in which we before lived in this World, then it would not be properly a *Resurrection*, but a Production of new things) and we believe that this *Resurrection* will be the fate of all Mankind, whether *just*, or *unjust*, according to that of St. Paul. *As in Adam*

Adam all died, so in Christ all shall be raised to Life again. (f)

(f) 1 Cor. c. i. v. 22

Heb. c. ix. v. 27.

To offer to prove to you, that *all Men* (as St. Paul says) *must once die*, is an unnecessary and needless Task ; since nothing can be more evident, nay the very Graves and Monuments of the dead which we daily see, tell us what we must all come to; and the Experience of so many past Ages, is a standing Proof and Confirmation of this great Truth, that all Mankind must taste of Death : Besides, among all the absurd Errors of Men, there never were any so foolish, as to think they should not die.

P. I.

What therefore I intend in this Discouse, is to treat upon Death, in order that we may better understand *the Resurrection of the Body*, and because there is no Consideration, that can contribute more to a good Life, than the Thought of Death ; but alas! the Misfortune is, the more profitable the Consideration of Death is, the greater Horror and Aversion many Sinners have to it. What Art of Persuasion then, shall I make use of, to prevail upon them to consider this Subject of Death, so as to make it both agreeable, and profitable ? All I can do is, to endeavour to treat this Subject in such a Manner, as not to cast a Damp upon any ones Spirits, but rather to raise them, and give new Life, so as not to disturb their Peace, but rather to encrease their happy Days; so as to teach them how to live, as well as to die ; in a Word, so as to moderate the Fear of Death, which Fear is the greatest Anxiety, that belongs to Man's Life, and damps more Courage, and chills more Blood, and extinguishes the Sense even

Art. XI. Disc. I.

even of innocent Pleasures, more than all other Causes whatsoever: If then I undertake to remove that Fear of Death, I hope this Discourse will be acceptable.

To judge by experience, of those who are mindful of their last End and prepare for Death by a good and pious Life, do we perceive that they have any disturbed Fancies, or Symptoms appear in them of uneasy or frightful Imaginations, for do they not converse as freely with their Friends as other Men do, who seldom or never think of Death? Since then all Men must certainly die, as well those who do not think or meditate on Death, as those who do; and since the Consideration or Meditation of Death, is the way to remove the Fear of it; and since those who do not think nor prepare for it, are most of all Men disturbed with the Fear of it; is it not better to imitate the wise in preparing for Death, than to imitate the unwise or imprudent, who never think so seriously of it, as to profit or amend their Lives thereby.

Now Dear Christians, I cannot render this Discourse profitable to you, without considering the Matter according to Truth: In the *first* place then, I must consider what the State of Death is, and lay before you all that is formidable in Death; *secondly*, I will give you a Description of a happy Death, and a sure means to arrive both at a happy Death, and by consequence at a happy Resurrection; so that you may be victorious over Death and the Grave; and even in this Life conquer the Fear of Death. I shall not here make any Account of unnatural, violent, or sudden Deaths, but only confider thofe, which are efteemed the eafieft and moft defirable, as when a Perfon dies in his Bed, and in the Arms of his Friends.

In the firft place, what is the Death of fuch a Man, but the Deftruction of the Man? For a Man there to lye and contemplate his own Deftruction, to know that not only his Friends, but that all Creatures together are not able to fuccour him, to feel the Revolution making in his Nature, to feel Death and the Diffolution of Nature feizing him, and to find the vital Union between Soul and Body break, and one half of himfelf depart from the other, is not this a very confiderable accident which concerns us all very nearly? It is being brought to the loweft State of all Mortals, and there is no King in this expiring Condition, but would willingly change with the vileft Slave in Health, that belongs to him; but through this low Condition of Mortals, the greateft Monarchs and their Subjects muft pafs, nay even lower than this, for their Bodies muft lye in the Grave, and not only lye, but rot there, fo that all will turn to Putrefaction, Worms, and Duft. O finful Man! defcend a little into the Sepulchres of the Dead, and there fee all the Pride of Life; Kings and their Subjects, Conquerors with the conquered all lying in the Duft ignoble together: See Bodies pampered with all the Delights of the Earth, and cloathed in all it's Riches, lying in Putrefaction: Strange Condition, and very fhocking to Nature! But there are other things to be confidered.

The Man by living in this World, has contracted many Affections to what he poffeffed

in

in it; he has contracted many Passions for what delighted him; now cruel Death, which breaks the Vital Union between Soul and Body, parts the dearest Friends too, and breaks with great Violence those strong Chains, whereby the Man had united himself to all he loved in this World; Death is the farewell of all; he loses all his usual Supports, his usual Comforts, all Help, all the Objects of his Passions and Desires in general; he loses all and finds nothing; every thing flies away with eternal flight, every thing sinks under him, every thing disappears. But this is not all.

Death is not only the farewell to this World, but a journey to another; and to go into another World, is to begin a new state of Life; to live without a Body; to enter into an unknown Region of Spirits, separated Souls; to converse with them, without a Body, without senses, without seeing or hearing; to go among those Spirits, without knowing what Entertainment one shall meet with; what kind of Habitation, what Employment, what Sense or Feeling? Sure there is nothing more amazing! But one surprising Object he will meet with here, will be to find the Presence of God, to feel him in his Power, after a new manner, quite different from what he felt him in this World, where the workings of God in nature are all hid; here he will find all immediately under the absolute Government of God himself; every Spirit fixed by an invariable order of Justice, without it's being possible for Time to alter his state. This furnishes us with

another

another Confideration of Death very formidable, which is.

That Death is the End of all Time, and the Beginning of Eternity, or a fatal Period between both, which on the one fide puts an End to all Time and Life, and confequently to all that this Life affords, and what is worfe, an End to the ſtate of meriting, and an End to good Works, and to the Days of Mercy, Grace, Pardon, and Repentance, the Lofs of which is much more confiderable, than the Lofs of a few empty Pleafures, and Vanities; and on the other fide, this fatal Hour defides our Eternity, and tranflates the Soul into an eternal ſtate, where all his eternal; his Manfion is eternal, his Employment eternal, his Action and his Paffion eternal, fixed by an invariable order of him who never alters.

Such is the ſtate, but what makes it more dreadful is, that we muſt every one try this ſtate, for tho' Death is of all things the moſt certain, yet we regard it at a Diſtance, and hope for a long Life; this is the grand Illufion of the Devil, he does not fuggeſt to a Man that he fhall never die, no that would be too grofs, but that he has a long Time to live, and therefore needs not yet undertake the Care of his Salvation; with this one Illufion, the Devil feduces the greater part of Mankind. Now tell me, you who propofe to yourfelves a long Life, how long do you propofe it, perhaps you will fay for forty or fifty Years longer, but this is rather too much, for the eſtimation of Man's Life is ufually valued but at ten Years in Contracts, and no Man will venture upon your

Life

Art. XI. *Disc.* I.

Life, for above ten Years, but we will suppose forty Years; you will then grant, that forty Years when past will be but short; and do you think that forty Years to come are longer, than forty Years past? Be not then deceived with this Illusion of the Devil; but why do you talk of forty or fifty Years, or even ten Years, for who can promise even ten Days? And this leads me to another Consideration concerning Death, which is it's Uncertainty. For

Our Bodies are so frail, that every trifle hurts and discomposes our Constitution, a little puff of bad Air; a little Gravel, or Stone, one Drop of Water, any of these situated in a wrong part of the Body, is enough to kill the strongest Man, for there is nothing in nature so little and inconsiderable, but may meet with mortal Men in such Circumstances, as to be too big for their Weakness, and may carry off the most valiant Hero. But what is more amazing is, that this frail Composition of ours, is placed among so many Causes, and Instruments of Death, which besets us on all sides; old Age and the Decays of Nature, Weakness, and Infirmity, Intemperances of Youth, wild Beasts, Prison, and the Sword, &c: Besides these Accidents, and innumerable other Chances, which make Death the most uncertain, as well as most certain thing in human Life, besides all these I say, (the sick Man is not sure of Death, nor the healthy Man sure of Life, since Men die without Rule, by accidental and hidden Causes) there is a fatal Blow given them, no one knows from what Hand; A Man for Example in a Consumption lies under an arrest of Death, and one at the

same

same time in a vigorous state of Health shall be nearer Death, than the consumptive Man, upon a more fatal, sudden, and less discerned Cause, because Men die without rule; and for the same Reason, no Age is secure; but every Age has a Gate for Death to enter; the Infant Age is as incurable by Art, as old Age by Nature; vigorous Youth itself has its Causes of Death, and a certain Fact it is, that more die young, than old beyond Comparison: But besides all this Mortality, there is one Cause of Death more surprising than the rest, viz. that Men should open a Gate to it themseves, by Viciousness, and Luxury; they pour in strong Drink and let out Life, they contract Diseases, and then cannot bear them, they strangle themselves with their own Intemperance, and suffer the Inflammations of their own lusts and Passions.

Thus Dear Christians, you see that snares are laid for our Lives, besides those we lay for ourselves; and our Death at all Hours is uncertain, the Hour is as uncertain as the Day, and the Day is as uncertain as the Week, and the Week as the Year. The Wisdom of God orders this uncertainty of Life, and his Wisdom is easily justifiable in this point, for it is a spur to our Industry, it makes Men watchful, sober, and wise, it makes them diligent in preparing for Death by a good Life, whereas if Men knew the Day of their Death, they would infallibly neglect the Practice of Virtue, till near the Day of their Death; besides, it would be no great Comfort to any Man to know the Day of his Death.

I have

Art. XI. Disc. I.

I have shewn you what Death is, that it is the Horror of Nature, but if we consider what is the Death of the Sinner, this will tell us what Death truly is, for Sin is properly the sting of Death, and as there is nothing more moving, so there is nothing more wholsome, than to consider the Sinner's End, that we ourselves may avoid it. There is nothing in this World so moving, as to see a Man so overcome with Sin as well as Infirmity, that in his Misery he cannot place his Hope in God : Such notwithstanding is the End of the impenitent Sinner ; see here a Discription of him, the Pains of his Body rack him, but the Pains of his Conscience still more ; his Sins that were his greatest Pleasure are now his greatest Pain, his dearest Friends are his greatest Grief, he has contracted violent Passions for this World, which joined with a Sense of his Guilt, gives him the utmost aversion of Death, which of all things is the most certain to him ; all human Consolations then utterly fail him ; the Helps of the Church which often afford succour, when all others fail, now fail him too; and what is worse, he cannot hope in the Goodness and Mercy of God, which is a Resource when all others are insufficient, but the Thought of God, is a Terror to him ; this is what he suffers in this World; and when he enters into the other, there he meets the Powers of Darkness ; and the Devil who seduced him, now seizes upon his Prey Insulting over him, and shewing him how he deceived him; and how he seconded the Devil in his own Destruction; so that instead of finding some Rest and Refreshment after his agonizing Pains, he finds fresh Sufferings, and

and thus sinks out of *temporal* Pains into *Eternal*. Sure nothing is more moving than such an End, yet such is the End of all Sinners who repent not; and those who wilfully continue in a wicked Life, are in very great Danger of coming to this End. These you will say are melancholy Considerations, and therefore I will continue no longer upon them, but endeavour to describe to you the Happiness of Death, as well as it's Terror, and shew you how you may Conquer the Fear of Death.

We are not called to Death but to Life; the Victory is gained over Death, by the Death of *Jesus Christ*, not for himself but for us; the Victory is gained, and Death is become even precious in the Saints, and desirable in the Just, for the Psalmist assures us, that *the Death of the Saints is precious in the Sight of God.* (*g*) This is the Victory of true Faith, and true Piety over Death. Why should we fear Death, if we lead a good Life? For do you not know, Dear Christians, that Death is reduced now to the Condition of Sleep? It is so called in holy Scripture, (*h*) it is there represented under the Notion of Rest and Sleep. For though the just Man tastes of Death as well as the impious, yet he does not suffer the Torments, Horror, and Anxiety of Death. The Death of the Just, is but a Passage to Resurrection, it is the first Day of Immortality, the Beginning of Rewards; a Change of Earth for Heaven; of Men for Angels; of Dangers for Safety; of Fight for Victory; of Labour for a Crown. We know not what are the Pleasures of the Immortal Life he is passed into; but if all things there are infinitely surprizing, as no doubt

(*g*) Pf.cxv. v. 15.

(*h*) 1 Cor. c. xv. v. 18. et St. John. c. xi v. 11.

doubt but they are, for St. Paul assures us, *that the Eye hath not seen, nor the Ear heard, nor hath it entered into the Heart of Man to conceive what God hath prepared for those who Love him.* (i) Hence we know that the State of the Just there, must be most agreeably surprizing. (i) 1 Cor. c. i. v. 9.

The Death of the Just is precious at all Ages of Life, for if he dies in his Youth, and leaves the World cause to lament his Loss. and promising Hopes of his Virtue; if he dies in the Flower of his Youth, he dies also in the Flower of his Virtue, and his precious Death is more desirable than mournful. And if he dies in a good old Age, as ripe in Virtue as in Years, grown old in Piety, in Faith, and good Works; having preserved his Life by his Sobriety and Temperance, and prolonged it by the Prayers and Blessings of the Poor, to whom he has been charitable and liberal, and so by a gentle Decay of Nature, drops off like the ripe Fruit from the Tree; nothing is more desireable than such a Death, it is what the Prophet Balaam wished for; *O let me die the Death of the Just, and let my End be like unto theirs.* (k) (k) Num. c. xxxiii. v. 10.

Let us now see what are the means we are to make use of in order to escape the dreadful, and terrible Death of the *wicked*, and how to arrrive at the happy Death of the *just*. I shall here prescribe but one Means to be made use of, and that is a good and pious Life; for generally speaking, we shall die as we have lived; if we spend our Life in the State of Grace, we shall in all appearance die in the State of Grace; or if we pass our Lives in the State of Sin, we shall in all likelihood die in the State of Sin. (l) P. II.

(l) See Proverb c. i. v. 24 Eccl. c. xli v. 1. Rom. c. ii. v. 5. 6. 7. 8.

There are two things which Death teaches us; in the *first* place, not to over-value Life, and *secondly*, not to under-value it; for things are valuable by their End; and Life is to be valued by the Sepulchre; it is of small Importance whether we lead our Lives a little more, or a little less conveniently; a little richer, or a little poorer; and yet for these small degrees of Advantage, how often do we see Men Sacrifice their all, their Conscience, their Faith, their Religion, and their Souls too; and the Poor are as Subject to over-value this Life, as the Rich; but surely both would do otherwise, if they saw the End of all in the Sepulchres of the dead; let us take heed how we over-value Life, lest we should go out of the World, with an eternal Passion for what we can never enjoy.

But then let us take care at the same time, not to undervalue Life by consuming one part of it in Idleness, and another in sinful Actions, and by shortening our Days by Intemperance and Excess; this is under valuing Life : When we consider how certain Death is, and on the other hand how short and frail Life is; these Considerations ought to make Men careful of their precious Life, and make them more assiduous to work while Time lasts, both for this World and the next; so far is the Thought of Death from making a Man regardless of Life, that it rather gives him Spirits, and adds a spur to Industry; and therefore a Man may make a diligent Preparation for Death, and yet answer all the Ends and Purposes of living; for it is those, who very seldom or never think of dying, that

that are commonly the most negligent and prodigal of Life, it is they who trifle away their precious Time more than others; and shorten their Lives by Debaucheries, Drunkenness, &c. and fear not by Rashness to expose them to every Hazard they meet with.

From what I have here said it plainly appears, that a right Preparation for Death, and the only one we can depend on, is a good and virtuous Life; we know there are Works, that will render us victorious over Death and the Grave; there are Works that will follow Men into the next World; there are Riches that may be sent before us; Treasures that may be laid up in Heaven; there is a good Work, which the holy Scripture tells us delivers a Man from Death, relieves him in the Day of his distress, which is the Day of Death, and will not permit his Soul to go into Darkness, (m) and that Work is *Almsdeeds*. There are also good Works which perpetuate our Memory, and in some sense prolong Life after Death; These are worthy Actions, by which Men benefit their Friends and Posterity, by good Institutions, charitable Foundations and the like; This is spending Life well, and not only doing good Works while living, but to continue them after Death.

Let us then be convinced that a good Life, is the only sure Preparation that can be depended on for a happy Death, that is, to obtain the Death of the just: A good Conscience takes away the Fear of Death both in our Life time, and at the hour of Death: For at that Time a good Conscience comes into our Relief, it makes Death comfortable, it raises the Spirits,

(m) Tob. c. iv. v. 11.

and gives life as I may say, to a dying Man; it gives the dying Person that Confidence to say within himself; *I have fought a good fight, I have finished my Course, I have kept my Faith,* and shewed it by good Works, now there is nothing remains for me but a *Crown of justice.* (n)

(n) Tim. c. iv. v. 7.

Thus Dear Christians you see, that a timely Preparation for Death, frees a Man from the Fears and Anxieties of Death; it is the Wicked, and those who make no Preparations for it, that are most of all disturbed with the fears of Death; for it is a Passion for this Life, joined with a sense of Guilt, that begets this Aversion to Death; from hence you cannot but see, that the Preparation for Death, rather tends to make Life happy, because this Preparation consists in the Practice of all Christian Virtues, which give Honour and Reputation in the World, and make you both beloved by God and Man. Let these Considerations then prevail upon you, to apply yourselves while you have Time to the Practice of Virtue, to set your Hands to work, to neglect no Duty, to slip no Opportunity, and to do even all your ordinary Actions for the Honour and Glory of God, and the eternal Salvation of your Souls; thus if you obey these Admonitions, you will imitate the wisest of Men, and it is what I heartily wish you may do.

ARTICLE.

ARTICLE, XI.

DISCOURSE. II.

The Resurrection of the Body.

This corruptible Body, must put on Incorruption; and this Mortal Body must put on Immortality. 1 Cor. c. xv. v. 53.

IN the last Discourse, I set before you the most evident Proof of the Mortality of human Bodies, viz. that we must all die; I also explained to you the state of Death, with all the Horrors which attend it. In this Discourse I shall treat concerning *the Resurrection of the Body* at the last Day of Judgement, which is the great *Hope* of all good Christians.

We must remember that Death does not put an End to us for ever, since it is a part of our *Faith* to believe, that the Separation of Soul and Body is not Eternal, for the Dust will return again into the same substance, which was turned into Dust before, so that the Union between Soul

Soul and Body will be knit again, the Graves must all yield forth their Dead, so we shall all rise again with the same *individual* Bodies, in which we lived before, tho' in some respects changed from their former state.*

---

* It is certain that this Article of our Faith, viz. The *Resurrection of the Dead*, has been always part of our Creed from the very beginning of Christianity; which appears not only from the ancient Creeds, but also from the Weight and Moment of the Doctrine itself, it being a Point on which the whole Christian Religion seems to depend.---For if there should be no Resurrection of the Dead, then the Christian Religion would be a mere Chimæra and Fable, and the grand Attractive, by which it was recommended to the World, would be no other than a downright Delusion. For when the Apostles dispersed themselves in order to convert the Heathen World, the method they took for that end, as we see by the example of St. Paul at Athens, as mentioned in the 17 Chapter of the Acts of the Apostles was to preach up *Jesus* and the *Resurrection*, that is to reveal a Saviour to them, who came to redeem them from their Sins, and to assure them of a *Resurrection* at the last Day. But we must here observe, that the *Epicurian* and *Stoick* Philosophers who encountered St. Paul at *Athens* when they heard of the *Resurrection* of the *Body*, they mocked and derided it, as an idle Fancy; and not only the Heathens, but also several pretended Christians did oppugn this necessary Truth, as *Hymenæus* and *Philetus*, mentioned by St. Paul in his 2 Epistle to Timothy, 2 chapter---We must likewise take notice, that there were certain Hereticks who did acknowledge the Resurrection of the *Body*, or of a *Body*, but they would not grant that the same Body, which we now have should be raised again, but instead thereof, they imagined that at the Resurrection Day, there should be framed by the Power of God thin and æreal Bodies, to which human Souls shall be joined, instead of those gross, material fleshly Bodies, which they now actuate and live in. Now against these Persons, both the *Greek* and *Latin* Creed make use of this Expression Σαϱϰὸς ἀνάστασιν, *Carnis Resurrectionem*, the Resurrection of the *Flesh*, and not of the *Body*, in which word Flesh

This is the *Hope* and *Faith* of all true Christians, for tho' many among the Heathens did believe the *Immortality* of the Soul, yet none among them did ever hope or believe *the Resurrection of the Body*; for this Doctrine was such a novelty at the first Promulgation of the Gospel, that it met with very considerable Opposition; for when St. Paul preached up at Athens, *the Resurrection of the Flesh*, many mocked at him, and even the Philosophers looked on him in the contemptible Light of a Babbler, or trifling Fellow. (*o*) Nay among the *Jews* themselves,

(*o*) Acts. c. xvii. v 18.

Flesh lies a particular Force and Emphasis, that latter Word being capable of more Subterfuges and equivocatory Explications, than the former word *Flesh*: of which *St. Jerom* gives us an instance in the *Origenists*, who espoused this Tenet; *they say*, faith he, *we believe the future Resurrection of the Body, which if it be sincerely said, is a pure Confession: but because there are celestial and terrestrial Bodies, and the Air and æther according to their Natures, are called Bodies, therefore they use the Word Body*, and not *Flesh*; that whilst the Orthodox Party hearing the Word *Body*, apprehended it to be *Flesh*; but the Hereticks understood it to be a *Spirit*, which is their first Evasion. See Tom. 2. ad Pammach. et Occan. Epist. 65. c. ii. p. 229.

Wherefore *Ruffinus*, who was accused of this Heresy, in the vindication of himself therefrom, alledges, that to remove all Suspicion of his being tainted therewith, he frequently affirmed, *that not only the Body, but that the Flesh also should rise again*. Invectiv. 1. in Hieron, inter. Oper. Hieron. T. 9. p. 162.---Now the primitive Fathers in order to prevent the equivocating Evasions of *Bardesanes, Origen*, and others; expressed this Article by the Resurrection of the *Flesh*, and not of the *Body*, as appears from *Gennadius Massiliensis, inter Oper. August. Tom.* 3. *de Ecclesiast. Dogmat.* p. 260. And the same is expressed by *St. Epiphanius*. advers. Heres. Compend. Fid. Cathol. p. 464---See also St. Augustin. in his City of God. Tom. 5. L. 13. c. xx. p. 30. And again in his 3 Tom. de Fide et Symbol. p. 196.

there

there was a whole Sect of Men, viz. *the Sadducees*, who said there was *no Resurrection;* but our Blessed Redeemer confuted them, and told them that they *erred, not knowing the Scriptures, nor the Power of God.* (*p*) They had neither attended to the clear Discoveries, with which they were supplied from Revelation, nor to those strong and conclusive Arguments in this behalf, which might have been drawn from Reason and the Nature of Things. Now this Charge must fall heavier upon the Christian *Sadducees*, if there are any yet so blind and senseless, as under the Gospel Dispensation to say, *there is no Resurrection*, it is evident that this Mistake must proceed, not for want of Attention, but from actually *not knowing the Scriptures and the Power of God*.

(*p*) Mat. c. xxii. v. 29.

Now since *the Resurrection of the Body*, is an Article of *Faith* peculiar to our Creed, we ought therefore to apply ourselves with greater diligence to reap the admirable Fruits of this our Faith. This great Mystery of our Belief, as St. Paul preaches to us, is this, that *we all shall rise again, but all shall not be changed*, (*q*) that is to say, all shall not be endowed with the Qualities of a glorified Body, for some will rise in the same state of Weakness, of Dishonour, in which they lay down, and these as Christ said, shall rise *unto a Resurrection of Judgment*, (*r*) But others shall rise and be changed; what is weak shall be changed into *Vigor*, and what is dishonour into *Glory*.

(*q*) 1 Cor. c. xv. v. 51.

(*r*) John. c. v. v. 29

This is the Mystery of our *Faith;* what therefore I intend in the *first* place, is to set before you the Proofs for our Belief of *the Resurrection;* and *Secondly*, to explain to you the state

The Divis*ion*

state of the *Just* and that of the *Reprobate* in the general Resurrection, according to the Scripture; how some will rise to a Resurrection of *Life;* and others to a Resurrection of *Judgment;* and how this is a great motive for us to lead a pious and holy Life.

The Resurrection of the Dead, is easily proved from the *Faith* or Belief of the Patriarchs, the Oracles of the Prophets. the Words of Christ, and the Doctrine of the Apostles; the *Patriarchs* hoped in it, as we may see from the Words of holy Job, *I know* says he, *that my Redeemer liveth, and in the last Day I shall rise out of the Earth, and I shall be cloathed again with my Skin, and in my Flesh I shall see my God, whom I myself shall see, and my own Eyes shall behold, and I and not another, this my hope is laid up in my Bosom.* (*f*) The *Prophets* foretold it, as we find from the Words of the Prophet Daniel, speaking of those who lay buried in the Earth, *some,* says he, *will rise to Life everlasting, and others to everlasting Confusion:* (*t*) Each one according to his Merits and Demerits in this Life, or as St. Paul expresses it, *according to what he has done,* whilest living in his Body, *whether it be good or Evil.* (*u*) Christ taught this great Truth against the *Sadducees*, who denied the Resurrection of the Body; but in order to prevent the like Mistake in any of his Disciples or Followers, he hath added such clear and perfect Declarations of the *Resurrection,* as to set it out of all Doubt; *The Hour is come,* says our Blessed Redeemer, *wherein all that are in the Grave, shall hear the Voice of the Son of God; and they that have done good things shall come*

P. I.

(*f*) Job. c. xix. v. 25. 26. 27.

(*t*) Dan. c. xii. v. 2.

(*u*) 2 Cor. c. v. v. 14.

come forth unto the *Resurrection of Life*, but they that have done *Evil unto the Resurrection of Judgment*. (w) The future Judgment which our Saviour Christ frequently makes mention of, is constantly ushered in with previous Circumstances of a Resurrection; the Rewards which he promises to his faithful Servants are founded solely in this, that they are not to be raised to Riches and Honours, but to *Life immortal*; and for all their Sufferings, all their Losses, and Self denials, they are to receive a Reward or *Recompence*, not in this frail and uncertain Life, but *at the Resurrection of the just*. (x)

(w) John c. v. v. 28. 29.

(x) Luke c. xiv. v. 15.

St. Paul sufficiently proves to the Corinthians *the Resurrection of the Body*, by this Argument, *if there be no Resurrection of the Dead*, upon account of the impossibility thereof, *then Christ is not risen again*, there being no more impossibility that one *mortal* Body should put on *immortality* than another, *and if Christ be not risen again, then is our Faith vain, and you are as yet in your Sins:* (y) And thus of Course the whole Scheme of your Christian Religion must fall to the Ground. But my present Design, is not so much to make a Defence of this our *Belief* from Scripture, (which some will not believe in, or attend to) as by some other Arguments.

(y) 1 Cor. c. xv. v. 13, 14, 18.

The *first* is, that Divine justice demands a *Resurrection*; that Judgment which is appointed at the last day, must be fully and compleatly just, as being the last; and the Distribution of Rewards and Punishments must be perfectly equitable, because eternal: How then can this Judgment be compleatly Just, without the whole Man be represented in Judgment at the last Day?

Day? For such as a Man was while he lived, so the same ought to be judged, because his Life is the Cause of his Judgment; now the Soul did not run the course of his Life alone, for his Body was it's constant Partner both in Vices and Virtues, in Sin and Merit, in Time and Place, in Action and Passion, in Pain and Pleasure; therefore these two inseparable Partners, and Accomplices in the same Guilt, constant shares of each others Joys and Sorrows, cannot be separated in Judgment, who were inseparable in Life, and in all those Actions which are the Cause of Judgment; this Judgment then is not compleatly just, except the Body and Soul both receive Judgment; and the Reason is, because the Judgment is not fully severe, without it punishes and rewards the Accomplices. Again in this last Judgment, the Laws of Retaliation, are to be executed with just Revenge, which renders like for like; but this does not seem possible except the Body rise and be represented in Judgment, for how can like for like be rendred, and the same kind of Punishment be returned, where there is not the same Person to suffer a return of it? How can the Persecutor endure or suffer the same, which he tyrannically made the Martyr suffer in the Flesh, except the Persecutor be represented in the Flesh? How can the Martyr receive his Reward by the Law of retaliation, if he is tormented in the Flesh, and without the Flesh rewarded? Divine Judgment then demands *a Resurrection of the Flesh*.

In the next place we are to examine and see, if God himself has sufficient Power to raise the Dead, or whether he be able to restore and rebuild

build the Tabernacle of a human Body that is putrified, or diffolved into duft, or by whatfoever Caufe made away. I anfwer firft, that the Power of God is not to be arraigned or called in Queftion, for he is all *Powerful*, *Almighty*, and can do all things what ever he pleafes, for as he made all things out of nothing, fo he can reftore the fame things if reduced into nothing; and as he made human Bodies out of the Elements, knowing what Parts and Parcels he chofe to frame their Structure, fo by the fame Knowledge he can find the fame Parts and Parcels again, and by the fame Power compofe them together again; for he who made the human Body out of thofe Parts at firft, and the Elements themfelves out of nothing, furely cannot want Knowledge to find the fame Parcels again. For why fays St. Paul, *fhould it be thought a thing incredible, that God fhould raife the Dead?* (z) Since the Refurrection of the Body is evident in the Similitude of feed, for do you not fee *that which thou fowefl, is not quickened, except it die firft.* (a) And do you not fee Refurrections through all Nature, and one fpringing from the Corruption of another, and nothing perifhes, but to give Birth to fome thing elfe. God preaching to us the Refurrection in his Works, before his Words, that we might believe him to be the Reftorer of human Bodies, whom we daily fee to be the Reftorer of all things.

Since then Juftice demands it, and God is able to do it, it remains to confider whether thefe Bodies of ours are worthy of a *Refurrection;* let us only obferve how God himfelf has honoured the

(z) Acts. c.xxvi.v. 8.

(a) 1 Cor. c. xv. v. 36.

the Flesh, that we may think it worthy to rise again from the dead. First, it was formed by the hand of God, made indeed out of Clay, but honoured as often as God had touched it when he gave it it's Form, and drew the Lineaments of a human Body: Let us consider the Wisdom, Care, Providence, Council, and Affection of Almighty God, knowing that his eternal Son *Jesus Christ* was to be born of that Flesh. Then consider again the Glory of the Flesh, because God himself appeared in the Flesh, was born, lived and died, rose and ascended, and sits at the right-hand of his eternal Father, in the Flesh; he worked Miracles in favour of the Flesh; he calls our Bodies the Members of his own; he sent the holy Spirit to inhabit in them, and to enrich them with all his Gifts.

There is still another Right or Privilege belonging to our Bodies, viz. the Soul can obtain no Merit, nor Sanctifying Grace, but while it is in the Body; besides, the Soul cannot be consecrated to God by the Sacraments but in the Flesh; the Flesh is washed in Baptism, that the Soul may be purified; the Flesh receives the Imposition of Hands, that the Soul may be enlightened with the Spirit of God; in a Word, all the Sacrifices of Christian Mortifications, Fastings, Penance, Charity, and Virginity, are all made in the Flesh: What will you say again of this human Body, when for the Name of Christ, for the Honour of God, for the sake of Justice, for the Belief of the true Christian Religion, it is dragged out and exposed to the Publick hatred; when it is starved in a Prison for want of Nourishment, or dies in Torture

for

for the fake of Chrift? That Flefh which has been confecrated by Sacraments, and in which the Living Soul has exerted all its pious Actions Virtues, and Merits; In a Word, whofe Purities God fo much loves; whofe Chaftifements God fo much approves; whofe Martyrdoms God fo highly prizes; what, fhall not that Flefh rife again, which by fo many Titles belongs to God? O Chriftians, let it never be faid, that the Members of Chrift, the Temple of the Holy Ghoft, the Inftruments of his Sacraments, the Tabernacle of his Gifts, the Organ of his Virtues, the Martyrs of his Faith, fhould lye deftitute for ever in the Duft. Give me now leave to afk you before I conclude this Point, what did Chrift undertake to fave? Was it not that which muft have perifhed; and what do you fay muft have perifhed? Man without doubt. I afk was it the whole Man or a Part? The whole Man without queftion, the whole then fhall be faved by Chrift; as the whole muft have perifhed, then moft certainly the Flefh will rife again, the fame and entire, and Chrift is the Surety for it, who will reprefent the whole Subftance in Judgment, that the fame may be judged and punifhed which finned; or that the whole Subftance may be faved, as the whole had perifhed: Thus far to confirm our Faith of the Refurrection.

Let us now fee what will be the State of the Refurrection, according to the Scripture; and how all this is a Motive for Chriftians to lead a holy and pious Life.

All mankind fhall rife from the Dead; and proceed forth out of their Graves, the very

fame

same *individual* Persons they were before, but their Countenances no doubt much changed; a Sense of Guilt in some, and a Sense of Innocence in others, will paint upon their Faces very different Aspects, of heavenly Joy, and hellish Sorrows.

St. Paul tells the Corrinthians, (*b*) that the Body is sown in *Corruption*, but it shall rise in *Incorruption;* it is sown in *Weakness*, it shall rise in *Vigour;* it is sown in *dishonour*, it shall rise in *Glory;* it is sown a *Natural* Body, it shall rise a *Spiritual* one. From hence you see in the *first* place, that the Body is sown in *Corruption*, with a natural Tendency to decay and putrify in the Grave; but it will *rise in Incorruption;* it hath no longer that Tendency. What an immortal Body is, who can tell? But it is enough for us to know that it will be *immortal,* that is above all the Causes of Death, and above the fear of it, that it can suffer and die no more, and that Death in that state will have no more Dominion over us, than over *Jesus Christ* Himself risen from the Dead. *Secondly,* the Body is sown in *Weakness,* heavy, dull, wrought upon with Labour and Difficulty, troublesome to itself, subject to almost innumerable Wants and Infirmities, and when laid in the Grave inanimate without Motion, but it shall rise in Power and *Vigour,* which no Youth can equal, or Age decay; with *Strength* which no force can resist, and which will need no Aid to strengthen it; whatsoever Action or Motion it undertakes, where the Soul moves it, its own strength will carry it; the sordid Parts are all subsided, even Air itself becomes too gross for it, through which

(*b*) 1 Cor. c. xv.

which by a specifick Levity, it shoots like a Meteor to meet its Lord in the Regions of a purer Æther. (c) *Thirdly*, the Body is sown in *Dishonour*, vile Earth, oftentimes deformed, and loathsome, and when in the Grave, deprived of Aspect and Figure. But it shall rise in *Glory*, beautiful, venerable, brighter than the Stars; (d) Resplendant as the Sun: (e) And like unto the glorious Body of Christ: (f) No longer the dark Prison of the Soul, but transmitting even her brightest Rays with additional Lustre. *Lastly*, it is sown a *Natural* Body, it shall rise a *Spiritual* Body; not a mere Spirit, but with Flesh and Bones, as our Saviour Christ had after his Resurrection: (g) The very same Body as before, but purified and refined from that which corrupted it's Nature; from the Rebellion of the Flesh; from all that is sensual, brutal and earthly; such are the Honours reserved for this now sordid, this unworthy Mass of Flesh.

(c) Thes. c.iv.v.16
(d) Dan. c.xii.v.3.
(e) Mat.c. xiii.v.43.
(f) Phil. c.iii.v.21.
(g) Luk. c. 24.v.39

But alas! this Honour will not extend to all the Dead, for some will rise to everlasting Life; and others to everlasting Shame and Contempt; yet even these shall be raised in *Incorruption* and Immortality, but to their Sorrow and eternal Curse; which I shall hereafter shew you. Let us now consider what an agreeable and surprising Change it will be, for the just Soul to enter into it's incorruptible and glorified Body; for a Man to see himself in an Instant recovered out of the Grave, and raised above the Power of Death and Hell: O Christians what Transport of joy must he feel This is the state of a happy

happy Refurrection, and this is the *Hope* of all good Chriftians.

For without this Hope and Faith, the Gofpel which recommends to us Mortification, felf-denial and fuffering, would but ferve to make Men miferable, if our Bodies were not to rife again; thofe who fuffer in them for the fake of *Jefus Chrift*, fuffer like the Criminals, and the Wicked carry off the Recompence. But the hopes of the *Refurrection* of the Body, make Death not only fupportable, but even comfortable to the good Chriftian; why then do we abhor Death? Why do we look pale at the Grave and Sepulchre? For do we not know that the Grain cannot fructify, without it firft perifhes; let our Bodies be turned into Duft, let them be putrified or devoured, if we find them again in the Refurrection of the Juft, all is well; in this Hope we courageoufly fupport Death, and the fame is our Comfort, when no other Confolation is left, in the lofs of our Friends, &c.

See here the glorious End of Chriftians; the fame is their End, as was the glorious End of *Jefus Chrift*. Who is not then animated to lead a Chriftian Life, who confiders his End? But remember this, that Man fhall never attain fo glorious an End, who does not keep the Commandments of God, who does not lead a pious and Chriftian Life, who does not live according to the Maxims of the Gofpel; *for what a Man fows that he fhall reap;* (*h*) let every one then take heed what he fows; for he that foweth Corruption, fhall reap no other. A Chriftian muft preferve himfelf from all Pain both of the Flefh and

(*h*) Gal. c. vi. v. 8.

the

the Spirit, if he hopes to arrive at this incorruptible Inheritance. O Dear Chriſtians be not deceived by others, nor deceive yourſelves ; for God has not prepared this incorruptible Inheritance for wilful Sinners who corrupt themſelves. Believe me Chriſtians, that neither thoſe who defile their Bodies with Luſt ; nor thoſe who deſtroy them with Intemperance ; nor thoſe who pamper them with Delicacies ; nor thoſe who make them Inſtruments of Senſuality and Iniquity, whatever has been their dead Faith, and Religion abuſed, ſhall not find their Place in the Reſurrecton of the Juſt. In a Word, thoſe who have made their Bodies partners with the Soul in pious and virtuous Actions, as Sufferings, Mortifications, Faſtings, Works of Mercy and the like, ſhall both be reunited, that both may be glorified through Jeſus Chriſt.

ARTICLE.

ARTICLE, XII.

DISCOURSE, I.

Life Everlasting.

The Wicked, shall go into everlasting Punishment, But the Just into Life everlasting. Mat. c. xxv. v. 46.

BY this last Article of our Creed, we are put in Mind of the glorious End, for which the Almighty created and redeemed Mankind; and that after the general Resurrection will succeed *Life Everlasting*, that is to say, a perpetual Existence of an immortal Life; we are also to believe, that there will be two Conditions or States of being after this Life; the one most *miserable*, the other most *Happy;* and that neither of them will ever have an End; and that all Mankind shall either be of the one or the other, either of the Number of the *Elect*, or of the Number of the *Reprobate*, of them that go to *Heaven*, or of those who go to *Hell*. Therefore now is the

Time

Time during this mortal Life to prepare ourselves so, as to be of the Number of the *Just*, in order to escape that of the *Wicked*; for after this Life, there will be no more Time for us: And doubtless we shall prepare ourselves, if we seriously consider well, what eternal *Misery*, and eternal *Happiness* is.

The Divis{.} And in order to this Preparation, I shall endeavour in this Discourse, to lay before you the *Everlasting Misery* of the Damned. In the *first* place we will consider the Torments of *Hell*; the Nature of them; their Violence; their Duration; and all that makes those Pains great, dreadful, and intolerable; and *Secondly*, I shall exhort you to avoid those Torments, by taking effectual means, in order to prevent your being plunged into those endless Miseries.

P. I. The Subject Dear Christians, I am now entering upon, is most dreadful and terrible. The Thoughts of Death, the Grave, the Corruption, the Worms, and the Dust, which all Mankind must turn into, are nothing to the Consideration of the Abyss of Hell, which all unrepenting Sinners must descend into. Wars, Famines, Plagues, Fires, or all that is painful among us here is but trifling, or rather a mere shadow, if compared to Hell Fire. My design is not to disturb my Neighbour's Peace, or to interrupt the innocent Enjoyment of Life by this Discourse; but rather to add more happy Days to their Lives; the Thoughts of Hell will make every Mans Life more Happy, because more Innocent, it will make all our Pains more tolerable. Virtue pleasanter, and Hardships easier, and moderate the worst of our Fears; but be this as it may, I cannot dissemble the

Truth

Truth. Hell is a supreme Evil, or Collection of all Miseries together, without the Mixture of any Good; Pains without any Rest; Sorrows without any Comfort; Pains intollerable beyond all Patience; not like the Pains we endure here, but Pains of an universal, perfect, and complete Misery. Who can dissemble so great a Truth? It is the Truth that makes me describe it; and the ardent desire I have, that none may fall into this Abyss of Torments will not suffer me to be silent; and especially so, as this Consideration has been the Cause of many Thousands escaping Damnation, and therefore may be of some Profit to you; remember that whether you will, or will not think of it, Hell, is Hell still, and wilful Sinners every Day descend into it; and it may be, because they did not reflect upon it with Attention in their Life time: But this, Dear Christians, is now in your Power at present, only think what the poor damned Souls would give for the same Opportunity, that is now offered you, and then make good use of it yourselves. *

Hell

* There were certain ancient Hereticks, viz. the Gnosticks, who denied this Article of *Life Everlasting*. They divided all Mankind into three parts, viz. *earthly*, *animal*, and *Spiritual*: the first of which, and part of the second, they affirmed, would be annihilated, or reduced to nothing by the general Conflagration at the end of the World, whilst only the *Spiritual* and part of the *animal*, should be made immortal and eternal. From whence we find, that *St. Irenæus* a Cotemporary with these Hereticks, and their greatest Antagonist and Confuter, doth in opposition to their Heresy, thus express in his Creed the final Determination of every Man; that after the Resurrection, *Christ* shall render a righteous

Judgment

Hell is often in the Scriptures reprefented to us under the Notion of Fire, *a Lake of burning Fire,* (*i*) *a Lake of Fire and Brimſtone,* (*k*) *a Land of burning Pitch,* (*l*) *a fiery Furnace,* (*m*) *Fire never to be ſquenched*; (*n*) Wherein the Bodies of the damned, are to burn for ever without confuming. Flames which after Millions and Millions of Years burning, are ſtill as lively, active, and vigorous as at the firſt Day. See here, Dear Chriſtians, a frightful Deſcription of Hell, at the firſt Entrance: I need not aggravate this Pain of Fire, I need not uſe Words and Figures of Amplification, to make you ſenſible of its Violence; for the very name of Fire at the firſt hearing, founds in our Ears ſomething inſupportable and beyond all Expreſſion; for *who of you,* crys out the Prophet, (*o*) *can dwell with devouring fire, or Everlaſting burnings?* To have no other Houſe to dwell in but Fire, burning, a red hot Priſon, no Ground to tread on but Fire, no Bed to lie on but Fire; no Air to breath in but Flames, who can ſupport even

(*i*) Revl. 14. et. 20:
(*k*) Iſa. c. 30.
(*l*) Job. c. x.
(*m*) Mat. c. xl.
(*n*) Mark. c. ix.

(*o*) Iſa. c. xxxiii. v. 14.

Judgment unto all. *The wicked, unjuſt, and ungodly Men, He will ſend into everlaſting Fire; but to the juſt and righteous, and thoſe who keep his Commandments, he will give immortality and eternal Glory.* Lib. 1. c. ii. n. 36. And to the ſame effect *Tertullian* lays in one of his Creeds, which he deſignedly repeats in oppoſition to the *Gnoſticks*, and other Hereticks of his time, that Chriſt ſhall come in *Glory* to receive the Saints into the Fruit of eternal Life, and to ſentence the prophane to everlaſting Fire. *Ad ſumendos Sanctos in vitæ æternæ fructum, et ad prophanos judicandos igni perpetuo. De Præſcript. adverſ. Hæret.* p. 73. See alſo St. Auguſtin, who ſays much the ſame in his Explication of this Article. Tom. 3. Enchrid. ad Laurent. c. cx. p. 252.

hits

Art. XII. *Disc.* I.

this Thought? Then consider that Hell is in the Nature of a Prison from whence there is no Redemption; in this Prison, the holy Scriptures tell us of Chains, not like those which bind our Criminals here, but woful Chains which confine the damned in their Torments, without leaving them any kind of Liberty; (*p*) but confining and binding them fast upon a Bed of Sorrow, where the Body is surrounded on all sides with Fire, not being able to make one Motion of Ease, but as the Scripture expresses it, must lie upon that Side where it falls for Eternity; for *which way soever the Tree falls, there it shall lie.* (*q*) Such are the Fires, Prisons, and Chains of Hell.

(*p*) Mat. c. xxii.

(*q*) Eccles. c. xi. v. 3.

Have you, Dear Christians, any Faith of this great Truth; is there any Fear of God amongst Men, when they commit Mortal or grievous Sins with so much Indifferency? Do you believe this, and shew so little Religion? And be so conceited with yourselves for the little Good you do, in comparison of so much Evil. And never think of the Hell reserved for the Wicked: O Christians, let us correct such insupportable Folly, and here once for all, think whether or no, there is not greater Reason to correct our own Lives, than censure other Men. I hope that some will grow wiser by this Consideration. But as yet I have shewn you nothing of the Torments of Hell; though this one Point of Fire, is enough to confound all our Thoughts; and you may see it is no Vision or Imagination of mine, but the Words and Expressions of holy Scripture.

Now

Now from the same holy Scripture, I will shew you what makes the pains of Hell so intolerably great, amazing, and excessive above all Weight and Measure of Suffering. There is no Pain in this Life but ceases sometimes; for either it is eased by a Medicine, or an interval, or by sleep; and the sharpness of one Pain deadens the Sense of another; but you may easily conceive, that this has no place in Hell: The Scripture tells us, that they have no Rest from Age to Age; there, Dear Christians, is no Rest by Day, no Sleep by Night; O insupportable! Pains without any Rest? Again the Pains of this Life cannot encrease to any extreme Violence, because our Bodies here are too Weak to suffer much; so that when the Pain encreases beyond the Measure of Mortal Man, it causes Death, and then the Pain ends; but it is not so in Hell, because there Men will be Immortal in their Pain, and for ever live in eternal Death, always dying with Pain, but never die, so that the Fire never going out, will exercise its full Violence upon the human Body, and pierce every Member, every Joint, every Bone, every Artery, every Nerve, every Sinew, every Fibre, with so many distinct and never ending Pains. Again what ever are the Pains of this Life, a Man has many Reliefs and Comforts; the Help of Physicians, the Compassion of Friends; the Support of a good Conscience; his own Patience, or at least the Hope of their ending in Death; which is the last Relief of the miserable. But the Pains of the damned, have their Continuance without ceasing or ever ending; so in those Pains they

are

Art. XII. Disc. 1.

are bereaved of all Comfort whatsoever, and all Refreshments universally; we have a Proof of this in the holy Scripture from the Mouth of Jesus Christ himself, in the Parable of *Dives* and *Lazarus* mentioned in St. Luke, (r) we are (r)c. xvi. there told, that the Rich Glutton in Hell, only v. 24. begged for one Drop of Water to cool his Tongue; and even this was denied him; if therefore he was refused, one Drop of Water, then it is evident as I said before, that there are no Reliefs, no Comforts, no Refreshments in Hell, but Pains without any Relief at all. Now to sum up all this, if a Man here in Pain, is apt to think the Time so long, as to count the Days, the Hours, and even the Minutes, may we not then make some Guess? How long and insupportable will these sad Hours in Hell seem, how long every Moment? Are not then those Pains of Hell, Torments enough to confound us, and to frighten us into a good Life, and to make all other Pains in this World tolerable?

I say nothing in particular of the Torments that will afflict every Sense, what hellish Objects will be presented to the Eyes, what Groans and Howlings will afflict the Ears, what Pains of Retaliation Justice has invented to punish the Senses, which were made the Organs of sensual Pleasures here, what Stenches to afflict the smell in this Land of Nauseousness, Pestilence, and Corruption, as Isaias calls it, (s) (s) c. xxxiv. in this dark Land covered over with the Shades of Death, as it is called by holy Job, (t) where (t)c. x. v. no Order, but where eternal Horror dwells. 22. I think I have said enough concerning the Pains of Senfe; and here I cannot but remind you again, that you be not deceived: Hell is full of People, who flattered themfelves they fhould never come there, but who fhall never go out from thence: Let me now tell you that there is no efcaping Hell, but by becoming innocent: O let us then become innocent! and look upon all, that is faid to the contrary for infupportable Folly, and this is growing Wife by the confideration of Hell Fire.

But I have only as yet defcribed one part of the Torments of Hell, viz. the Pain of *Senfe;* but there is another great Pain in Hell, which is called the Pain of *Lofs,* which is the Pain of the Mind, and which is faid to be more grievous and intolerable, than the Pain of *Senfe.* The holy Scripture tells us how the Damned in Hell lament the Lofs of Heaven, and envy the Glory of the Saints: *Thefe are the Men,* fay they, *whom we once held in Derifion; we thought their Lives Madnefs, and their End without Honour;* but fee they are *now numbered among the Children of God, and with the Saints is their eternal lot.* (*u*) They fee the fovereign Good they have loft in God; and this irrecoverable Lofs is the Torment of their Mind; hence come the Weeping and gnafhing of Teeth in thofe horrid Dungeons; Groans and Lamentations of Men that fuffer the Torment of Mind; as well as Cries and Shrieks of thofe, that fuffer Pain in the Body: Tones of the deepeft Affliction, of the moft doleful Melancholy, of eternal Sorrow: Who can recount the Difcourfes, in which thofe unfortunate Perfons will pafs their melancholy Hours in Hell, in the fight of what they have loft, and what they have got

(*u*) Wifd. c. v.

for

for it? remembering their paſt Pleaſures the Cauſe of all their Wo; what horrid Crimes they committed, and for how little Gain, and with how little Pains all might have been avoided; thus they will paſs their melancholy Hours, in thinking of the Loſs of God, in the deepeſt Afflictions, Reſentments, Griefs, and Sorrows, in anxious and unprofitable Thoughts, and Remembrances, in Tears that are eternal and unfruitful.

But this is not the only Pain of their Souls; their Paſſions which they ſo indulged in this Life, will prove to be ſome of the greateſt Pains in Hell; for every one in Hell will have the ſame Paſſions he indulged in this Life, and what more juſt? Now in Hell, the Sinner will find no Objects to gratify thoſe Paſſions, being out of the Poſſeſſion of all Good, he will find nothing to gratify one Paſſion, one Appetite, one Deſire, either of Pride, Luſt, Gluttony, Envy, or Revenge; but he will find himſelf in a State, where he miſſes of all his Aims, and his Deſires are all croſſed, and ſtill he cannot curb his Paſſion, but feels an eternal Paſſion for that, which he can never, never more enjoy. This, Dear Chriſtians, is the Puniſhment of Paſſion indulged, and this ſo great a Hell, that ſome have though fooliſhly affirmed, there is no other; but to this we muſt add many others, viz. the Hell that every one will ſuffer from the Company which is there; from the Company of Devils, who hate the Damned, and the Damned them; and yet are in the Devils Slavery; from the Company of the other Damned, who are all troubleſome and irkſome to each other, by Mockeries and

Railery, and Infults, and all the Difagreement of Humour and Temper, and all the Difagreement that Spirits can be capable of; which will caufe fuch Curfes, Imprecations, Blafphemies and Revilings, and fuch abufive Difcourfe, as the Wicked make ufe of here on Earth, which they uttered in Defiance of the Gofpel, and which they have now juftly brought upon their own Heads. But the greateft Pain of all is yet to come.

I mean the Thoughts of Eternity, that Worm which never dies, this one Thought confounds them for ever, and is enough to amaze all underftanding; for as Eternity is infinite, fo it adds an incredible and infinite Weight to every Torment in Hell; to feel fuch Pains, and then to think, that every diftinct Pain is eternal; that their State is unchangeable, that the Decrees of God are irreverfible, and their Torments never, never more to End; though every Sand on the Sea Shore, every drop of Water, every Leaf of the Trees, fhould ftand for ten Thoufand Millions of Years; that at the End of all this immenfe Time, they are ftill at the beginning of Eternity which never ends, but ever begins: This Thought I fay, is abfolutely the greateft Torment of Hell. For as the greateft Evil, is made tolerable by *Hope*, fo the leaft Evil, is made grievous and intolerable by *Defpair;* Defpair is the moft compleat of all Torments, and we fee it, that in temporal Evils which are Pleafures in comparifon of Hell, and may even become Pleafures in Heaven, it often drives Men into Diftraction, or unto voluntary Death; now the Defpair of the Damned is not like our Defpair,

Despair, but a true and perfect Despair; for our Despair has still the Hopes of Death, but theirs has no Hope, not the least Hopes of ever ending; and as they have no Hope, so they have no Patience, which is the only thing that can make Pain supportable; but Patience in that State is impossible, and the Reason is, because Patience proceeds from a certain Knowledge, that their Pain, or Evil will end, and that at the End, there will be a Recompence for the patient Suffering: But alas! the Damned have a certain Knowledge, that their Pains will never end, nor be rewarded, but are Sufferings without End, or without Fruit, and so all Patience in this State, by fatal Necessity, turns into Despair. I have here, Dear Christians, given you a short Description of Hell and eternal Evils; see if it be not the supreme Evil, an universal Misery, so extensive, as to leave no part of the Body free; and to seize every Power of the Soul: Pains of Devils, Pains intollerable, amazing, enough to confound all Understanding; in a Word, a perfect and compleat Misery, where all Evils and no Good is. Who can take a View of this Lake of Misery without Pity for Mankind? Who can survey the Woes prepared for mortal Man, without Eyes of Compassion for the Frailty of his Condition? O Eternal God have Mercy on mortal Man! Stop the Hand that strikes them: Let Mercy prevent them from falling there, where Mercy itself will never deliver them.

Now Dear Christians, perhaps you will say, why do I propose such terrible Objects? My Answer is, for no other End but to induce you to serve God, and that you may escape Hell, by leading a good Life, this is my Design, and ardent Desire; and I am persuaded a serious Thought of Hell, is a great Motive to avoid it; all my Design by this Consideration, is to make Men Sober, Just, and Pious; what remains then, is, to shew you how you may escape these dreadful Woes and Punishments of the Wicked.

All this dreadful Pain in Hell, is caused by the Evil of Sin, and yet we commit mortal or deadly Sin with as much Indifferency, as we drink Water, or eat our Bread; grievous Sins are become the ordinary and daily Actions of human Life, the Matter of a Joke and Jest: Tell me now, whither think you are gone all our lustful Thoughts or Desires, Gluttonies and Drunkenness, all our Oaths, Perjuries, Curses, opprobious Language, Slanders, Detractions, Calumnies, which publick Conversation, and private Friendships are made up of, and which are every Day uttered, but chiefly on Sabbath-Days; and the most outragious Slanders of all, are frequently uttered from the very Pulpit, by Pretenders to Devotion, who defame the Innocent out of an Act of Charity, as they pretend: Whither think you is all this Iniquity gone? I will tell you, to Hell from whence it came, to light the Fires and prepare the Torments for all the Guilty. These vices have only served to prove these Reprobates, who are Guilty; and all those who suffer by them with Patience, merit a Crown of eternal Glory. O Christians, forsake these Paths of Iniquity, which are grown so widened and beaten with Use and Custom

tom of many Thoufands, who are gone to Hell through them; let me now befeech you to think frequently of Hell, and not only to think of it, but of the great Danger you are in of falling into it: For to this Place of Torments are fent all the Impious, thofe who commit Luft or Gluttony; and the Cheat and the Deceiver; and thofe who commit Injuftice of any kind; and the Covetous and the Envious; the Ambitious and Contentious; the Proud and Prophane; the Sacrilegious and Irreligious who do not adore and love God; the Perjured and the Detractor; the Reviler and Difobedient; and all and every one of the vicious, who do not truly and fincerely repent; for there is no effectual way to efcape Hell, but to become Innocent, fince all the Pains of Hell, are caufed by the Evil of Sin.

P. II. Here, Dear Chriftians, I cannot but admonifh you of a great and certain Truth, which is, that Hell may be avoided with very little Pains. Is it not a very obfervable thing, that almoft all Men have but one Paffion to conquer, which if not conquered will conquer them? A Luft, a Gluttony, an Anger, a Detraction, a Sloth, an Envy, a Vanity, &c. and if that one prevailing, and unruly Appetite was conquered, you would fee that their Lives would be innocent, their Confcience eafy, their End happy. Thus you fee what is requifite in order to efcape Hell. The fmall Pains of mortifying one Paffion, which God leaves us for our Trial, the fmall Pains of refifting a Temptation or the like, is the Mortification which God demands of us, and it is this, which moft Men carry unmortified

unmortified to the Grave; and excuse themselves in it all their Lives, throwing the Blame upon frail Nature, or the Temptation of the Devil, and so say they cannot conquer it; but I say, they may and can, for Thousands have done it; and Thousands by the Grace of God will do it again, and every Man can, if his Will be but strong enough. Secure then your Souls by Innocence: Hell may be escaped by very little Pains; by the Mortification of that Passion which tempts you to Sin; but those, who will carry their Passion unmortified to the Grave, are in great Danger of being buried in Hell. Only examine the holy Scriptures, and see if what I say, be not true. Think once more of all these Truths together. First how intollerable the Pains of Hell are; then how many and great our Sins; then for what little Gain we commit them; then from what little Causes they generally proceed; and then with how little Pains all may be avoided.

You see, Dear Christians, the Tendency and Aim of this Discourse; 'tis in order to make Mans Life more Innocent, and as I think more Happy; for what if the Thought and Consideration of Hell should induce a Man to become Sober, Wise, and Just? Where is the Harm? Take notice and reflect what kind of Means, I propose to you in order to escape Hell; see it here all laid before your Eyes: The *first* thing, is to quit those Vices which ruin your Soul, Health, Estate, Reputation, and Families; *Secondly*, to practise those Virtues which will prolong your Lives, preserve your Health, Fortunes, and Honour, and make you beloved ed both by God and Man; is this then disturbing your Peace? No, my Design is rather to increase it, and that you would love your own and other Mens Peace; is this interrupting your Happiness? No certainly, for I prescribe to you the very means in which a happy Life consists; I desire to add happy Days to your Lives; by adding the Peace of a good Conscience to all the rest; to remove by the Thought of Hell, the Guilt of Sin out of Mans Life, and the sting of remorse out of your Consciences, which will moderate the Fear of Hell, and all other Fears; that being set free from the Fears of Hell, you may with perfect Liberty aspire to Heaven: Keep the Commandments of God, and let no Passion overcome you to transgress them; keep the Precepts of the Church, and let no Sloth serve you for an Excuse; these are the means to escape Hell, these are the means to gain the Happiness of this Life, and the Felicity of the Kingdom of Heaven. Besides this, in order to atone and satisfy for our Sins, let us offer up daily to Almighty God all our Sufferings, Mortifications, Losses, Crosses, and Contradictions, which are sent us, not only to punish our Sins, but even to merit Heaven: Only consider how great a Reward attends the least Christian suffering in this Life, and how unfruitful are the Tears and Sufferings of the Damned; and yet alas! for Fear of suffering the least temporal Loss or Inconvenience, we see Men forsake God, their Conscience, and their Religion; and Thousands are backward in embracing the Truth, for fear of some small Suffering, or Inconvenience, which is the very means alloted by God both to escape Hell, and merit Heaven. And what then ; shall we, who know the Merits of such Sufferings repine at them? Ought we not rather to bless God, and render him our Thanks, that as we have so often deserved Hell, we are still preserved from it, and have it in our Power as yet to obtain Heaven.

Let us then grow wise by these Considerations, let us grow more innocent, let us grow more virtuous, more exact Observers both of God's Commandments and his Church; more punctual in all Christian Duties; more mortified and patient in sufferings, more sober, just, temperate, and charitable in thought, word, and deed; more zealous, religious, and devout in the Divine Service; and more diligent in frequenting the Sacraments: Remember and call to Mind frequently, the dreadful Torments of Hell; nothing is more proper to correct our Follies, nothing will induce Sinners sooner to Repentance, and all Mankind to the Practice of an Innocent Life, and consequently will sooner lead us to Heaven; and therefore, the Thought and Consideration of Hell, is the way of Sanctity, Beatitude, and eternal Life; which is what I intend to treat of in the next Discourse, wishing at the same time we may all arrive at it.

ARTICLE,

ARTICLE, XII.

DISCOURSE. II.

Life Everlasting.

The Wicked, *shall go into Everlasting Punishment, But the Just into Life Everlasting.* Mat. c. xxv. v. 46.

IN the preceding Discourse, I laid before you a small sketch of the horrible, and endless Woes, the *Wicked* must suffer for all Eternity, in the Kingdom of Darkness, the Flames of Hell. What then I intend in this (which ends the Creed), is *first*, to describe to you the Felicity and Happiness, which the *just* shall enjoy forever in the Kingdom of Heaven; and so let you see how ravishing are it's Joys, and how glorious the Crown. *Secondly*, I shall encourage you to live in such a manner, as to merit it by a virtuous Life, and not to lose it for mere Shadows. But this, Dear Christians, is a Subject so sublime, that the true Nature thereof cannot possibly be comprehended by any human means; so that to describe it, nothing less than the Eloquence of an Angel, is capable of it; since nothing here on Earth, bears the least Proportion to the Glory and Happiness of that eternal Kingdom; for whatever I can say of it, falls infinitely short of the Subject; and therefore I am under a necessity of shewing you, *what it is not*, in order to supply my inability of demonstrating to you, *what it really* is. All I can then do, is to let you see, what the Scripture reveals to us concerning this eternal Beatitude, where we shall see enough to make this World a Thousand times contemptible.

The Happiness of Heaven is to see God: This is *everlasting Life*, this is essential Beatitude.

P. I. Now concerning the clear Sight and Vision of God, let us see what the holy Scripture says of it. First, St. Paul says, that we *now behold him in a Glass, in Obscurity; then* we shall see him *Face to Face; now I know* him only *imperfectly, but then I shall know him as I am known by him.* (w) And (w) 1 Cor. c. xiii. v. 12 in another place he says, when we shall behold the Glory of God, by the clear Sight of it, we shall be transfigur'd, and pass on from Brightness into Brightness; approaching still nearer and nearer in likeness to God. Let us hear what St. John the Evangelist says of it, *we are already made Sons of God; but it does not appear we shall be like to him, because we shall see him as he is in himself;* here Christians, you see what is promised us, a clear Sight of the living God, of the Almighty, Eternal, and Infinite God. Now the Sight of God, is the sovereign Felicity of the Saints; for he who sees what is worthy of Love, and

1 Ep. St. John. c. iii. v. 2.

and loves what he sees, and desires to possess what he loves, and possesses what he desires, and is disquieted with no anxious Fear of losing the Possession, this Man is what we call Happy, this is what we count Felicity upon Earth: Now this Vision or Sight of God, causes this in the utmost degree; here you see all Good; as when Moses prayed to see God, it was answered him, *I will shew thee all Good;* here then you see the sovereign Good, you eternally love all you see, eternally desire all you love, and eternally possess all you desire, and are not disquieted with any Fear of losing the Possession; therefore the Vision of God is supreme Beatitude. I do not pretend to make you comprehend this, the carnal, the sensual, the voluptuous, the sinful, the worldly Man, will understand nothing of it; but give me, says St. Augustin, a Man who loves, a Man who desires, a Man who sighs for Heaven, and he will understand. (x) So far at least we know, that to see God, is to see the sovereign Good; and the sovereign Good does not only satiate some of our Desires, but all our Desires; which is a Pleasure quite unknown in this World: And that it does not only set you free from some, but from all Miseries, which is another Pleasure quite unexperienced upon Earth. This we know again, that if the Enjoyment of Creatures here in this Life, can cause so great a Sense of Pleasure in Man; that which is increated, eternal, and infinite; and that which is the Substance of these Shadows, the Truth and Reality of these Dreams, will make quite different Impressions, will affect you after a much
more

Exod. c. xxxiii. v. 19.

(x) de Civ. dei. L. xv.

more lively and active Manner; will cause a far different Sense of Pleasure: Pleasures wholly unexperienced, new Ravishments, new Joys, new Tranquility, of which there can be no Experience upon Earth: Joys amazingly great, full of surprize, and a thousand Astonishments, being what surpasses all Experience, Thought, Desire, Hope, and Expectation; for as St. Paul says, *(y) the Eye has not seen nor the Ear heard, nor has it entered into the Heart of Man,* to conceive, *what God has prepared for those who Love him.*

(y) 1 Cor. c. ii. v. 9.

There are three things which make up all the Felicity, or Happiness of this World, and these are *Riches, Honours,* and *Pleasures.* There are in Heaven all *Riches,* not like ours which are perishable, but incorruptible, because the Possessors shall live eternally to enjoy them; not like ours which impoverish one to enrich another; which breed Covetousness in the Mind; which are acquired with Labour and Toil; possessed with Cares and Fears, and lost with Grief and Anxieties: But true Riches, a hidden Treasure that is unknown to Men, a precious Pearl. Riches that are free from Covetousness, free from Cares and Strife, free from Envy, Tears and Loss; and therefore the only true, real, substantial, permanent, and eternal Goods. There are also in Heaven, *Honours,* Crowns of Glory, not like our Honours, where Calumnies are mixed with Praises; where Vice is rewarded with Virtue; not like our Fame, which is the Voice of Men subject to Error and Flattery; but Honours of the Just; true Honours which are neither denied to true

Merit

Merit, nor granted to the unworthy. There also dwells eternal *Pleasure*, not like our Pleasures, which are interrupted with many intervals of Sorrow, Grief, and Pain, which only satiate one Desire, only affect one Sense, and which grow tedious in the Enjoyment; but a Torrent of Pleasure, as the Royal Prophet says, which satiates every Desire, affects every Sense, and every Power of the Soul, overflowing all like a Torrent broke loose; Joy which wipes all Grief out of the Mind, and Tears from the Eyes; all Pleasures that belong either to the Happiness of the mind, or perfect state of the Body; a Will without Propension to Evil, Understanding without Error, Memory without Oblivion, Thought without wandering, all Health without any Disease, Blessings in every part, Blessings in the Understanding, Blessings in the Will, Blessings in the Memory, Blessings in the Sight, Blessings in the Hearing, Blessings in all the Senses; therefore this Life cannot be called properly Life, where so few Hours are passed in Pleasure, and the greatest part of our Days in Cares, Fears, Labour, Pains, Sleep, and Insensibility; but that is a true and perfect Life, where every Power of Man's Soul, and every Sense, and all that is Man, lives in perpetual Joy and Beatitude.

What shall I say of the Glory of this Place, the Glory of Heaven? Glorious things are said of the Pity of God, (In the Apocalypse of St. John). Now to frame some faint Idea of the Magnificence of Heaven, only consider that it is the Place made for eternal Pleasure, it is the House

c. xxi.

House, the City, the Kingdom of God, made to shew his Glory; let us then frame to our Imagination an earthly Paradise, where Nature pours out all her Charms, where Magnificence seems exhausted by an unbounded Profuseness, and where Art has left no Room for the least Improvement. But let us pass from the Place to the Blessedness of the Inhabitants: There Quires of Angels of infinite Varieties dwell; there you will discover different Brightnesses in the Saints, different Honours according to their different Merits, Variety of Crowns for variety of glorious Actions; no Envy in the lowest, no Pride in the highest, all delighted and transported with their Crowns, because delighted with that Justice, which bestowed them. Out of this Company are banished all the Impious, no Envier, no Detracter, not one of the Proud, not one of the Ambitious there, for there could be no Heaven where they are: But there dwells Peace and Security, perfect Concord and universal Agreement of Spirit. O blessed Inhabitants in this City of God! Blessed Society among such great and illustrious Persons, all Sons of God, and Spirits of the just and perfect.

Now there are three things, which compleat this Beatitude of the Saints in Heaven; the *first* is, that all these Felicities are pure Felicities, without Mixture of the least Evil; no Miseries exterior or interior, to afflict either Mind or Body; no Labour, Sickness, or Pain; no Fears, Cares, Anxieties, Losses, Sorrows, Griefs, or Tears; because all this is gone and past; no Snares for Innocence, no Precipices for

for Virtue, no fear of Death, but security without Fear, Safety without Danger, Rest without Anxiety, Peace without the least Dissention, Virtue praised without Obloquy, Merit crowned without Envy, Joy succeeded by no Sorrow, Life never ended by Death. The *second* Condition which compleats this Felicity, is their Perpetuity and Eternity; *Perpetuity*, because the Happiness has no Intervals, no Interruption, no change or Shadow of change, all the change there in this Beatitude, if there be any, is, that it shall receive new encrease, and still grow greater and greater, as long as God shall be God: This then compleats the Happiness, its being continual without Interruption ; and eternal without End, and the certainty of that Eternity. This is an entire Possession, when the Felicity is supreme, and the Duration of it eternal; we can have no Sentiments of this here, because our Happiness is all temporal; the Thoughts of Eternity in Heaven will cause quite other Ravishments, other Joys than ours, and a Peace of Mind quite unknown and inconceiveable to us. The *third* Condition, which still augments and compleats this Happiness is, that it is a Happiness which succeeds after so much Misery; so much the sweeter, because it is Rest after hard Labour, Victory after a long and doubtful Combat, Refreshment after Sorrow, Pleasure after Pain, Safety succeeding Danger; O Christians, what an agreeable and surprizing Change! so total and compleat a Happiness, such high honours! This must certainly be an agreeable and surprizing Change, to those who have known little
else

else but Misery, and have felt the State of Suffering; to the Poor, the Injured, the Afflicted, the Despised, and Oppressed. Consider then, Dear Christians, in one view, and see if this be not a compleat and perfect Felicity. *First*, sovereign Good possessed. *Secondly*, Felicity in every Power of the Soul, and every Sense. *Thirdly*, each Felicity in the utmost Degree of Perfection. *Fourthly*, pure Pleasure without the Mixture of any Ill. *Fifthly*, Happiness succeeding many Miseries. *Lastly*, Eternity of that Happiness, and Certainty of that Eternity.

O happy Day, a thousand times happy! when we shall find our Souls to have made this great change! when we shall find ourselves translated into Paradise! when we shall arrive in an instant at the clear Vision of God, for ever fixt in the Possession of the sovereign Good; when we shall look about us, and consider the Haven of Security, in which we are arrived; when we shall cast an Eye back, and view the dangerous Precipices we have past; the doubtful Combats we have sustained; the Jaws of Devils we have escaped; the Miseries from which we are translated; the Dangers in which other Men are labouring; the Damnation into which, many of our Companions and Acquaintance are fallen head-long; the singular Favour and Mercy God has shewn to us; all which must needs augment our Joy and Peace; and makes us value our own most fortunate Lot.

But let us now turn our Consideration upon this Life, and see for what Trifles, what Shadows

dows, Men forfeit so immense a Felicity; let us suppose (as our Saviour Christ says) a Man should gain the whole World; suppose him the most prosperous Man in the World; his Fortune the most splendid, yet Weariness and Tediousness of Spirits, attend the Great, as well as those of a meaner Condition; but make if you please the most of his Gain, for the Loss of his Soul, I will uphold he has lost Heaven to gain a Trifle, and my Reason is this, because all human Felicity is built upon Man's Life, and Life is the Basis, upon which all the Grandeur of his Fortune must depend: For his Felicity must end with his Life, and his Life must end in Death, and therefore all his Felicities must end and conclude in Nothing: I appeal to every Man's Sense if that which ends in Nothing, when set in Balance with the supreme Happiness, which never ends, be not in the proper Language of Truth, a mere Trifle or Shadow. But why do I talk of gaining the World? No Mortal Man can arrive at that Fortune; and those few who attempted *it* (as an Alexander, Cæsar, &c.) fell in the Enterprize, and got nothing but an untimely Grave.

Let us apply the Supposition, made by our Saviour, of gaining the whole World to practice, because this selling of Heaven for temporal Gain is no Fiction, but a Bargain which Men, too many, God knows, make; let us see then, how much Men do really gain for the Loss of Heaven, and I will allow they may gain some temporal Felicites, and sensual Pleasures, but then we must not forget, that these Felicities are often not better than Dreams, since the Possessors do not always find that Content they expected; we must not forget their Toil and Labour, and that Life perchance for many Years, is to be unpleasant, troublesome and vexatious, before the Possession of these Pleasures can be had; don't forget that these Men are mortal still, and that there is no Felicity in this Life, which is not counterpoised with Mortifications and common Misery; again we must not forget, that temporal Prosperity is subject to changes, and often ends in Adversity, which is worse than nothing; and then we must not forget, that these sinful Satisfactions make the Possessors vile, base, and contemptible, and upon many Considerations, are found to be so much diminished in their Value, that there is scarce any thing left to the Possessor: But why do I speak of Gain, the greatest part of Men lose Heaven and gain nothing, nay the greatest part gain worse than nothing, for after a weary, base, and sinful Life, loss of ease and quiet, worn out with Disorders, they at last lie down in their Graves, and this is the Gain for the Loss of Heaven.

P. II. You here see, Dear Christians, for what Trifles Heaven is lost; let us now see for how little Labour it may be gained. This incorruptible Crown is won by Virtue, so highly prized is Virtue with God, that Heaven is not thought a Reward too great, tho' it is sometimes rewarded and honoured even here upon Earth, but it's just Reward, it's Seat, it's Dignity, Merit, and Favour are all in Heaven. But
one

one thing is certain, that the Occasions of meriting Heaven are almost infinite; Virtue is interwoven with all our daily Employments, and we may if we please make it the Matter of continual Action, there is not one Day, nay scarce an Hour, but we may perform Actions worthy of eternal Life, and those who are disabled from acting, may still merit the same Crown by suffering, and what is still more, these precious Occasions of *Merit* and *Virtue*, can by no Power be taken from us; whether a Man be Rich or Poor, whether he lives in Peace or Persecution, whether he is in Health or Sickness, whether he has Friends or Enemies; nothing of all this can hinder him from being virtuous if he will; they may raise Persecution against him, they may injure and oppress him, and make him lead his Life through a great Variety of Sorrows; but then you must observe, that Variety of Sorrows will still afford him Matter for a new Variety of Virtues, and changing the State of his Life, does but change the Virtue; and certain I am, that neither Men nor Devils can hinder a Man from being virtuous, if he has a Mind so to be; no Power whatever can ravish or take from him, the Opportunities of meriting the Crown of eternal Felicity every Day of his Life. What Excuse then can we make for not doing it? The Crown is glorious; the Labour small; Opportunies innumerable; Virtue does not only gain a Crown of Glory for us hereafter; but it even Crowns us with Felicities in this Life, and creates a Happiness in the Mind unknown to the Wicked; the Care of our Salvation is no ways inconsistent,

ent, with a prudent Care and wife Management for this Life, but it will rather make us more active and induftrious in all Good; what Excufe then have we? Are not thofe who lofe Heaven inexcufable, certainly they are? However, as eafy and familiar as the Occafions of Virtue are, almoft all neglect them; and the Gofpel is verified, that the Way to Heaven is ftrait and narrow, by reafon of the few that pafs through it; and the Way to Perdition wide, (z)tho the Occafions of Salvation are infinite, by reafon of the great Number who neglect them, which ought to make every one folicitous for themfelves, efpecially all thofe, who know they are not in the way to Everlafting Life.

(z) Mat. c.vii.v.13

There are two great Caufes that exclude from the Kingdom of Heaven, viz. *Vicioufnefs*, and *Sloth*; Vice by drawing Men into thofe actions which deferve Hell fire; and *Sloth* by hindering the Performance of thofe actions, which are worthy of eternal Life; I know there are many, who flatter themfelves they fhall gain Heaven time enough after all their Diforders; but let me befeech you, Dear Chriftians, not to deceive yourfelves in a matter of fo great Confequence as your eternal Salvation; only give Ear to what St. Paul writes to the Corinthians, who had the fame falfe Hopes; *do not deceive your felves*, fays he, for *neither the Adulterer, nor Fornicator, nor Thieves, nor the Covetous, nor Drunkards, nor Extortioners, fhall poffefs the Kingdom of God.* (a) You hear from holy Scripture, which is infallible Truth, what Vices exclude from the Kingdom of Heaven; fhun then thofe Vices if you hope to be faved; do not deceive

(a)1 Cor. c. vi.v. 9 10.

deceive yourselves, for Heaven was never made for the flothful, it is a Reward of too great a Price to be granted to the unworthy; but the Truth is, we must act and suffer too, if we hope to carry the Prize of eternal Life; found the holy Scriptures and you will find, that Heaven is the Reward of true Virtue, an Honour granted for glorious Actions; a Crown of Justice, the Reward of sufferings, Mortifications, and self-denials; the Fruit of long labour; a Crown of Victory; a Kingdom taken by Violence; no Man shall carry off the Prize, who has not run out his Course; the Crown is his, who gains the Victory; and none shall be crowned, who has not fought out the Battle.

I have here laid before you great Motives to a good Life, and I beseech you once more to consider them well all in one View. I have given you a Description of the Beatitude or Happiness, which the Just enjoy in the Kingdom of Heaven, viz. sovereign Good possessed; Felicity in every Power of the Soul, and every Sense; all the Happiness that belongs to the Mind, or perfect State of the Body; pure Pleasure without the Mixture of any evil; Eternity of that Happiness; and Certainty of that Eternity; and that we have infinite Occasions of losing this Crown; and also infinite Occasions of gaining it, which nothing but our own Sloth can take from us; and that it is lost for mere Trifles; and may be gained by small Labour; and that Virtue at the same Time it gains Heaven, renders Men happier even in this Life; and that labouring for Heaven does not hinder, a prudent Diligence in our temporal Affairs; from
hence

hence you may see, that it is in your Power to obtain an eternal Crown in the Kingdom of Heaven.

Arm yourselves then, Dear Christians, to this glorious Combat, by the example of Thousands who are gone before you, and have gained the Crown; who were once mortal Men as we are, they had the same corrupt Nature to overcome, and they conquered it; the same Passions to mortify, the same Difficulties to labour with, and some much greater; they were made of the same Flesh and Blood as we, and we have the same Helps as they had, the same Opportunities, nay more than many of them; they met with the same Crosses and Sufferings as we, but by their Patience, they have won a Crown of Glory, which will never fade; they had the same Actions and Employments upon Earth as we now have, and therefore we may if we please, behave our selves as virtuously in them, as they did. Give Ear then to those Persons, who by their Example here upon Earth now speak to you from Heaven, and loudly call you both to the Fight and the Crown; animate yourselves even by the Example of Sinners, that is, let their labouring and toiling for corruptible Gain, encourage you to labour for an incorruptible Crown; consider how much you toil and labour for this World, and do not then judge eternal Life unworthy of some of your Pains. Believe me, Dear Christians, Heaven is worth all you can do and suffer; set the Crown then continually before your Eyes, in every Action and every suffering; and consider that if you will, you may make that Action and suffering

ing worth eternal Life; take off your Affections from temporal Felicities, which make you forget Heaven; for it is to the poor in Spirit to whom Heaven belongs; take Injuries in the Spirit of Meekness, which becomes Christians, and such shall possess the Land of Promise: Blessed are they that mourn in Tears of Penance, for they shall be ravished with the joys of Heaven; keep your Hearts free from the Love of impure, vain, and unlawful Things, for none but the clean of Heart shall see God in his Glory; shew Mercy to other Men: Such are worthy to live in Heaven, from whence all Dissension and Strife is banished; if you will be a Disciple of Christ, suffer for Justice sake; to such Heaven belongs: Be constant in Prayer, in the wholsome use of the Sacraments, and all the Duties of your holy Catholick Religion; be punctual in all the Duties of your State and calling, and Patient in all Sufferings, such will infallibly arrive at Life Everlasting. Amen.

F I N I S.

Y y   A TABLE

A TABLE OF THE CONTENTS.

ON the Necessity of Faith, as also on the Properties, and Requisites thereof. See the Intro. Disc.

On the Existence of a God. Page. 22
On the Unity of God. 25
On the Nature and Attributes of God. 28
On the Divinity of Jesus Christ. 72
On the Incarnation of the Son of God. 81
On the Fruits and Benefits of his Incarnation. 92
On the means how to partake of those Benefits 93
On the Sufferings of Christ. 98
On the Mystery of his Passion. 102
On his Crucifixion. 121
On his Death. 128
On his Burial. 131
On his Descent into Hell. 134
On his Resurrection. 140
On how we ought to imitate his Resurrection 156
On his Ascension into Heaven. 161
On the Reasons of his Ascension. 173
On the meaning of those Words, *he sitteth at the right hand of God.* 180
On the particular Judgment at Death. 189
On the general Judgment at the last Day. 197
On what we ought to believe of the Blessed Trinity. 215
On what we ought to believe of the Holy Ghost

CONTENTS.

Ghost.	216
On what it is to live by the Spirit of the Holy Ghost.	222
On what is meant by the *Term* Church.	230
On the true Church of Christ.	240
On the Unity of the Church.	233
On the Perpetuity of the Church.	239
On the Visibility of the Church.	240
On the Holiness of the Church.	242
On the Universality of the Church.	243
On the Infallibility of the Church.	253
On the Communion of Saints.	247
On the Intercession of the Saints.	250
On praying for the Dead.	251
On the Power of absolving from Sin.	267
On the Disposition the Sinner ought to be in before he can be absolved from his Sins.	274
On the Remission of Sins.	276
On Confession.	278
On the Mercy and Goodness of God towards Sinners.	280
On Death.	288
On the Means how to escape the Death of the Wicked.	297
On the Means how to obtain the Death of the Just.	299
On the Resurrection of the Body at the last Day.	301
On the different State of the *Just*, and that of the *Reprobate* at the last Day.	310
On the Torments of Hell, and the Nature and Duration of them.	315
On the Means how to avoid those dreadful Torments.	327
On the eternal Joys of Heaven.	331
On the Means how to obtain those Joys.	340

ERRATA.

Page.	Line:	Errata.	Correct.
12,	35	were	where
22,	14	every	even,
27,	22	founded	founded,
29,	9	call	calls,
41,	11	menandians	menandrians,
45,	30	adrirble	admirable,
47,	3	as were	as it were,
53,	26	quedem	quidem,
54,	10	born	borne,
68,	22	fynagouge	fynagogue,
72,	20	Arain	Arian,
131,	27	dele	Anacephal,
135,	25	were	where,
135,	27	Origin	Origen,
143,	28	reected	rejected,
149.	8	moſt	muſt,
150,	8.	to be gardener	to be the Gardener,
163,	32	as	and,
170,	26	ut vaginam exempto Chriſto Sedere	Sine Chriſto ut vaginam exempto gladio Sedere,
282,	27	inferior	is inferior,
211,	8	hoping for	hoped for,
212,	12	aſſerting	aſſenting,
112,	18	to	or,
216,	26	their	the,
219,	28	for on	that on,
223,	17	Council	Counſel,
236,	10	for	but,
254,	33	tell	tells,
280,	4	Phort	Short,
292,	13	ſ	c,
	15	his	is,
302,	41	Σαδχες	Σαρχος,

The courteous Reader will pleaſe to correct the reſt.

www.ingramcontent.com/pod-product-compliance
Lightning Source LLC
Chambersburg PA
CBHW020228240426
43672CB00006B/459